# Man and Metropolis

Lewis Mumford's provocative views on urban planning are expressed with vigor and clarity in these intriguing essays. Using examples from Europe and America, the author points out some of the marvels and many of the follies of modern architecture and engineering. He discusses specific buildings— the Guggenheim Museum, Coventry Cathedral, Pennsylvania Station, Maison de l'Unité d'Habitation—with such clarity and perception that the reader comes to understand the architect's purpose, the execution of his work, and his ultimate success or failure.

# Expressways to Nowhere

*In discussing highways and skyways, Mr. Mumford analyzes the shortsighted efforts of contemporary city planners, which result in traffic congestion and the tyranny of the truck or car. He advocates the building of "greenbelts" with self-contained cities outside the major metropolis—areas where people may live and work in leisure and beauty.*

## Other MENTOR Books of Special Interest

**American Skyline**
*by Christopher Tunnard and Henry Hope Reed*
A fascinating panorama of American civilization as
shown in the growth and form of our cities and towns.
Profusely illustrated. (#MD175—50¢)

**The Living City** *by Frank Lloyd Wright*
Wright unfolds his revolutionary plan for a city of the
future. Profusely illustrated with fifty-five photographs,
drawings, sketches, and plans. (#MT470—75¢)

**The Natural House** *by Frank Lloyd Wright*
Wright's plans for the design and structure of moderate
cost homes. Illustrated with one hundred and sixteen
photographs, plans, and drawings. (#MT469—75¢)

**The Future of Architecture** *by Frank Lloyd Wright*
Wright looks back over his career and explains his aims,
ideas, and art. Includes some of Wright's most contro-
versial papers, and forty-six drawings and photographs.
(#MQ471—95¢)

# THE HIGHWAY
# AND THE CITY

*by Lewis Mumford*

A MENTOR BOOK

Published by The New American Library

*Published as a MENTOR BOOK*
*by arrangement with Harcourt, Brace & World, Inc.,*
*who have authorized this softcover edition.*

FIRST PRINTING, MAY, 1964

"The Case Against 'Modern Architecture'" and "The Highway and the City" originally appeared in *Architectural Record;* "Landscape and Townscape," in *Landscape,* as "The Social Function of Open Spaces"; "Postscript: In Memoriam: 1869-1959," in *The Proceedings of the American Academy of Arts and Letters and the National Institute of Arts and Letters,* as "Frank Lloyd Wright." All the other essays appeared in *The New Yorker,* "London—to the Skies!" as "London and the Laocoön," "The Pennsylvania Station Nightmare" as "The Disappearance of Pennsylvania Station," "Frozen-Faced Embassy" as "False Front or Cold-War Image."

# Preface

*This book deals with a wide range of cities, buildings, and monuments. The period it covers coincides with the years I spent in preparing and writing* The City in History. *Some of the underlying themes of that book are here stated in concrete, contemporary terms; while in turn the problems of the contemporary city, which I analyzed in* The Highway and the City, *threw a vivid light on earlier modes of planning, and revealed advantages that must be recaptured in new forms, as we are now recapturing the market place in the pedestrian shopping mall, as well as persistent defects that we may now easily overcome.*

*From its inception* The City in History *called for a companion volume dealing with the contemporary city and its further transformations, actual and potential. I have still to carry through that work, though a perceptive reader will find it foreshadowed on almost every page of the history; and I will not pretend that the present book can serve as a satisfactory substitute. But at least these chapters will indicate by concrete example some of the fashionable blind alleys we must avoid, and some of the desirable goals toward which we may profitably direct our efforts.*

*When these essays first appeared, many forces that were at once regimenting and disintegrating the city had not yet been challenged. The high-rise slab was looked upon as the very paragon of modern architectural form: the glass curtain wall was still a pat symbol of modernity, and the words 'modern' or 'contemporary' were still used as an unqualified term of praise and edification. So, too, the preposterous plans of the highway engineers for gouging*

v

*out the living cores of great cities with expressways, inter-
changes, and parking lots, whilst draining off the working
population into scattered nondescript suburban housing,
were widely regarded as the last word in urban progress.*

*In the course of a decade, that situation has changed.
The issues that I raised have proved discussable; and the
rigid methods and regimented goals that once seemed as
inevitable as they were ominous, since they were based on
the latest findings of science and technology, have begun
to collapse like pricked balloons under rational examination. They are as bankrupt as our nuclear policy of 'sur-
vival' by competitive mass extermination.*

*Perhaps the best reason for bringing out this book now
is that it may still further widen the circle of public discussion, and thus prepare the ground for a more humane
order of building and living than that which a money-
centered and power-intoxicated economy has seen fit to
impose.*

# Contents

## *Part Two*  UNITED STATES

PART 1

*Europe*

ONE

Babel in Europe

After having spent four months in Europe, I should find it easy to give an account of its present state of town planning and architecture, but this is an impossible task today. Thirty years ago, the lines were clear and the direction was obvious; the tide of historical imitation had ebbed, and the turn toward a clean, bright, austere, efficient modern form had begun. The modern was then easily defined; it was that which did justice to the virtues of the machine—the precise, the calculable, the economic. At the beginning of the century, Adolph Loos, the Viennese architect, had proclaimed that ornament was a crime—a statement that put him in opposition to both the eclectic traditionalists and the "secessionists," who, like Louis Sullivan here, sought to create a new system of ornament. Later, in the early nineteen-twenties, Le Corbusier had demonstrated that a new esthetic, as free from caprice and fantasy as an ocean steamship or an English smoker's pipe, set up a criterion for every form. Architecture, cleansed of fantasy, would concentrate henceforth on the utilitarian and the constructive; the great cylinders of an American silo were the Doric columns of the new age.

On that basis, a few simple clichés served to identify a modern building. The smooth façade, without cornices or columns; the wide expanse of horizontal windows; the external curtain wall supported on cantilevers from an interior row of columns—these were enough to establish the authentically modern, and any departure from them was a violation, indeed an unthinkable regression. There were still very few modern buildings in 1930, and their contrast with the tourist souvenirs of eclecticism was so refreshing that no one suspected that an urban quarter designed on these restrictive principles alone might be an appalling monument of esthetic dullness.

And in town planning the same new clarification, the same austerity and simplicity, prevailed. In reaction against the often arbitrary overemphasis of topographical irregularities and curved streets in suburban planning, the planners restored rectangular blocks and straight, parallel rows in an ecstasy of schematic rigor. Long, continuous palisades of single-family houses or apartment buildings, whose straight lines made possible the use of travelling cranes and miniature railroads in building operations, became *ipso facto* the desirable modern form. Conformance with this rectitude was partly rationalized by accepting as an absolute the "new" principle of orientation, which held that streets should run north and south, and houses face east and west—without regard to view, to prevailing winds, or to the fact that if winter sun is what is desired, the major orientation of houses in the northern hemisphere, as Xenophon pointed out more than two thousand years ago, should be south.

In 1930, a few dozen buildings and housing estates summed up modern architecture and town planning; a student who had diligently visited Hamburg, Berlin, Stuttgart, Dessau, the Paris suburbs, Rotterdam, and Zurich could without a twinge of conscience feel that he had pretty well covered the whole ground—unless he thought he should add Mies van der Rohe's Barcelona pavilion (1929) and his dwelling house in the Czechoslovakian town of Brno (1930). Electicism was dead; the regional had seemingly succumbed to the rational; the architecture and town planning of the past, everyone agreed, had nothing to teach the modern architect. Long before the bombings of the Second World War had destroyed the historic cores of London, Rotterdam, and Berlin, Le Corbusier, acting on these notions, had theoretically wiped out the center of Paris and made it over on a Cartesian plan—high buildings separated by large areas of empty space, an arrangement making pretentious claims to sunlight and modernity but devoid of any urban character except excessive density of population.

Those plans of Le Corbusier's are today, ironically, the principal holdovers of that period, perhaps because they now unconsciously symbolize the inflation of money, the deflation of human hopes, and what one must perhaps call the "normalization of the irrational." This last is a characteristic of an age that is busily engaged in the exploitation of atomic energy without first pausing to find a safe way to dispose of its lethal peacetime by-products: an age that in order to insure abundant crops is recklessly poisoning with deadly insecticides and pesticides those who consume the food that has been "scientifically" so saved.

Many of the buildings of this early modern era, though they have become commonplace, seem as fresh now as when they were breathtaking innovations. Looking idly out the train window on the way from Rotterdam to The Hague, I recognized with a pleasurable start the handsome van Nelle factory, a paragon in its day and still unspotted by time; its concrete frame and glass walls and compact organization would make it a model for factories whose production needs do not require them to follow the current mode of one-floor sprawl. But there is hardly a single esthetic dogma that has carried over from those early days without severe revision; even the glass wall is open to vigorous challenge. Now that a thousand buildings have been constructed with curtain walls so arranged that their windows must be covered with Venetian blinds as protection from the sun, producing even blanker walls, we are aware of the sheer dullness as well as the functional contradiction of this solution, to say nothing of the costly housekeeping these dust-catchers exact.

To the pain and consternation of his earlier disciples, that great innovator Le Corbusier has turned his back on the axioms and principles that made his Esprit Nouveau pavilion, in Paris, so famous in 1925, and has designed a child's-story-book church in Ronchamp in which the windows are peep-holes, as capriciously spattered over its face as a five-year-old might spatter them on a drawing—and with about as much discipline of form. This repentance with a vengeance has the violence of caricature, but however the Master's more pious admirers try to disguise it, his reaction points to a serious lack in the old credo.

In short, the modern movement no longer presents a united front; it has already divided into two wings—the formalists (sometimes still known in America as the practitioners of the International Style) and the organicists, the two of them being merely our old friends the classicists and the romanticists, doing business in new quarters. This suggests that architecture is in effect back where it started in the twenties, which would be sad if it were true.

\* \* \*

In a recent survey of postwar architecture in Europe, the editors of the London *Architectural Review* found it impossible to make any valid generalizations about the course of contemporary architecture, and were plainly disconcerted by its lack of direction. Though I, too, find myself unable to make generalizations, I believe that the present confusion and lack of direction are due partly to a not unsound effort to reacquire some of the architectural qualities that were cast aside by the somewhat naïve formulations of the nineteen-twenties. Not long ago, one of the most voluminous exponents of modern architecture, who established some of the European clichés of the twenties, privately justified his return to stone facing, as opposed to facing of concrete, plastics, metal, or glass, by observing that more than one fine façade has been spoiled by materials that weathered badly or simply got unpleasantly dirty. Defiantly—but properly—he felt that his status as an exponent of the modern should not be lowered because of his sensible reversion to stone. Forms native to our age are a necessity, if our lives are to be lived with integrity, but the fact that the forms or materials employed are peculiar to the twentieth century does not by itself insure their beauty or their usefulness. Atomic energy is native to our age, too, but it may poison the soil and pollute the atmosphere beyond repair before we are intelligent enough to control it.

A good architectural solution today cannot be a mere mechanical solution, however brilliant or original, any more than it can be a mere cellophane package, wrapped in Mondrian strings, that ignores or denies its contents. Yet the revolt against a purely utilitarian functionalism begun by some of the younger architects, under the leadership of the venerable Mies van der Rohe, has already brought forth a formalism equally one-sided and even more sterile. What we still lack is an order of architecture capable of expressing in appropriate constructional form our many-faceted human needs, esthetic and social, and of cultivating economy as a means to an inner grace—the sort of order exhibited by the Italian Pier Luigi Nervi, the outstanding structural engineer of our generation, in the new Sport Palace now going up on the outskirts of Rome, with a dome of thinnest concrete "floating" above the arena. (It is one of the handsomest structures I came upon in Europe this summer.)

What modern architecture needs if it is to achieve the richness of form its earlier machine-minded program denied is a matching and molding of formal order, physical functions, and human feelings, both within and without, which means arranging *all* the mechanical, biological, social, and personal aspects of a building in the rank of their importance and significance for the human purpose in mind. This recalls Louis Sullivan's demand for an order "so inclusive that it will admit of no exceptions." So the present confusion in architecture is perhaps a prelude to a new effort to accomplish just this. The International Style of the twenties certainly did not embody that kind of order.

This change in the approach to a modern design is admirably illustrated by a minor building that has evoked controversy in England: a small, six-story office building—or, rather, two separately owned buildings treated as one—at 45 and 46 Albemarle Street, just off Piccadilly, in London. Though the architect, Ernö Goldfinger, has utilized the materials and resources of modern techniques to create openness and good light where they are needed, he has also respected the historic tone of the quarter and produced a structure that, though more brilliant than its muted, shabby neighbors, conforms to their scale and to the rhythm of the street. To overcome the dullness of its flat façade, composed of concrete, Portland stone, gray Vitrolite, and glass, he has scandalized some of his pedantic contemporaries by using sharp contrasts of light and shadow to give it color and distinction. All the windows have reveals, instead of being flush with the wall, and the upper parts of these windows, arranged in panels of three, form a kind of clerestory, whose even deeper reveals create a strong band of shadow; in addition, at the third floor, and again at the fifth, there jut out two shallow glass bays; their main esthetic purpose, like that of a Regency balcony, is to relieve the otherwise monotonous front with still heavier shadows, which are delicately emphasized by the thin black frames, top and bottom, of the windows. (In his new National Dock Labour Board Building, on the Thames Embankment, Frederick Gibberd has used a similar device.)

The final scandal of this design is the parapet, which is curved outward to form the bold line of a cornice; the shadow it casts firmly says "Finis" at the top. To make matters worse —that is, better—the concrete members are covered with Portland stone. Here is a building that has not merely learned the lessons of modern form but has learned them thoroughly enough to feel free to learn, too, from the eighteenth century and the Regency, how to create a lively façade for a street that must be modernized. Here the past has been neither externally imitated nor crassly rejected but inwardly absorbed and re-created, and contemporary form, instead of being confined to a handful of easily recognized clichés, is a fresh, supple, and many-toned orchestration of varied instruments. When this attitude becomes more common among architects, the problem of adapting historic quarters to new uses without effacing their identity will be easier, and modern design will have come of age.

The clearest line of development in contemporary European architecture unfortunately is in some ways the most depressing, for it involves a repetition of many of the mistakes made in the development of the skyscraper in America during the last two generations. As in a small American town, the skyscraper, almost anywhere in Europe, is a sign of having arrived and of being up to date; it is also an attempt to escape from the drab and the commonplace, which are often reinforced by bureaucratic building regulations that seek merely to produce an outward uniformity of façade or roof line.

Under the delusion that the skyscraper dwelling is more economical and efficient than lower buildings, great tenement skyscrapers have gone up on the outskirts of nearly every city of the Continent, from Antwerp to Milan. I even found one lonely specimen, twenty stories high, on the outskirts of ancient Avignon, while in London, on the London County Council's new Roehampton Estate—in some respects a brilliant job—such buildings have raised their heads above the hitherto inviolate rural landscape of Richmond Park. Sometimes these buildings are as gay, at least in the colors of their stucco and their shutters, as they are along the Italian Riviera, but when they dominate a whole quarter, they form a singularly unpleasant kind of urban space, gigantic in scale, procrustean in feeling, empty in human content.

Only trees and gardens of the grandest order, as at Roehampton, can redeem such urban deserts. The silly fashionable term, "vertical garden cities," is mainly sales talk for "overcrowding."

This sort of skyscraper apartment appeared well before the war—for example, the dismal towers in Drancy, outside Paris, which were long unoccupied but have now been taken over, I believe, by families of the metropolitan police forces. But the skyscraper that has set the pace for contemporary efforts and has had the most unfortunate hypnotic influence upon the younger architects is Le Corbusier's famous apartment house on stilts, in Marseille, whose atrocious plan corrupts all its superficial esthetic vitality. Perhaps the only big city that has kept consistently to a human scale of building in its new quarters is Amsterdam, but, partly because of the stringent limitation on costs in Dutch housing and partly because of oversimplified site planning, these low buildings are a little grim by contrast with the still ingratiating façades of Haussmann's middle-class Paris boulevards of a century ago, though all that architecture was, unfortunately, concentrated in the façades.

So far, the most sensible effort to exercise public control over the skyscraper, to keep it from becoming a major nuisance in already crowded cities, was recently made by the London County Council. It sets maximum population densities for all buildings in various parts of London, according to the function of the neighborhood, but allows the builder to choose between putting up a low building that covers an entire plot and getting the same amount of floor space by going into the air and leaving part of the plot uncovered, as our own Lever House does. This is a more rational method of control than the imposition of a uniform roof line or uniform setbacks, for it allows cubic space to be provided in accordance with the purpose of the building. Whereas department stores and garages, which function best on a basis of horizontal movement, may need to cover a whole block, offices and hospitals may be more conveniently and salubriously housed in towers or slabs, with plenty of open space on every side. This new form of control was forecast in the model prepared last year by Sir William Holford for the precinct around St. Paul's, in London—an assemblage of free-standing buildings of varying heights, accessible and visible from many directions. This picture is the precise opposite of that created by the wall of solid

masonry that constitutes the traditional city block, but it is
the form appropriate to the outsize superblock, which seeks
to isolate a large area from through vehicular traffic and offers
ample provision for unhindered pedestrian movement. Until
whole blocks, or even neighborhoods, are so disposed, however,
isolated buildings or clusters of buildings laid out in this fashion will be mere gaps in the orderly frame of the old-fashioned
street, as the Seagram Building is on Park Avenue.

In neither form nor content did I see any striking departure
in Europe from the contemporary American concepts of skyscraper design, though Werner Moser, in Zurich, has in some
respects improved upon Lever House in his projected office
building, and Gio Ponti and Pier Luigi Nervi are making an
outwardly radical departure in Milan, in the form of a thirty-
two-story skyscraper with a cigar-shaped ground plan—the
new headquarters of the Pirelli rubber company. Everywhere,
the glass wall, with continuous windows and opaque glass
spandrels, has become fashionable; there are postwar examples
as far apart as London and Geneva. But this is a dead end of
glossy architectural boredom, against which a reaction is already overdue.

Certain things have happened in Europe since the last war
that run counter to the Continent's emotional need, deepened
by the destructions of war, to refurbish and conserve its
historic past in architecture while creating a modern environment more favorable to the demands of our own period. The
most corrosive of these influences is the motorcar, which
brings mobility to the countryside but congestion and frustra-
tion, plus a threat of stagnation and blight, to the city. For
a generation, Europeans consoled themselves with the thought
that since the motorcar was an upper-class privilege, they need
not attempt to adapt their cities to motor traffic or the motorcar to their cities. The ubiquity of their chief vehicle of private transportation, the bicycle, and the mild congestion it
produced, should have warned them. When Hitler made his
one contribution to respectable fame by commissioning the
Volkswagen for the man in the street, it was already too late.
Since the war, and especially in the last few years, every town
in Europe (like every town in the United States) has become
clogged with motor traffic. The old market squares, which
once or twice a week were cluttered with peddlers' carts and
stands, are now cluttered every day with motorcars, since they

are the cheapest of central parking lots. To behold the venerable buildings that surround these squares, one now needs stilts. Half of the Grand Place, in Brussels, a glorious composition in gray and black and gold, is given over to motorcars, though a flower market keeps a tenuous grip on the other half; in Paris, the Place Vendôme has entirely lost its serenity and order to the parked and moving vehicles. And what is true of these cities is true of all the other cities famed for their beauty. In Amsterdam, the parked cars so effectively line the canals of the central city that they completely spoil the townscape. The quays are so crowded with vehicles and parking so tricky that the municipality has had to give instructions to motorists for escaping when the car has tumbled into the water, as cars frequently do. (The dodge is to keep calm till the water has risen high enough inside the car to equalize the pressures and permit one to open the door.)

Grandiose projects, modelled on American lines, have been suggested in Europe—midtown garages, arterial highways, and overpasses and underpasses, like those Brussels recently built to cope with the traffic its International Exposition will draw. No one, it seems, pays heed to our own grim experience, which is that the more facilities are provided for the motorcar, the more cars appear. The only thing that keeps this flood from being even worse in Europe is the shorter length and breadth of European cars; European manufacturers have intelligently developed a series of small vehicles —notably, the Isetta and the Goggomobil—that fit admirably into a tight urban pattern. These cars are sized to the human frame, not to the human ego. But what the man in the street lacks in the size of his car he compensates for—at least in Italy—in deliberately ostentatious noise, so that in every Italian city the delights for the eye are spoiled by the assaults on the ear. What is worse, pride and vanity lead wealthy Europeans to import American cars or to demand similar dimensions in the local product. So a race is going on between the rationalities of technology and the irrationalities of style.

European city planners and administrators are still as reluctant as our own to treat the problem of the motorcar on the only terms that will prevent it from making city life first unendurable and finally impossible. The solution demands at least four intermeshing steps: the vigorous restoration and improvement of public transportation within the city; the replanning of both the central and the residential neighborhoods to encourage pedestrian movement and restrict access by automobile; the designing of private cars, mainly for town use, no bigger than an Isetta, preferably powered by electric batteries of an efficient type still to be invented, along with the restriction of huge cars within the core of the city; and the relocation of metropolitan industry, business, and administration in outlying subcenters, to favor cross-transportation rather than the swollen tides of one-way traffic that now flow into midtown by day and ebb in the evening. The Europeans are one up on us by having invented a tolerable type of small car. London has made a further move by encouraging the construction of upper-income apartments, along with office buildings, in the ancient City of London, a central area whose nighttime population, aside from watchmen and rats, was negligible even before the Blitz.

These measures are only palliatives. The main issue is that the right to have access to every building in the city by private motorcar, in an age when everyone possesses such a vehicle, is actually the right to destroy the city. We still habitually sacrifice all the special values of the city to the function of motor transportation, as during the nineteenth century they were sacrificed to the railroad and the factory. In many of our expressways and viaducts and cloverleaf intersections, our highway engineers, in defiance of the lessons the past should have taught them, are butchering good urban land as recklessly as the railroad builders did in laying out their terminals and marshalling yards. But the notion that you can free the motorcar from all restrictions in the city without devastating the city's living spaces is a delusion that will probably cause a lot more damage before it dies. Meanwhile, the explosion of population in the central areas is producing a suburban fallout that is polluting the metropolitan countryside almost as effectively as strontium 90. This goes for Europe as well as America, though there it has not yet reached the proportions that now confront us along the whole Atlantic seaboard.

One final note, on a minor aspect of urbanism. Europe, which is copying our mistakes in handling the skyscraper and transportation, is likewise the victim of the lighting engineer, who, under the guise of providing scientific illumination, has been lining our streets and avenues with the gawky lamp standards and the ghastly modes of illumination that reflect his bad taste, turning human beings into green corpses with sodium lights, and making it impossible for anyone to sleep if his window faces the stabbing glare of a fluorescent tube. The chief merit of these batons of light is their cheapness, but they have not yet achieved a decent form. All honor to Robert Louis Stevenson, who back in the eighties, foretold this miscarriage of technics. "The word electricity," he noted, "now sounds the note of danger. In Paris, at the mouth of the Passage des Princes, in the place before the Opéra portico, and in the Rue Drouot at the *Figaro* office, a new sort of urban star now shines out nightly, horrible, unearthly, obnoxious to the human eye: a lamp for a nightmare. Such a light as this should shine only on murders and public crime, or along the corridors of lunatic asylums, a horror to heighten horror."

Stevenson could hardly guess that these esthetic misdemeanors would multiply under the specious banner of "progress." Whatever lighting engineers may think, it is not the intensity but the quality of light and the pleasantness of its form that count in an urban street, and these designers should confine their technical improvements to apparatus that can be put in a round globe or hemisphere and placed, at least in residential quarters, on a low standard. It is the use of hemispherical forms, on tall, thin posts, that gives the plaza before the new Rotterdam railway station a cheerful quality that streets lighted by long fluorescent tubes do not have. Lighting, like transportation, is too important a matter to be left to the experts.

*1957*

# TWO

# East End Urbanity

One of the impressive things about present-day England (1953) is that everywhere one sees evidence of brisk rebuilding, not merely in the bombed areas but out in the open country, where new factories, which England forgot to build in the days of her unevenly distributed prosperity, have appeared. In fact, today England looks the way Germany did at the end of the twenties, when French, English, and American bankers were squandering their clients' funds by pouring money into ill-fated investments in German municipal utilities.

But the basis for this English industrial construction is sound, since one of England's notorious handicaps in prewar days was her mass of obsolete mills and equipment. Most of these postwar factories, not least the ones in the New Towns (the British term for the dozen self-contained cities that have been built from scratch since the war) like Harlow and Hemel Hempstead, are as clean-cut, straightforward, and handsome as one could wish. The English are never so sure esthetically as when they are doing something practical, like building a ship or a jet plane, and this has been true in architecture from the days of the great Liverpool docks of the eighteen-twenties—more classic in form than any merely imitative classicism and still worth a pilgrimage—down to the present. The new London power stations, which have been dressed up with pseudo-classic smokestacks, are miracles of turgid inanity, and the new business buildings in the City of London represent British philistinism in its most crass and shortsighted form; but the bulk of recent British architecture —particularly the schools and the factories—can be put alongside the best that is being produced anywhere in the world.

In housing, the situation is more complicated. At the end of the First World War, the Ministry of Health sought to fulfill the promise, made in the exaltation of fighting it, to provide houses "fit for heroes to live in." A decade later, a million two hundred thousand subsidized houses had been built, largely in new suburban estates, on the fringes of the growing cities. In construction, interior space, and external amenities, including ample private gardens, the standard set by these houses was higher than any other country, even America, has yet achieved—allowing for differences in taste and habit, which gives us central heating and refrigerators and television sets in quarters too small for human occupancy. Sir Raymond Unwin, the original technical administrator of that scheme, succeeded in establishing a density of no more than twelve houses to the acre, on the assumption that every workman wanted room to grow vegetables—even potatoes—as well as flowers. The houses were usually grouped in rows of from three to six, and when done by imaginative planners like him and Barry Parker the result was often comely and sometimes good-looking. But the over-all pattern was needlessly uniform, needlessly dull, and an excess of space was devoted to front lawns, as well as to access streets that were usually far too wide.

England ameliorated its housing problem, but in doing so it produced a standardized suburban brick house in a standardized open layout, the same in industrial town as in country village, and almost the same for the working-class renter and the middle-class owner. The latter's house ran to bowed windows and half timbers, but that was simply evidence of his standardized freedom to choose exactly what his neighbor chose.

Thus, at the end of the Second World War, the English awoke to find that they no longer had an urban tradition of building, though London was still a vast museum of civic form, full of historic experiments, with its handsome squares and terraces, markets and shopping parades, from seventeenth-century Covent Garden to the two great squares, each with a church in its central green, that Sir Edwin Lutyens designed as the core of Unwin's magnificent twentieth-century plan for Hampstead Garden Suburb, which was built some forty years ago. This loss of the urban tradition was a loss not merely of form but of social compactness and facility, and all this has made more difficult both the replanning of the great bombed areas of London and the building of new towns. In reaction against suburban stodginess—after Hampstead Garden Suburb, nothing so fresh and inventive had been done anywhere in England—the younger architects of the thirties chose the high building in the mode of Le Corbusier as the symbol of the modern urban form. So there is now a violent quarrel between those who advocate the single-family house and garden, which at least ninety per cent of the British of every class prefer, and a group of architects who, apparently unmindful of the needs of family life, advocate tall flats, whether any large number of people want to live in them or not. The extremists on one side will not settle for more than twelve houses (thirty-six to forty-eight people) to the acre; the extremists on the other side welcome two hundred or even more people to the acre, provided they can be encased in a big, high building, with visual open space surrounding them but no private gardens. The quarrel is irrational, because these are purely arbitrary alternatives. It is a war that has been going on in nearly every country, under various slogans and battle cries. In New York, the argument for congestion is that the land is too expensive for low buildings, and so the New York City Housing Authority has been clearing sites in the Bronx and Brooklyn that were occupied by two- and three-story buildings and erecting thirteen-story barracks on them.

Being a family man, I am ranged with the opponents of the skyscraper apartment (a naïve modernism that was new way back in 1880), which requires a far greater original investment and, because of such items as janitorial work, upkeep, and elevator service, imposes a permanent heavy financial burden. It has, by the way, been unofficially estimated that in London a single-family dwelling can be built for not much more than half of what a flat of comparable size and amenities—but without a private garden—costs. In England, the advocates of congestion have on their side the powerful Conservative landed interests, which have rallied to their support under the impression that single-family dwellings withdraw too much land from agriculture. Yet one has only to look out of a train window anywhere except in the cindery Black Country to see that the garden space behind the British one-family house is always intensively cultivated. This sort of gardening often produces more vegetables and fruit than the land did when it was being professionally farmed. But the areas around the tall new apartments, such as the big public development in London's Pimlico section, are automatically sterilized against agriculture by the density of the population—two hundred or more souls to an acre—which makes it impossible even to keep any grass growing. Such open space, as Emerson put it, is "not to eat, not for love." The sole truly human touch in the Pimlico dwellings is a literary one; each has been given a historic name, such as Jane Austen House, Coleridge House, Martineau House, and —as a graceful acknowledgment to America—Hawthorne House. Unhappily, literature is not a substitute for sound architecture.

Many English critics say that the Pimlico development is one of the high points of all postwar housing, but I found it singularly depressing. Though its idiom is a little fresher than that of similar public housing in New York, and though occasional balconies grace its tall façades, Pimlico is one of those architectural dreams that always look much better on the drawing board than in real life. It consists of great rows of nine-story apartments, mostly grouped around the perimeter of a large block, within which are three-, four-, and seven-story buildings containing two-story maisonettes as well as conventional apartments. An interesting departure from the norm is the placing of the fire stairs of the tall buildings. Instead of being wound around central elevator shafts, as is our custom, they are glass-enclosed cages on the outside of the buildings—a fresh note, to be sure, though not so fresh when the cost of keeping those glass cages reasonably transparent is considered. The details, such as windows and balconies, are on the whole excellent; so is the occasional use of strong colors, and, for the moment, the contrast of gray concrete and yellow London brick, though this has been spoiled by the housewives' passion for pink and blue curtains. But the close-up effect is grim even now, and it will become grimmer as accumulating dirt lessens this contrast. These tenements (since that is the rightful name for them), creating a density of two hundred people to the acre, follow the English tradition established in the heyday of Victorianism by the Peabody

Model Dwellings, sternly hygienic but dismal, of doing the better thing in a worse way. Though the floor plans and the fittings are decided improvements on the ones in the cramped two-story houses that still surround this bombed-out area, the latter nevertheless have the intimacy and snugness, along with a tiny patch of green or a back-yard tree, that one associates with a home, and the finest of barracks architecture is no answer. This Pimlico project, which took first prize in a postwar competition, is possibly as much as can be done at such a density, even with a large subsidy. Yet anything above a hundred people an acre produces not merely bad housing but the sort of traffic congestion that is already strangling the great cities all over the world.

Fortunately, one does not even have to leave London to find a better way of life and a better kind of architecture. In Poplar, which was one of the most heavily bombed boroughs of London, since it adjoins the great dock area of the port, the County Council has turned out, on a small scale, a splendid example of urban building, the best I have found in England, and perhaps the best thing that has yet been done for lower-income groups anywhere. This is the still incomplete but now partly inhabited development called Lansbury Neighbourhood, which, in a much less complete stage, was one of the features of the 1951 Festival of Britain in London. Here is space without social dispersion, urbanity without social stultification, variety without empty caprice, and, as far as design goes, a fresh form based on a traditional pattern but reinterpreted in terms of modern needs. More adventurous architecturally even than our own Fresh Meadows housing project, near Flushing, and more varied in layout, it gives an excellent hint of what a good sectional development in a big city should look like.

The London County Council has elected to reconstruct eleven areas in the city. These Neighbourhoods, as they are called, are being planned to house from fifty-five hundred to eleven thousand people each—in effect, small cities. Lansbury Neighborhood is one of several in the East End, once the most drab and foully overcrowded quarter of town, despite the fact that many of the houses were only two stories high. The area being rehabilitated there totals three square miles. Some of the old buildings in Lansbury Neighbourhood are still standing—too sound, in tight times

like these, to be pulled down yet. Its main roads and canals, since they serve the port industry that fringes it, cannot be arbitrarily recast, so any new buildings must be fitted
into a pattern that presents a few difficulties. The main
shopping center of this district, serving three of these developments, is at the east end of Lansbury, on Chrisp Street,
which has been the local market street from Victorian
times. This market gives the district a bit of life and color
that is sadly invisible in New York City's housing schemes.
It is an irregular square, open on two sides, closed in by
the short flank of an L-shaped block of apartments and shops
on another side, and closed in on the fourth side by a row
of three-story buildings with an arcade of shops on the
ground floor. The apartments on the upper floors project
over the arcade to the curb line, to form a cheerful covered
walk punctuated by sustaining columns.

In the middle of this square is a one-story hall, designed
mainly for the sale of perishable foods, but the barrows
venders, finding the rents too high, have taken to the stalls
adjacent to it, in the open air. Also in the square is an
enclosure with benches, where shopping mothers may leave
their children under the eye of a friend, or rest their own
weary feet. This market, which is closed to wheeled traffic,
is, in short, a little masterpiece of planning, and the architect of this portion of the project, Frederick Gibberd,
deserves the acclaim he has received.

The common yellow London brick, rich in color and texture, which darkens in time to the sobriety of Bloomsbury,
has been used almost exclusively in Lansbury Neighbourhood.
The only exceptions are the panels of strong blue tile that
frame the stair wells in some of the apartment houses, and
the rather too pallid blue tile on one side of a borough
building. These simple expedients, as well as differences in
heights and in the sizes of windows to give variation to the
façades, and the avoiding of long, straight walls and rigid
rectangularity by slightly slanting the axis of a group of
buildings away from the line of a street, have enabled the
planners and architects to achieve a remarkable degree of
liveliness.

Now, the important point is that these variations are
not arbitrary; in ranging from two-story houses and two-story
blocks of flats to three-story buildings, containing two-story
maisonettes and one-story apartments, and on up to six-

story blocks of flats, they have sought to take account of every need. The people occupying single houses or ground-floor apartments have sizable gardens, and what is more, they are all in fervid cultivation. By now, even a rockery, that strange passion in a land of velvety meadows and lush gardens, has had time to raise its quaint hump. One of the happiest touches in this very human design is the placing of a small group of apartments for old people within hearten-ing sight of one of the schools. The size, the scale, and the site of this part of the project are all that they should be. In the housing and care of the aged, England is well ahead of us, putting into practice measures we are still gingerly discussing, and it is doing this now with a fine regard for individual privacy and self-reliance; indeed, this "welfare state" has de-institutionalized the care of the aged far more effectively than we have.

Though the East End of London had long been one of the most congested areas in the metropolis, it was nevertheless an area of two- and three-story houses; the congestion came about not merely because the houses were too close back to back—a device for squeezing profits out of lower-class housing discovered in the seventeeth century—but because too many people were forced to live together in one room in order to pay the rent. When, in the early Victorian days, model-housing associations tried to improve conditions, they held fast to the principle of congestion and simply attempted to make it a little more orderly, to which end they introduced five-story walkup tenements—grimly hygienic, hideously de-cent.

Lansbury Neighbourhood has ignored this dismal compro-mise, a modish 1953 example of which is the Pimlico de-velopment, and gone back to the human scale of the earlier houses, but with a variety of form that puts to shame the jerry-builders who made vast segments of London a night-mare of two-story monotony. In pleasing contrast to Pimlico, Lansbury houses only a hundred and thirty-six people to the residential acre. Though that is above the highest standard, it is reasonably near to it for a necessarily urban design, since the generous open spaces provided for its schools and its playgrounds, its market, and its future green pedestrian walks bring the over-all density down to around seventy-five people to the acre. When one contrasts this with the three hundred to four hundred and fifty an acre provided for by the New York City Housing Authority, one can only shake one's head over our addiction to congestion—itself originally the product of the slum-owner's greed. The present doldrums in public housing, which is a result of the official policy in Washington, may be a boon if our housing experts and administrators spend a little of their idle time prayerfully reconsidering their own achievements, so inhuman in scale, so dull in content, so lacking in gracious sociable touches in comparison with the variety and the attractiveness of Lansbury Neighbourhood.

I have not looked at all that Europe has to offer since the war, but I shall be surprised if Lansbury is not one of the best bits of housing and urban planning anywhere—far more significant and inviting than the work that has been done in Amsterdam, which Dr. Sigfried Giedion has strangely overpraised in his *Space, Time and Architecture.* Indeed, Lansbury is probably the freshest piece of design since Ernst May's Römerstadt housing estate in Frankfort-on-the-Main, built at the beginning of the thirties. And the reason Lansbury Neighbourhood has turned out to be so good is simple. Its design has been based not solely on abstract esthetic principles, or on the economics of commercial construction, or on the techniques of mass production, but on the social constitution of the community itself, with its diversity of human interests and human needs. Thus the architects and planners have avoided not merely the clichés of "high rise" building but the dreary, prisonlike order that results from forgetting the very purpose of housing and the necessities of neighborhood living. But the esthetic side was not forgotten, and the results are remarkably good. In Lansbury—if one excepts its overmonumental Roman Catholic church, an odd mixture of pompous traditionalism and expressionism—the freshness of the design as a whole reaffirms the basic decencies of the individual buildings. The old inhabitants of the district who are now housed in these quarters are delighted with them, according to reports, and I must say that I never before encountered such a healthy and relaxed lot of children in this part of London. The only drawback is that, even with subsidies, the rents are so high that they press hard against every other item in the family budget. But that is a matter for which there is no architectural solution, since as soon as one tries to fit housing to insufficient incomes, one can only re-create the slums one is seeking to abolish. While public housing is catching its breath in America and becoming conscious, I trust, of its sins, we might profitably consider this masterly effort as a guide to our own thinking. The planners of the London County Council and their architectural collaborators have much to teach us.

*1953*

# THREE

# Old Forms for New Towns

The London County Council has been replacing the old two-and three-story houses in the city's heavily bombed areas mainly with high (six- to nine-story) elevator apartments, usually in the form of slabs, with open corridors running across their fronts. These buildings show considerably more imagination in dealing with balconies, window openings, and the superficial patterns of wall, window, and balustrade than our dreary New York and Chicago counterparts: but in essence they are still barracks, and a continued large-scale rebuilding of residential London at a density of two hundred people to the acre would even further congeal traffic and impede the business and social activities of the metropolis. Already its trampled parks show the effect of excessive use (because of overpopulation) almost as badly as Central Park does, though the floral plantings, miraculously untouched by vandals, are as sightly as ever.

By contrast, since 1946 the British national government has attempted to deal with the problem of urban deterioration in more positive fashion—not by congesting the great cities' central areas further or by building new housing on their suburban fringes but by setting up a series of what it calls New Towns in the open country, thirty to fifty miles out of London. These New Towns are not suburbs filled with commuters, who must sacrifice an hour or more a day in shuttling between home and office. They are independent and fairly self-sufficient towns, with their own markets and shops, their own recreation centers and schools, their own (projected) theatres, hospitals, and other public institutions, and— most important of all—their own industries, lifted out of the crowded cities. Each of these communities possesses, in addition to broad stretches of park and playing fields within itself, a wide encircling belt of permanently agricultural land, which will prevent spreading from within or encroachments from without.

The 1946 act providing for these towns established a series of Development Corporations, which have roughly the initiative and power of our Port of New York Authority. Eight sites near London were selected, most of them close to or surrounding small country towns. Plans were laid down to provide, in all, houses and work for four hundred and eighty-three thousand people, in towns ranging in size from ten thousand (Aycliffe) to eighty thousand (Basildon and Harlow). A third of the construction job has so far been carried out. If it is no further advanced, it is because of the slowing down of the whole tempo of housing and building during the late forties, in deference to Britain's need for increasing her exports. But twelve thousand houses, or housing for forty thousand people, are now being completed in these towns every year.

The notion of relieving the congestion of big cities by building new towns of limited population is not wholly a recent one. This experiment is, however, the largest and most concentrated town-building venture since the seventeenth century, after Richelieu planted a small town in rural France and all the absolute princes of Europe began founding new capitals for themselves. There is another precedent, too; four hundred and fifty years ago, Leonardo da Vinci proposed to the Duke of Milan that he build ten cities, each of thirty thousand population, to ease the overcrowding of Milan. But the concept of the modern New Town is nevertheless a distinctly British invention—exactly the sort of sensible innovation one might expect from a robust little man with red cheeks and a walrus mustache who spent a good part of his life and modest income improving the typewriter and inventing a stenotype machine. Just fifty-five years ago, this urban innovator, Ebenezer Howard, a true Londoner, born within the sound of Bow Bells, published a book, written in an earnest, pedestrian style, called in its first edition *Tomorrow: A Peaceful Path to Real Reform* and later and prophetically *Garden Cities of Tomorrow*. One has to know this book to understand the New Towns policy; and this is important, since it is easy for an innocent American to be thoroughly confused by the issues that the New Towns policy and the New Towns have raised in England. Thus, an American social scientist, Harold Orlans, has written a book, called *Utopia Limited*, which developed the curious thesis that these communities must be a disappointment because they turn out to be living towns, full of the tensions, conflicts, difficulties, and compromises of life elsewhere, instead of perfectionists' utopias. Howard was too sensible a man to entertain the illusions his critics impute to him. His Victorian optimism was always ballasted with his sense of the practicable, though he demonstrated in Letchworth and Welwyn that what his contemporaries considered practical fell far short of the achievable.

Howard was the first person to apply political intelligence to the problem of the overgrowth and congestion of cities and to set up not a fanciful paper scheme, without the faintest conception of economic or social realities, but a new way of approaching the problem. He sought to replace the planless overexpansion of the big city with a planned "colonization" to draw off the surplus population. To achieve this, he proposed to build largely self-sufficient communities, limited in size and density of population but big enough to sustain a variety of industries and to satisfy the everyday wants of the population. In these towns the land is held and controlled by a public authority. He also made one of the few major contributions to the art of city building since the Stone Age invention of the city wall by suggesting that each of these towns be surrounded by a horizontal wall of agricultural land, or "greenbelt."

Howard called this new urban form the "garden city," a name he may have picked up from A. T. Stewart's Garden City experiment, on Long Island, during the few years he spent in America, though Chicago, which he also knew, had been called, once upon a time, the Garden City.

In a chapter called "Social Cities," Howard recognized that a single garden city, though indispensable as a pilot project, could not do the full job of a bigger city with its small population. He recognized that there are some wants—a college, a specialized hospital, a symphony orchestra—that no community of his proposed maximum (thirty-two thousand people) could support, so he suggested that a group of garden cities connected by rapid transit could sustain such specialized institutions and also provide for a diversification of industries and employment opportunities that only the congested big cities had hitherto offered. A whole group of garden cities is now at last coming into being, north of London, around the nucleus provided by Letchworth and Welwyn, the two garden cities Howard helped to found. The new political structure for this collection of related urban communities is still lacking, but the physical outlines are plainly visible.

Like any good inventor, Ebenezer Howard wished to test his idea by building a full-scale model. He felt that if a few such private ventures proved successful, then the garden city might, like the experimental railway lines of the eighteen-thirties, be organized on a greater national scale. This apple-cheeked little man had the faith that moves real estate, if it does not move mountains, and—what is even more remarkable—opens the pockets of socially disposed investors and secures the cooperation of hardfisted businessmen. Less than five years after the book's publication, the First Garden City Limited was organized to build the first actual New Town, Letchworth, thirty-five miles from London; its fiftieth anniversary, in fact, came in September, 1953. But the idea did not catch on at once. Letchworth grew slowly, and it had not reached more than a third of its planned population and industry in 1919 when the impatient Howard decided to build a second one, Welwyn Garden City, fifteen miles nearer London.

Welwyn grew faster than Letchworth, but for a long time it, too, had no influence on government policy. Both private and public investors continued to foster the wasteful, uneconomic growth of London by expanding the city outward, removing its inhabitants farther and farther from contact with the country, lengthening many a depressing journey to work, obliterating what open spaces existed in town, and building costly arterial roads to make it possible for more people to escape more quickly from the very metropolis that supposedly embraced all the blessings of civilization.

Thus Howard's invention, despite its two successful demonstrations, seemed a dud. England did bestow a knighthood on him in 1927, shortly before his death, but he was aware that while he had created a new concept of the city, which was to influence town planners throughout the world, he would not live to see it achieve real recognition. So the idea marked time: snobs condemned the garden city as "middle class" whilst the fashionable Communists of the thirties, following Moscow, dismissed it as a "left"—or was it "right"? —deviation. [Postscript, 1962: The USSR has now, with admiration, embraced the garden-city principle, after a visit by their town planners. "Seeing was believing."] Howard's fulfillment did not even begin till 1939, when a Parliamentary committee on industrial decentralization decided that the garden city was the most effective answer to the dangerous overconcentration of London's industries.

Then the Blitz of 1940, which demonstrated the vulnerability of London, provided the perfect reason for the change. Almost without dissension, all political parties accepted, after the war, the necessity of reducing the congestion in the big cities by building new towns. It was to Howard's invention that they turned. The best of the younger generation of town designers, such as William (now Sir William) Holford and Gordon Stephenson, flocked at once to the new Ministry of Town and Country Planning, and it seemed as if the New Towns would be new not merely in political and social constitution but also in architectural expression. So far, this last hope has been partly frustrated. For reasons it is difficult to trace, the more creative minds dropped out of the Ministry, and, even though some able architects were called in, only here and there do the New Towns express the new principles of planning or the new needs and possibilities of contemporary life.

The New Towns nevertheless embody several positive achievements, and I can best demonstrate what they are— as well as what they lack—by presenting a composite picture. This hypothetical town is situated in open country, near a main-line railroad, and it includes an already existing village, which helps feed and serve the new community while it is being built. Because of government priorities on materials, the civic center is unfortunately at present the least devel-

oped portion, and this tends to diminish the beholder's
esthetic impression. On the other hand, the industrial zone, in
both its layout and especially in its buildings, shows great
architectural vitality; whether the factories are owned by corporations or built by the town's Development Corporation
and leased, they occupy spacious sites, with well-planted approaches to the administration buildings, and the architecture
is often technically inventive—fresh, vigorous, gay. If one
comes to a New Town from the appalling Black Country
or from the more sordid industrial areas of London, the contrast is almost unbelievable. England's experience in planning
Trading Estates, its name for industrial areas like our own
more recent industrial parks, specially designed to facilitate
both production and transportation, has stood the New Town
in good stead. The industrial zone of the town is no more
than fifteen minutes by bicycle from the remotest residential
area, even though the low density of population spreads the
inhabitants fairly thin.

The plans for the New Town frequently incorporate an idea
barely suggested by Ebenezer Howard—designing it as a series of neighborhoods, each with its own elementary schools
and playing fields, and generally separated from one another
by belts or wedges of green. This neighborhood idea, first
clearly defined by an American, Clarence Perry, is a large
and radical departure, but because the pattern is essentially
a loose one, the innovation is both practically and visually
less effective than it should be. The second distinguishing mark
is the large amount of land devoted not merely to schools
and playing fields, which is mandatory under the new Education Act, but to parks or commons. This would be highly
laudable if so much space were not frittered away on streets
that are much wider than is necessary, as well as on wide
borders along the street and private front gardens. As a result, the two-story houses are often placed as far apart as
eight-story apartments should be.

In its revolt against congestion and sordor, a space-hun-
gry generation has, I fear, developed eyes that are bigger
than its stomach. Such openness not merely reduces urbanity,
but it also reduces social amenity and is economically wasteful. Unhappily, the standardized open layout developed in
England in the twenties—straight rows of houses with front
gardens big enough to preserve privacy, and back gardens
big enough to grow vegetables—has been almost universally

adhered to. But even assuming that a uniform density of twelve houses to the acre were desirable, there could be many variations on the pattern, as the town planner Sir Raymond Unwin demonstrated in his Hampstead Garden Suburb, in northwest London, more than forty years ago.

The ignoring of Unwin's later lessons, to say nothing of those of such American equivalents of the New Towns as Radburn and Greenbelt, and the apparent unreadiness to devise alternative layouts, make the New Towns needlessly monotonous. Even in other contemporary British housing schemes, such as the one in Wrexham, in Wales, I have seen innovations in community design that are lacking in the New Towns. Indeed, ancient Oxford, with its collegiate superblocks and playing fields, has more to teach the modern planner. Admittedly, the residential neighborhoods achieve a high standard of civic decency. Two-story houses, usually of brick and sometimes faced with stucco or tile, are arranged in short rows, of four to eight apiece, with garages or a high garden wall joining them into a group. Sometimes there are knots of three- or even six-story apartments; in the New Town of Harlow there is a ten-story building, set on a bit of high ground and surrounded by a sweep of green, that dominates the whole site as a castle or church would have done in the Middle Ages. But in general, two-story dwellings prevail. Sometimes it has a gabled roof, sometimes a single-pitch roof, but either way it manages to look just about the same. Even the grounds are standardized. In front of each house, there is usually a garden, often taking up four hundred square feet; behind, hidden from the passerby, is another garden of almost two thousand square feet. Twenty by a hundred feet is the size of many a Manhattan house lot, so these lots are around half again as large for houses of about the same surface dimensions. Gardens of this size provide plenty of room to grow a considerable quantity of vegetables, and they satisfy the Briton's admirable passion for shrubs and flowers. The administrators of these towns say that the migration of industry has been aided by such spacious gardens, which have persuaded workers who would not have been tempted to leave the cities if they were offered merely a better-equipped apartment. This explanation is probably sound, but it hardly justifies the uniformity of treatment.

This standard pattern of housing, though far superior to anything offered to most people in England before 1920, and though still superior in the main to the best American housing for similar income groups, has the defects of its virtues. It was devised as an escape from the dingy, overcrowded, smoky city, and it is planned for privacy rather than sociability, for spacious solitude and domestic isolation rather than for easy communication and cooperation with one's neighbors. And while all sorts of clubs and associations flourish in the New Towns, there is little in the plan to facilitate their functioning on an informal basis. One of the things that this salubrious housing ignores is the fact that today, because of a shortage of paid help, Englishwomen of all classes need to share services as much as the women of America; and to make possible baby-sitting, child-minding, washing-machine sharing, and all other sorts of informal cooperation, better ways of grouping houses must be invented. Not only that, but facilities for caring for illness and childbearing that are more accessible than big, overcentralized hospitals must be devised.

To achieve new form is not a matter of occasionally exchanging gabled roofs for flat ones, small windows for wide ones, or a horizontal row of single dwellings for a dozen rows of them, one on top of the other, in a tall building. Those are superficial changes, and in the case of high-rise apartments they are far from being improvements. When more essential matters are neglected, that kind of surface modernism and urbanism is a sham. What these planners need is to take a fresh look at the needs and desires and hopes of men and women today, and to find a form that will meet these needs in all their diversity. It is the lack of this kind of thinking that makes the housing in the New Towns too much like a hundred other British suburban developments.

Possibly it is unfair to criticize the few shopping centers and markets I have seen in these New Towns, for better ones are in process of building. They usually provide arcaded walks beside the shops, but aside from that even the best seem to me to have been conceived without reference to the exigencies of the motor age or of future traffic. Nowhere is there the separation of pedestrian precincts from parking lots and motor avenues one would expect in a mid-twentieth century New Town; nowhere is there sufficient use of the superblock or the cul-de-sac street to separate foot and wheeled traffic; rarely are there any of the internal parks and internal pedestrian ways such as the pioneering Unwin provided in Hampstead Garden Suburb.

As a result, the New Towns, though more hygienic and pleasanter than any other such quarters for people of comparable income, are brightly commonplace. But the fashionable English criticism—that they take too much land out of agriculture—is economically blind; I never saw so much urban space so highly cultivated, so rich in crops. The yield in vegetable foods is in fact far higher than when the land was in open field dedicated solely to agriculture. A more valid criticism is that they take too much land out of social use and that in overcoming congestion they forget the social virtues of concentration. Prudent administrators might well hesitate to make expensive experiments with purely theoretical schemes, lest they squander as much money as the French did on Le Corbusier's monument to Le Corbusier in Marseille, a piece of abstract sculpture cunningly disguised as a housing project. But the men who are putting the New Towns together have overlooked too many proved devices of urban planning or have only halfheartedly applied them. The result is monotony and sprawling suburbanism—not the exhilarating fresh city forms that might have been conceived, or even such sober excellences as Lansbury Neighbourhood has already achieved in London.

In the first batch of New Towns, then, Howard's fertile and significant idea has only partly come alive. The technical and political feasibility of large-scale decentralization is admittedly demonstrated. That in itself is no small contribution to urban statesmanship. In their main structural outlines, the New Towns are indeed new—the neighborhood greenbelt, the neighborhoods themselves, the well-insulated industrial zone, the civic center, above all a better balance of human functions in a partly self-contained urban unit with an economic base detached from London. In social structure and function the New Town is unmistakably a city, not a mere segment like a residential suburb. Unfortunately these social innovations have not yet found their equivalent architectural form, which in turn would reflect and enhance the daily activities of the inhabitants. A relatively good standardized plan has been an enemy of a more supple, a more varied and imaginative, in short a better form, to say nothing of an ideally conceivable best.

Something important in the old towns and villages that these New Towns often surround has been lost in the new designs —something that needs to be understood and adapted. The fact is that a city is not primarily a way of providing a vegetable garden for every inhabitant, though gardens should be an integral part of every modern city. Above everything else, a city is a means of providing a maximum number of social contacts and satisfactions. When the open spaces gape too widely, and dispersal is too constant, the people lack a stage for their activities and the drama of their daily life lacks sharp focus. Like every other amenity, public open spaces and private gardens must be scaled to the whole for which they are planned. Because the new planners were mainly in revolt against congestion and squalor, rather than in love with urban order and cooperation, the New Towns do not yet adequately reveal what the modern city should be.

*1953*

# FOUR

# A Walk Through Rotterdam

Everyone says Rotterdam is the one city in Europe that has turned the disasters of war and occupation into a triumph. For once, everyone is right. Rotterdam was—after Warsaw— the first victim of the Nazi policy of extermination bombing, almost three years before the Allied powers adopted the same barbarous military policies. In the Blitz of May, 1940, the Germans in a few minutes wiped out the historic triangular core of Rotterdam, along with many acres to the east and west of it—in all, some twenty-eight million square feet. This included twenty-five thousand homes, twenty-three hundred stores, two thousand factories and workshops, sixty-two schools, and thirteen hospitals. The nations were not yet conditioned to complacently accepting the possible extermination of the human race by nuclear warfare, so Rotterdam's sudden destruction was a traumatic experience. One desirable consequence of this injury—nobody would dare to think that in any sense it was a compensation—was to engender a cooperation that has made bold urban planning and building on a large scale possible. A week after the German assault, the citizens of Rotterdam decided to pool the land in the center of the city and to replan the whole quarter. The municipal authorities respected property interests as a basis for compensation, but they wiped out old property lines. The

fact that the war lasted so long had its ironic advantages, for
it enabled better second thoughts to make over the rather
timid and old-fashioned plan that was first put forward. Under the new planning director, Dr. Cornelius van Traa, Rotterdam is not merely replanning its interior district but is
dispersing its population in nearby subcenters—not an easy
job in the Netherlands, where the cities are close together,
the population is dense, and good agricultural land is precious.

Before the war, Rotterdam was a somewhat bedraggled
cosmopolitan version of a typical Dutch town, boasting an
ancient church; a rather handsome modern fish market; a
thriving port; an ancestral native son, Erasmus; and J. J. P.
Oud, one of the early leaders of modern architecture. The
church, battered by the Blitz, is now under reconstruction;
the port, vengefully ruined by the Nazis in their hour of defeat, has been restored; Oud, who renounced the purism of
the twenties before Le Corbusier did, is at work again; and
Erasmus, that lonely, smiling humanist, is still ensconced in
the heart of the city, among tough traders and shipbuilders
whose spirit seems closer to a boisterous Rabelais.

Though in 1940 inner Rotterdam still had a few pleasant
canals, lined with grassy banks and offering occasional
vistas, from a bridge, of gardens embowered in poplars and
willows, all as idyllic as Oxford's Cherwell above Magdalen
Bridge, the city had become unpleasantly overcrowded and
grimy. Rotterdam spreads along the broad estuary of the
Nieuwe Maas, which forms its southern border. Its blasted
center is bounded on the north and east by the railway
that leads from the new Central Station, which is at the
northeast corner, and on the west by the remains of an old
residential, hotel, and business quarter. The German demolition was a brutal remedy, but a wholesale slum clearance
was long overdue, as in London and Berlin.

This central area is bisected, north to south, by the Coolsingel, a canal long ago filled in and paved to form a
broad business avenue, which stretches between the railroad
line that partly encircles the old city and the river port. On
the east side of the Coolsingel stand the Town Hall, the
Central Post Office, and the new Bourse. Thanks perhaps
to their ponderous masonry as well as their position, the
first two buildings were practically unscathed by the Blitz,
and so was the Atlanta Hotel, on the opposite side of the

Coolsingel. But the rebuilding of central Rotterdam might have been more felicitous if these survivors could have been rebuilt on other sites. Apart from these buildings and a few trees, whose miraculous escape has given them the sentimental value of shrines, the area was reduced to rubble. Another survivor stood at the southern end of the Coolsingel, toward the harbor—the Beehive department store. This building, the work of the Dutch modern architect Willem Dudok, was hailed, when it opened, as the last word in modern design, because of its striking use of the continuous glass window. But even in 1932, when I saw it first, the windows had been largely covered, since the store had found that exposure to sunlight and air ruined certain merchandise. The Beehive survived the Blitz, but it did not survive the replanning. Dudok's work is slated for demolition, to permit the straightening of the Coolsingel, and a new Beehive, designed on quite opposite lines, with almost no windows, has already arisen across from the Bourse, in the midst of a new shopping area.

By now, enough building has been done to suggest the texture and the outlines of the reconstruction. This job of replanning has a positive and a negative side. The positive side is that of conceiving the best possible building types and the best possible grouping of functions to further the life of the community. The negative task is the avoidance of congestion and strangulation through the increase in vehicular traffic as a result of inept planning and greedy overbuilding, like what is now so merrily taking place on our own Park Avenue. In this respect, Rotterdam has made some notable departures; one is to reverse the process of specializing and separating urban functions, which has steadily increased the distance and the volume of vehicular transportation between the places where people work and the places where they eat, sleep, reproduce, and relax. Though the Coolsingel is the principal axis of Rotterdam's business quarter, whose office buildings, some high, some low, march right down to the harbor, the planners have built apartment houses in the neighborhood, many within easy walking distance; from afar, it is hard to tell whether a group of buildings ten to fourteen stories high are offices or apartments. Only thirty-one per cent of the area is now occupied by buildings, as opposed to fifty-five per cent before, but—American banks and insurance companies take note—the property values are

twice as high. The density of the dwelling areas in central
Rotterdam, eighty to a hundred people an acre, compares
happily with the density of four hundred people an acre that
Le Corbusier, in his apartment housing, considers reasonable.

This mingling of dwellings and business buildings anticipated similar proposals of the London County Council for the
rebuilding of the inner areas of London. Meanwhile, our own
public authorities and private enterprisers, lacking a Blitz,
have been gutting out the hotels and the apartment houses
of our midtown area in a last desperate effort, which has
excellent prospects for success, to bring wheeled traffic to
a complete standstill. The planners of Rotterdam realize
that the principle of single-use zoning, reserving large areas
severally and exclusively for industry, business, multifamily
apartment buildings, or single-family houses, will have to be
modified; certain urban functions must indeed be strictly
isolated, since no one can live comfortably next to a steel-
works or a printing plant, but certain others must be
combined again, not higgledy-piggledy but with a firm sense
of their needs and interrelationships.

Unfortunately, Rotterdam's planners have taken only a
partial step toward improving pedestrian movement to the
center of the city and thus easing the pressure on the transportation system. Apart from the new shopping mall, their
main improvement has been to greatly widen the sidewalks
around the conventional-size midtown blocks. What is needed,
however, is a throwing together of these small blocks into
much larger superblocks almost completely shut away from
traffic but traversed in all directions by pedestrians. The new
buildings should be insulated from traffic streets, setting up
domestic precincts—or *"Cités,"* as they call them in Paris—
that turn their backs to the noise and stir of traffic and create little pools of domestic silence and order, open up to a
point, but only to local delivery wagons, ambulances, hearses,
or such other occasional vehicles.

Two stereotypes, one old and one new, still curb the
imaginations of planners. The old stereotype is the street
and blockfront, lined on both sides with a continuous palisade of buildings, a usage going back to the archetypal cities
of Mesopotamia and India. The new stereotype is the monumental slab, high and shallow, though free-standing on all
sides, as the ideal unit for apartments or offices. In Rotter-

dam, these two stereotypes are combined in the new housing quarter—nine-story slab apartment houses, whose ground plan forms an L, grouped in small blocks, plus a row of low houses that turns the L into a right-angled U. Despite the balconies, the spacious windows, and the open spaces, the result is a little forbidding, for the small inner court formed by the U is dominated by the high slabs and the pedestrian is dwarfed. The new dwellings in Rotterdam have even more hygienic virtues than the buildings in a New York Housing Authority's superblock, but they have not, it seems to me, achieved the right scale, the right layout, or the right combination of forms in buildings and open spaces to create the fresh urban pattern one would like to see in every new central development. Row houses overshadowed by a series of slab skyscrapers are not the answer.

The achievement of a fresh form is not a mere external matter to be determined by a new system of construction, or by calculations of the most economic height for an elevator installation or of the distances between buildings necessary to permit sunlight to enter the lowest floor. These factors should all be subservient to the daily contents of modern living and to the effort to find a comprehensive form for these contents. The open space in a residential quarter should be treated as a series of outdoor rooms, complementary to the indoor space, planned to add color to indoor tasks and give a focus, as well as a background, to outdoor activities. Hence the need for an intimate scale, which a rank of high buildings destroys. In turn, the public and private indoor space should not fit human activities into a rigid and mechanically arbitrary structure but should fit the structure to the purposes it serves. So far, the only residential buildings that truly respect the contents of living are suburban houses; too often, modern architecture ceases to be humane or efficient when it leaves the open spaces and gardens of the suburb. This failure to achieve a new form for an urban residential quarter is as evident in the British New Towns, which started from scratch, as it is in the rebuilding of the most congested metropolis. In Rotterdam, it is all the more conspicuous because of the successful design of the Lijnbaan, a mall that runs north to south, parallel to the Coolsingel and a bit to the west of it. The Lijnbaan, by the way, is part of the new shopping area.

The basic feature of this area is its treatment of pedestrian traffic, not merely to lessen the congestion of cars, buses, and trolleys but to make daily life more enjoyable to that forgotten man, the pedestrian, whose life and limb are equally endangered by careless drivers and by sheer muscular atrophy. Pedestrians, as the satiric authors of *The Little Golden Calf* remind us, should be loved; they make up the greater part of humanity. Yet their natural freedom of movement is progressively confined, while the car, which pedestrians invented, is invited everywhere. In America, we have pushed the elimination of the pedestrian to its ultimate conclusion—the drive-in market, the drive-in movie theatre, and the drive-in bank. (We lack only a drive-in cemetery.) The Lijnbaan has moved in the opposite direction. You can pass freely through it without once being nuzzled by a motorcar. In planning it, the architects have made a dramatic contribution to the modern city, for they have shown that the advantages we associate in America with the suburban or regional shopping center may also be made available in the heart of a metropolis.

On the south, the Lijnbaan terminates in the Binnenweg, a street, running west to east, that has been widened at this point to make a small square. Here the larger stores are grouped, with sidewalks in front of them broad enough not merely to accommodate showcases but to tempt shoppers to loiter, without impeding the flow of traffic. The Lijnbaan itself, on the other hand, is dedicated to small specialty shops, plus an occasional café or restaurant or tourist office, like the Fifth Avenue approach to Rockefeller Center. The planners had originally proposed to set these little shops in a series of new streets, parallel to the Coolsingel, with shops on the ground floor and three floors of flats above. But the architects persuaded the shopkeepers to make a bolder move and establish a special thoroughfare of their own, a pedestrian mall, separated from both street-bound pedestrians and vehicles.

As in similar English shopping malls in Coventry and the New Town of Crawley, the architects of the Lijnbaan had to break down a prejudice shopkeepers have clung to for two centuries, ever since the periodic weekly function of marketing, concentrated in a compact market place, gave way to the daily process of "shopping" in stores that stretched indefinitely along an avenue. This prejudice had substance in the days of the "carriage trade," when fashionable ladies went forth in coaches to visit shops just to kill time, and the placing of transportation systems on these same avenues completed the tieup between wheeled traffic and sales. So intent were merchants on ignoring the pedestrian during the last hundred years that in most American cities shade trees on shopping avenues were slaughtered to make them more amenable to rapid transit.

But the long shopping thoroughfare never achieved an unqualified victory. The most successful specialty-shopping streets are short and narrow, like Old Bond Street in London and the Kalverstraat in Amsterdam, and sometimes, as in the latter case, virtually reserved for the pedestrian. During the nineteenth century, a whole series of glass-covered shopping arcades were built, from the Burlington Arcade off Piccadilly to the more monumental Galleria in Milan. The architects of the Lijnbaan carried this tradition further; though they rejected the glass arcade, they have provided a covered way for shoppers, as on the Rue de Rivoli in Paris and in many medieval arcades. But by cantilevering the overhang of the arcade, they eliminated obstructive columns. Wisely, the planners favored the narrow street over the open market place, following the principle, first practiced in medieval Venice, of completely separating movement on foot from other modes of traffic. But the feature that distinguishes our own suburban shopping centers was not forgotten; space has been set aside nearby for a big car park, which also serves the neighboring concert hall and the movie theatres.

The Lijnbaan forms an inverted L, the corner of which abuts on the plaza that runs west from the City Hall, while the long arm, which extends toward the department stores on the Binnenweg, is interrupted—perhaps unnecessarily—by a cross street. (The short arm of the L is, in a way, a continuation of the plaza.) Access streets behind the shops provide for deliveries. All the buildings are uniform in height (two stories), though some of the shops have several levels, and no high building overshadows the area. The shops form a continuous front, with display windows on the ground level and panels of three windows, separated by vertical fins set in a dark wood frame, above. A wide overhang along the shop fronts, unpunctuated by any posts except the flagpoles that edge it at intervals, provides a covered way, and it is joined here and there by covered crosswalks. One might question the use of the dark wood sheathing above the concrete frames of the shops, and the sometimes raucous lettering of the shop signs, but the effect of the Lijnbaan is warm, lively, almost gay: the daylight, the waving flags, the delicate acacia trees, the rectangular flower beds, the occasional benches, even a glass-enclosed café area plump in the middle of the mall—and, not least, the human figures, moving in and out between the shadows of the covered way and the open sunlight, in an area that is entirely their own. The unity and harmony of all this delight the eye, with just the right combination of the artful and the natural, the intimate detail and the clear over-all pattern.

Through sedulous respect for the human scale and for pedestrian movement—the mall is only about fifty feet wide from window to window—these modest means have produced magnificent effects. Nothing in this whole composition depends upon hugeness, upon acrobatic technological exploits, or upon costly materials. Here is a sound urban form that could be adapted anywhere. The plan might be carried through, with great ease and happy effect, in the back alleys and minor streets of Philadelphia, Baltimore, and Washington. In addition, the Lijnbaan gains from the blessed absence of mechanical noises, carbon-monoxide poisoning, gasoline stench, impatient waits at traffic lights, and any sense of congestion even when the mall is thronged with people. Because of the fullest exploitation of the entire methodology of shopping—not just buying but inspecting, daydreaming, ruminating, eating, drinking, meeting people, stretching one's legs—this is a more convincing modern urban form than has yet been produced in residential quarters. Merely being *in* the Lijnbaan is a pleasure, even if one has no shopping to do. That fact is attested to by the pedestrians who use it to get from one part of the business area to another. So pervasive and ingratiating is it that the one major error of the sponsors and designers may turn out to be their failure to provide enough eating places; it is only in such an insulated and protected place that the traditional delights of the outdoor café, now ruined by constant assaults on nose, eyes, and ears, can become real again.

The shops and department stores in the rest of the shopping area front on streets in the conventional fashion, but the planners have still not forgotten the pedestrian, for there are wide sidewalks here, too. Big stone troughs are filled in spring with peonies, marigolds, pansies, and geraniums that enchant the eye; colored tiles and mosaics have been used to relieve the sometimes dry façades. Even the bolder use of sculpture on blank building walls, like the gay abstractions in high relief on the Thalia Theatre, which closes the north end of the Lijnbaan, makes sense when one approaches it from a distance on foot; indeed, the whole area invites outdoor sculpture, though not enough sculptors know how to take advantage of such an opportunity. In addition to the homely esthetic touches visible all through the town—of contrasting textures in paving, tiled ornament, flowers, and avenues of trees—there are more striking exploitations of the possibilities opened by a daring plan. For one, there is the superb monumental sculpture in steel and stone and bronze, the work of Naum Gabo, that stands outside the new Beehive, and there is Ossip Zadkine's moving symbolic statue of Rotterdam's ordeal, which occupies in solitude the great plaza by the waterfront.

The effect of this urban transformation is one of untrammelled confidence and of energy sufficiently released from purely sordid calculations to create art. Except in the Bourse, there is no effort in the new buildings toward the Palatial or the Monumental or the Showy. Even the five-story Beehive, on a prominent corner of the Coolsingel, has a certain reticence. Its show windows are overhung by a flat façade almost entirely sheathed in travertine stone, cut in hexagons on the Coolsingel side, and pierced (above the ground floor) by narrow vertical windows—mere oblong slits, chiefly for a gay lighting effect at night—as well as by three large horizontal openings. Why the architect abandoned the symbolic hexagon, the classic form of the beehive, for the oblong on the flanking façades, I cannot fathom; this seems to come under the rhetorical sin of the meaningless variation. But this shell, severe to the point of emptiness, has some obvious merits, for it is a studious attempt to find the right form for a building visited by large crowds and ventilated and lighted by artificial means. The three horizontal openings, one for a loggia at the top, two for restaurant windows below, give some outlook to the patrons. There is perhaps a psychological need for such breaks, but the effect of these sudden black oblongs is esthetically so disturbing and seems so arbitrary that one wishes the architect had lessened the breaches by

perhaps carrying the hexagon motifs clear across the openings in the form of a grille, to give some feeling of surface
continuity. Happily, the building serves as a foil to Gabo's
statue, whose dynamism gains by contrast with the static
façade.

At the rear of this four-square structure, facing north, the
architect Marcel Breuer has produced one of the best office-
building façades I have seen anywhere. By using a sort of val-
ance of opaque glass in the upper part of the windows,
he has achieved a maximum of useful light with a minimum
of glare. A solution equally integral has still to be found
for façades exposed to the sun, but Breuer has made a step
in the right direction to rescue modern buildings from the
dust-collecting Venetian blind and the icicle-collecting *brise-
soleil,* or external sun screen.

But it is by its spirited, resourceful planning as a whole,
not by this or that individual building, that Rotterdam makes
a profound impression. Here again it is true that the whole
is greater, and certainly more significant, than the parts. Already some of the mistakes that originally were made have
been digested; inquiry by Rotterdam housing authorities disclosed, for example, that the inmates of the tall apartment
houses, at least those with families, would have preferred
low buildings. As a result, a new course is being set. As
far as I know, the work of the London County Council
alone is Rotterdam's rival in the quality of its thinking and
the extent of its postwar reconstruction of a devastated area.

*1957*

# FIVE

# The Cave, the City, and the Flower

One of the oddities of the postwar period in Europe is that none of the new buildings is half as impressive as a group of sober-eloquent public monuments. Though architecture seems now to be in a period of internal contradiction and indecision, the older schools of sculpture have, at the end of forty years of experiment, produced public works of great vitality and distinction, in which the original purpose and program of the various new movements have been carried, each in its own way, to a significant conclusion. With the exception of the Cave Ardeatine, near Rome, each of the monuments I shall discuss is the work of a single master—Ossip Zadkine, Naum Gabo, or Jacob Epstein. Two of them are in the classification of war memorials, which usually deny the sentiments that prompted their construction by sculptural platitudes as emotionally unconvincing as they are esthetically banal. But there is more esthetic life in these monuments, dedicated to the dead, than there is in most of the recent multi-storied housing developments, dedicated (supposedly) to the living. If anything today seems emptily grandiose, it is not the monument but the big slab apartment house.

The Cave Ardeatine, sometimes misnamed the Fosse Ardeatine, is less known than it should be, for it lies outside Rome, along the Appian Way, just beyond one of the most famous Christian catacombs, and the tourist is not so likely to stumble upon it as he is upon the fountains of Bernini. Moreover, a reticence about treating this sad memorial as a mere spectacle doubtless keeps the Romans from listing it as a show place. The three hundred graves in the Cave Ardeatine, the final focus of this monument, are still visited by relatives and friends of the slain victims, bringing flowers to the dead where they lie under their heavy concrete canopy. In retaliation for a wartime partisan ambush of a detachment of German soldiers, the Nazis rounded up three hundred Romans at random in a public square—the young and the old, the destitute and the comfortable, the amiable and the inimical—and took them to one of the caves that honeycomb the hills of Rome. There they machine-gunned their captives; then, perhaps appalled by thoughts of the effect this massacre would produce on the populace, they concealed the bodies by the simple expedient of blowing in the roof of the cave with the same notable technical ability they applied to other forms of extermination. To give honorable burial to the dead, and to remind us, in today's Purgatory, of the Inferno they had passed through, this monument was conceived, after the war, by a team of five architects and landscapists, and two sculptors. The names of these artists should be perpetuated, for they brought to the task not only skill and esthetic discernment but a human sensibility that is foreign to many contemporary artists, seemingly bent on capturing the incoherent noises of prehuman unconscious processes, as if recorded in a decapitated brain, severed from heart and guts, from feeling and meaning. The sculptors are Mirko Basaldella, who wrought the wide bronze gate at the entrance to the cave, and Francesco Coccia, who did the figures that stand above the entrance; the architects and landscapists are Nello Aprile, Cino Calcaprina, Aldo Cardelli, Mario Fiorentino, and Giuseppe Perugini. The dead may well be grateful to them for the clarity of their feeling and the forthrightness of their interpretation.

On the road leading to it, this cemetery—for that is what the monument is—is first announced by a wall of brown volcanic stone that rises gradually to a height of fifteen feet at the entrance. This serves as both a visual boundary and a retaining wall for the lower part of the hill over the cave; in addition, the great flat field stones that compose this wall form a dark, rought-textured base for the three white marble figures, about twice the human scale, that stand just inside and above the entrance—three victims bound together, back to back. The effect of these figures in the sunlight is of a silver horn above the brooding beat of a bass drum. The rightness of this contrast diminishes one's disappointment in the figures themselves; the absurd costume of modern man, baggy and formless, is hardly redeemed by the naked torso of one of the figures. Only a master could have risen above the tepid realism of this sculpture without losing the pathos and tenderness that were a necessary part of the artist's intention. Except for Ernst Barlach and Jacob Epstein, one might look in vain for a modern sculptor capable of doing justice to both the formal and the emotional elements of such a monument. But if the detail is weak, the concept is sound: so well placed is this vertical accent, so just is the scale, that the figures, almost in spite of themselves, match up to the rest of the design as an organic part of the composition. The whole, by its unity of spirit, has turned the transient victims by way of art into enduring victors.

The entrance gate is at the inside corner of a right-angle indentation in the wall, and this achieves the double purpose of creating a pocket of parking space beside the road and indicating the point of entry. The bronze gate, in which, at one side, a small door is set, strikes, even more definitely than the sculpture, the opening note of the martyrdom here recorded; the jagged pattern of the heavy rods that are interlaced to make the gate gives a feeling of the inimical, of the bound and the chained, without forfeiting the language of abstraction or the function that an entrance must serve. Basaldella's achievement here is a firm one. Entering, with the sculptured figures hovering above one on the left, one crosses a broad, irregular open area, paved with small stones and edged by grassy slopes planted with laurels and cedars, toward the high opening of the cavernous passage to the site of the massacre. The two cedars near the entrance and the rich green ivy that covers it perhaps unduly soften the austerity proper to the whole design; the landscape gardener's natural desire to overcome by plantings the desolation of the bare slopes seems at odds with the expressive grimness of the rest of the composition.

But once one has crossed this open space and entered the cave beyond, all is circumspection and restraint—the interior has been kept rough and dark, with only covered lights at shoulder height to guide one over the earthen floor and through a long, high passage that terminates in a humble chapel, from which another and equally dark passage takes one back to the entrance and to the sunken burial ground to which the bodies of the victims have been removed. The chapel is, like the Pantheon in Rome, open to the sky, but its utterly artless simplicity says more than the Pantheon in all its grandeur. For here is where the roof of the cave was blasted by the Germans to bury the victims, and the sudden exposure to the air and light stabs one, by contrast to the enveloping darkness from which one has just emerged. At the rough edges of this high opening, grasses and bushes have taken hold; when I made this pilgrimage, the petals of wild roses were fluttering downward through a shaft of sunlight, and that accidental contribution of nature deepened one's sense of the coldly calculated violence and horror that had been committed here.

In designing the cemetery itself, architects of less imagination might have been tempted to say, in stone or sculpture, what is unsayable. But these artists were wise enough to let the dead have the last word: their building is in the most elemental of forms—an oblong, horizontal slab of concrete, gigantic in scale, without a touch of molding or lettering to relieve its surface. That slab stretches flatly over the graves, which are arrayed in a wide, low chamber with dark stone walls. The dead are banked in double rows, enclosed in seemingly solid granite, each stone coffin separated by a narrow channel from its neighbor, the tops of the double rows slanting gently upward to form a low-pitched gable. The space beneath the roof is unbroken by columns, and the sole illumination is the daylight that enters through the crack, apparently not more than a foot high, that separates the walls and the roof. The starkness, the pervading gloom, the oppressive monotony of the composition are relieved only by the contrast in texture of the wall, the rough concrete ceiling, and the pitted granite surface of the graves, with their bronze wreaths and the names of the identifiable dead.

In this cavelike structure, one is not merely alone with the dead; one is close to their final moment of agony. So, far from making that moment easier for the visitor, the architects have sought to intensify it—though their desire to keep the whole space free of votive offerings has been humanely ignored, and now bouquets and vases of flowers provide a tender contrast to this solemn moment of encounter. Here the severity of truth chastely curbs any kind of esthetic glorification. Mere pictures and words cannot do justic to such a monument; one has to go through the experience, in its contrasts, in its eloquent omissions, and even to repeat the pilgrimage, observing its cumulative effect on oneself, to feel the depths of the artists' imagination and the quality of their execution. This is like the descent into hell in ancient times as practiced by the mystery religions, a descent followed by a promise of redemption as one returns to the daylight world. To say that the passage through the Cave Ardeatine is unforgettable is merely to say that art has done all it can do to bring the dead back to life in the very place that gave their life its tragic significance.

One must go to Rotterdam to find a war memorial that compares with the Cave Ardeatine in intensity of feeling. The phony war ended on May 14, 1940, with the German air assault on this Dutch city, which wiped out the commercial center and killed many of its inhabitants. The citizens of Rotterdam have not forgotten that sudden savagery or the grim occupation that followed, but the resentment that might have smoldered for years has now crystallized, in visible form, in a monument that translates their historic trial into a work of art. One of the Jewish business families in Rotterdam, whose wealth survived the war, thanks to their Christian friends and faithful employees, desired in gratitude to erect a public monument, and the director of the firm, Dr. G. van der Wal, himself a collector of modern art, had the inspiration to commission Ossip Zadkine to create one that would remind even those who had not suffered of what the city had gone through. Who could have been sure that such an undertaking would find, in the Expressionism of Zadkine, an effective interpretation of this experience, or that the right spot would be secured for it? War memorials too often miscarry. But in Zadkine's creation all the human lacerations and disruptions that had been prophetically symbolized in the work of the Expressionists and the Surrealists found at last an appropriate occasion for public use.

Zadkine's monument, a human figure at least twice human size, stands by itself, toward the waterfront end of an oblong plaza, at a point where the business district and one of the inlets of the busy port meet. It rests upon a granite base, and its long arms, angularly raised to the sky, identify it at a considerable distance. To the right, as one approaches it from the city, a long quay for small craft, with a parked embankment and promenade alongside it, sweeps southward in a slow curve to the outer harbor. Zadkine's dark bronze figure is male in head and torso, almost female in pelvis and flank, the trunk and head thrown back, the face deformed with pain and the mouth shrieking, the arms gigantic, the hands supplicating, the whole figure contorted and maimed yet overpoweringly alive. To one side, the blasted stump of a tree completes the image of life desecrated. The torso itself has been riven in the middle, as if by an explosion, and that opening translates with almost unbearable poignancy the agony of Rotterdam. This is an image as terrible, in its immediacy, as Picasso's "Guernica," yet conceived with a power that promises the resurrection Rotterdam has experienced. Sculpture with such a weight of emotion and meaning cannot be received lightly as just another titillating horror, like a gruesome murder tale. The moment that Zadkine's figure recalls is not to be encountered thoughtlessly or remembered frequently, as if it were the sculptured equivalent of background music. Hence the setting of the monument deserves special commendation; though business buildings surround the plaza, a wide thoroughfare and a stretch of verdure insulate it, so that really to see the monument one must go a little out of one's way and visit it on foot. Beyond it, in the port, the uplifted arms of the loading cranes underscore and carry through, with subtle congruence, the pattern of the uplifted arms of Zadkine's Rotterdam.

Zadkine's earliest sculptures, in which the influence of Brancusi was often visible, were locked within the wood or stone he used; his archaic, proto-Cubist images were often no less warped in shape than this Rotterdam memorial, but the warping was to fit the material form of the medium. In this figure of the destroyed city, the liberation—and the disruption—of the form does not spring from such an external condition; it arises directly out of the subjective contents. Here one aspect of modern art has come to a climax—that which dredges into the brutal images of the unconscious, which deliberately confronts the "existential nausea" of our time, which attempts to give formal expression to the frightfulness that made the destruction of Rotterdam an actuality and now makes the destruction of mankind in a nuclear holocaust a possibility. It is a tribute to the courage and sanity of Rotterdam that it has dared to face these realities and has given Zadkine's sculpture the dramatic setting it deserves. That spirit links this work to the Cave Ardeatine and sets it off from all the blander sepulchres and memorials that flinch, like television sponsors, from any allusion to mankind's perilous state.

At the opposite pole is the work of another contemporary, of the same age and originally, too, from Russia—the new monument in Rotterdam by Naum Gabo, the surviving leader and almost solitary exponent of the Constructivists. This abstraction, which dominates the midtown thoroughfare called the Coolsingel, has Marcel Breuer's new flat-façaded, five-story Beehive department store as a neutral background, and is very nearly as tall as the store itself. In this creation, another aspect of the modern movement in art has come to a magnificent consummation. Gabo's work was called into existence, inadvertently, by Dr. Cornelius van Traa, the man in charge of the replanning of bombed-out Rotterdam. His scheme called for a widening of the Coolsingel, and accordingly the new Beehive was set back on the new building line. One of the few survivors of the bombing, however, is the old Atlanta Hotel, which occupies the next corner on the Coolsingel and juts out beyond the new building line. To counterbalance this brick mass, Dr. van Traa suggested another bay, projecting thirteen feet from the far end of the department store. Having no need for extra space (having, in fact, designed the store as a four-square box), the architect decided to meet Dr. van Traa halfway by calling in Gabo to produce an abstract monument that would serve the purpose of interrupting, if only partly and diaphanously, the long vista. So the town planner at last agreed to a freestanding vertical construction, of parabolic steel ribs, as unlike the design of the store as a flower is unlike a beehive. The building of this huge abstraction was a challenge to the sculptor's technical insight and to Dutch engineering skill. Most of Gabo's constructions are small and delicate fabrications of exquisite craftsmanship and originality of form, in glass, plastics, and metal, but this monument is over eighty feet high, and it had to be executed in a shipyard, for the whole mass of metal weighs forty-three tons. Who can describe a purely abstract figure, especially when, as Gabo explains,

"This sculpture is the form of itself"? In a desire to characterize this abstract form, to pin it down to some analogous
object, it has been nicknamed The Flower, The Banana, The
Gold Tower, and, perhaps in resignation, The Thing. Some
have even read into it the suggestion of a pair of upended
oar blades, and have seen in the black interior figure, in
the cage formed by the shafts, a ship's anchor. But what is
true of the Cave Ardeatine is true of this work—no photograph, no static view, no single word can do justice to such
a complex form. This lithe figure is composed of two pairs
of curving metal shafts, coated with gloden bronze, rising
out of two bases of concrete sheathed with black granite.
But the curve begins most subtly, not at the visible base
but as if it started a considerable distance below, the visible
and the invisible portions suggesting the shaft of a flattened
S curve. At the top, the shafts, instead of coming together all
too obviously in a point, end, before they have reached the
climax of the inward curve, in a horizontal metal network,
interlacing like the bottom strings of a tennis racket and
capped by a flat top that carries out the flat line of the Beehive's roof.

The putting together of this fabric demanded more than
usual mechanical intelligence and ingenuity. The scale of this
structure required calculations of stresses and strains that
play no part in any small-size model—all the more because
the unbuttressed form had to be capable of surviving high
winds and the weight of ice, to say nothing of the expansion
and contraction of metals with changes of temperature. The
work was constructed on its side, so to judge the engineer's
success in laying out the curving members, the artist had
to be hoisted by derrick a hundred feet in the air to gain
an over-all view of the work in progress. There are thousands of years of technical experience behind the casting of
big bronze figures, but the only process that compares to the
building of Gabo's sculpture is the building of an airplane.

The artist's shaping of this image was comparable to
Michelangelo's painting the Sistine Chapel lying on his back.
In fact, Gabo's presence was needed at every stage of the
work; during the finishing of the great ribs, he actually held
the arm of the workman who manipulated the polishing machine, to make sure that the surface was neither too rough
nor too smooth. Disaster hovered over this project throughout
its execution; until it was finally set in its concrete base, a

mistaken command might have caused a crash that would have undone a year's work. Even the transportation of the statue was a chancy business—by barge from the shipyard to the dock at Rotterdam, then by trucks (one of which started to buckle under the weight) to the site, where at first the derrick provided proved too feeble to raise the prostrate form. When the monument was moved through the streets of Rotterdam, many of the trolley wires had to be taken down at the intersecting streets. On the second night of its journey, two thousand people accompanied it through the cold, windy May night till five in the morning, when the job was over. Not since the high days of the Renaissance, as far as I can recall, has a new work of art drawn forth so much public interest. The Dutch architect Henric Wijdeveld gave me a memorable picture of the procession, headed by Gabo, dizzy with anxiety and elation, dancing in front of his construction almost as David danced before the Ark, sure at last, after repeated inspection, that the men in the shipyard had captured his subtle curves. As a constructive achievement, as a symbol, and as a pure esthetic form, this noble and beautiful image is in a class by itself—peace to those who flinch from these unfashionable words!—proclaiming the dominance of the human spirit, through technology, over the forces that would cripple man and even nullify his technology. The size of this monument, feasible only because of our technical resources, is one of the reasons for its esthetic success; that is, it is now possible to do what only those with Gabo's own special imagination could accomplish when viewing his smaller works of art—penetrate within the space he creates and behold the form from the inside, looking outward and upward, as one inspects a work of architecture.

This sculpture is the fulfillment of a lifetime dedicated to Constructivism—a life unshaken by the more popular fashions of Expressionism, Archaicism, Surrealism, Brutalism, and Disintegrationism, but bent on creating truly human symbols for the form-creating processes of modern science and industry. And the main success of Gabo's new work is not in its exhibition of technical virtuosity, for that is more than counterweighted by the seemingly effortless perfection of the image. Though it has not a single moving part, if one excepts the vibrating lacework of springs that holds the vertical elements in tension as the metal expands and contracts, the whole structure seems in constant motion as one walks toward it and around it, and it undergoes further changes as the light in the sky dims or brightens. Even at a distance every aspect registers.

If the common man often calls Gabo's monumental figure The Thing, the shipyard workers referred to it, perhaps ironically, perhaps affectionately, as The Flower. Though there is no hint of a plant in this structure, the instinct that associates it with organic forms capable of life, growth, and movement is not an unsound one, for life and movement are exactly what this monument has. An eminent British art critic has compared it to an Egyptian pyramid, but that geometric mountain, the very image of immobility and static repose, of dead matter protecting a dead body, is emphatically what this sculpture is not. The unique quality of Gabo's art is that it is literally inconceivable in any culture but our own. If that keeps it within certain limitations, it also releases precisely those dynamic features that have hitherto been creatively used only for practical purposes.

In The Flower, what is positive, healthy, organically creative, confidently in command of our new energies and eager to plumb new potentialities, has come together in an original design. What we have achieved through mathematical calculation, the physical sciences, the skills and audacities of engineering has here become a visible structure, under the sway of a formative human purpose that transcends mere utilitarian ways and means. In that high confidence, this sculpture, which "is the form of itself," is also a most fitting symbol of the city in which it stands, whose unflagging energies restored in four years most of the technical equipment the Germans destroyed. When the project was under discussion, the municipal officials took Gabo on a tour of the waterfront and proudly indicated the "abstract" utilitarian forms their technicians had already created, and his sculpture, in its own turn, has given these qualities the fullest possible expression. As Zadkine's monument recalls the panic moment of anxiety and fear, of agony and despair, so Gabo's evokes the moment of liberation, rebirth, creative potency.

The last piece of architectural sculpture I have to discuss is Sir Jacob Epstein's bronze "Virgin and Child," in London's Cavendish Square. Among Epstein's earliest works are the figures that punctuate the upper façade of the British Medical Association's building in the Strand, now Rhodesia House;

unfortunately, these examples of muted cooperation between sculptor and architect have, over the years, lost their heads, and they now suggest the victims of an iconoclastic crusade, though this decapitation took place naturally, without benefit of wartime bombing. "Virgin and Child," one of Epstein's most recent works, was done for the Convent of the Holy Child Jesus, whose buildings, flanking a street that enters the Square, are connected by a central structure that spans the street with a wide, low round arch. A neutral stone wall, set back from the façades of the other buildings and running across the arch, here provides an ideal frame for the figures. The Virgin is an upright figure, enfolding and giving, a mother of mothers; the partly swaddled Child, also upright, is sturdy, large-eyed, his legs close together, his arms outstretched to make the figure of the Cross, but transforming it from a symbol of dolor into a symbol of faith. The surface roughness of Epstein's earlier figures, modelled in clay and presenting in bronze a disconcerting exaggeration of texture, has yielded to the more reticent strength of carving. The subdued classicism of the setting is a perfect background, and by transforming a blank wall into a highly expressive one, it gives an idea of what might be done elsewhere to vivify many all too impassive and anonymous street fronts. It is significant, I believe, that this traditional work on a traditional theme in a traditional medium should have appeared at the same moment as Zadkine's and Gabo's climactic sculptures. It occupies the middle space between the lacerated subjective art of Zadkine, so characteristic of our troubled times, and the more serene objective forms, as confidently rational and experimental as science itself, but passionately humane and life-enhancing, that grow out of Gabo's illumined mind. All three approaches to form and meaning are valid. None of them can alone represent the total experience of modern man, yet each of them must be respected and absorbed if that experience is not to remain fragmentary and abortive. Eventually, perhaps in a single work of art such as Herman Melville foreshadowed in *Moby Dick,* all three may be wrought together in an organic whole.

This hope, it is true, dates the critic almost as much as it dates the sculptors under discussion, who were born in 1890 or even before—long enough ago to bring to this period of spiritual depression and disillusion some of the hope that men breathed as unconsciously before 1914 as they breathed the air. Today those most busily concerned with works of contemporary art, such as critics or museum directors, have no criterion for judging esthetic merit except newness and nihilism. In their denial of form and value, in their absorption in the incoherent, the infantile, the pathological, the prehuman, they find the only forms and values acceptable to their generation.

But the fact that these current preoccupations may be as painfully unavoidable as a neurosis does not dispose of the need for a sounder and more durable criterion of value and a saner appreciation of life's possibilities. It is too easy to absolve decadent and psychotic tendencies in modern art by identifying those who reject these tendencies with creatures like Hitler and Stalin, who once denounced every manifestation of modern art: but the childishness of this logic only brings out the weakness of the esthetic position it defends. Epstein's sculpture in Cavendish Square, if offered by an unknown name for an exhibition of contemporary sculpture, would probably be peremptorily rejected; fortunately, the nuns appear to have judged Epstein's work by a human norm that the sophisticated now deny. Even Gabo's Rotterdam monument might easily have been turned back by a cowardly museum director, not because Gabo's sculpture is insufficiently abstract but because its abstraction is too sturdily organized, too coherent, too resourcefully integrated to be countenanced as a sufficiently "modern" form. As for Zadkine's sculpture, which recalls various early Cubist experiments, to say nothing of its outward semblance to a human being, its form is now old-fashioned, too, but it might squeeze by purely on the basis of its harrowing contents, provided the allusion to an actual event or a specific occasion for human suffering were politely concealed. Yet all three sculptures have come into existence and found a place for themselves—a witness to the reserves of health and energy that still survive even within the world of art, at least among the older generation, and whether this is a dawn or a sunset, it is at least a manifestation of light in a murky world.

*1957*

# SIX

# The Marseille "Folly"

There are many reasons for going to Marseille besides inspecting Le Corbusier's first Maison de l'Unité d'Habitation and I was impelled there recently by several of them. This ancient port, founded by the Phoenicians twenty-five hundred years ago, and occupied at one time or another by the Greeks, the Romans, the Provençals, and all the races of the Levant, is a pungent bouillabaisse of a city. Today, it is the center of bold regional-planning schemes that are involved with the harnessing of the water power of the Lower Rhone and the redemption of the local swamps, or the Camargue, as rice fields—an improvement that will probably remove the primitive, picturesque folk, somewhat resembling our cowboys, who have clung for centuries to a precarious trapper's life. A bred-in-the-bone New Yorker, I have a feeling of kinship, deeper than mere liking, with seaports like Rotterdam, Genoa, and Marseille, full of scheming, energetic men, hearty eaters and drinkers, generous gamblers, who like to carry out big ideas in a big way, if they get their share of the rakeoff. Writers of guidebooks, licking their chops over the vices of Marseille, have never done justice to the natural beauties of its harbor, or to the marvellous pink stone of the old fortifications, dominated by the steep hill where the towers of Notre Dame de la Garde shoot farther upward. One sees these beauties more clearly now, and the grosser sexual displays more dimly, because the red-light quarter was razed by the Nazis. (Those efficient people, hating any criminality or perversion less loathsome than their own, cleared out twenty-four thousand inhabitants in a few hours, before going to work on the buildings.) Now this area is covered by a comely palisade of office buildings and presumably respectable municipal apartment houses, all part of a scheme of bringing order and space for public promenades into the Old Port.

The raffish vitality of Marseille may explain why this was the first place in which, after the Second World War, Le Corbusier was given a chance to carry out his ideas about urban housing. He was offered a site for a working-class project near the heart of the city, where the land was rugged, and the opportunity for using several levels of ground might well have stirred him, but he preferred a tamer suburban area, to the south of town, in a tract zoned for middle-class housing. With reluctance, I tore myself away from the great constructions of the port, about which so little has been heard, to make a pilgrimage to his Unity House, as I translate its somewhat pretentious title—Maison de l'Unité d'Habitation. Unity House is a seventeen-story apartment building in the shape of a domino set on its long edge, its axis running north and south. It embodies all the features Le Corbusier regards as essential for seemly urban living. If he left anything out, it was not because his sponsors were unwilling to pay for it. This project was broached in 1945, during the acute postwar housing shortage; it was begun in 1947; and it was opened in 1952, for it took twice as long to erect as a building of more conventional construction. Both the national Ministry of Reconstruction and the municipality of Marseille showed considerable courage in authorizing this experimental building: whatever its merits, there was nothing in the plan or the method of construction to promise that it would be a cheap one. Unity House provides quarters for sixteen hundred people, but it proved so outrageously expensive that even with a heavy subsidy it could be offered only to people in high-income groups or public officials whose apartments are part of their salary. (Must employees of the state try in the line of duty to salvage the government's errors in housing by living in them?)

All this has brought down a heavy fire from the French

critics, but had Unity House proved a notably good building, it might in the long run have easily justified the heavy first costs. So I prefer to deal with this project purely on architectural and social terms, the only terms Le Corbusier himself took into consideration. The extravagant cost could be excused on the ground that a bold gesture is sometimes necessary to restore morale after a national disaster—like a man buying his wife flowers instead of bread after being fired from his job. Since then, more than a score of other French cities have commissioned Le Corbusier to design similar buildings, thus expiating prewar timidity with postwar recklessness.

To reach Unity House, one takes a fifteen-minute ride in a tram or a taxi from the Old Port, with its open promenade, where the fishermen sell their catch of eels, squid, and sardines, and the cranes along the docks load seagoing vessels. The color of the city weakens as one leaves the central area, and the land becomes flat as the tree-lined Boulevard Michelet leads into a rather heavily wooded area surrounding little cottages and market gardens. Suddenly Unity House bulks up —a powerful slab of concrete, a man-made mountain, some four hundred and fifty feet long, sixty or seventy feet wide, and some hundred and eighty feet high, standing alone in four acres of parkland and orchard, where the older children of the community, evading the supervised playground on the roof, like to roam. This building has three hundred and thirty-seven apartments of twenty-three types, from a few domiciles for a family with eight children to simple bachelor quarters and cubicles for guests.

The most striking feature of the building is that it is raised twenty-four feet aboveground on a double row of cyclopean, wedge-shaped concrete columns, or *pilotis,* which uphold the hollow canopy of concrete that forms the basement of the building proper, a basement that contains the machinery for running the elevators and the air-conditioning plant. This exposed foundation, massive in form, positive in texture, establishes dramatically the scale and style of the whole structure, and its bold forms are repeated, with variations, in the ventilator towers on the roof.

The technical feat of lifting a building above the earth in this fashion is dear to Le Corbusier; he used it quite rationally once, in a suburban house, to straddle a cul-de-sac and disclose a view of the greenery beyond, but he has also used it without any special justification, simply as a hallmark of the modern, in the Villa Savoye, in Poissy, and in the Swiss Pavilion at the Cité Universitaire, in Paris. So closely is the method identified with him that many people fancy he invented it. Actually, pile dwellings became fashionable among the lake dwellers of Switzerland in the Neolithic period, and all over Europe medieval market halls were built in the same fashion, to provide a covered storeroom above and space continuous with the open market below. In Unity House, the cost of the handsome underpinning came to more than ten per cent of the total cost of the structure, and in his second Unity House, in Nantes, Le Corbusier prudently returned to ordinary columns, less bulky and more widely spaced.

But it is only when one draws away from this building and sees its domino form against the long, jagged rhythms of the mountains in the distance that one discovers that the façade, not merely the columns or the entrance canopy, was conceived in depth, as a piece of abstract sculpture in high relief. For Le Corbusier, this is a revolutionary about-face. During the twenties, the esthetic of Le Corbusier's buildings was formulated in terms of smooth planes of glass and stucco, or concrete, as nearly two-dimensional in effect as was possible. Their façades had the elemental order of a Mondrian painting, a rectangular arrangement of lines and planes; and they also had the happy property, very useful in publicity, of looking good in black-and-white photographs. Only on the inside of these shells was the third dimension visible, so their exaggerated external simplicity deserved Frank Lloyd Wright's gibe of "paper-box architecture."

Le Corbusier's revolutionary step in the design of Unity House was not his resurrection of Charles Fourier's century-old scheme for a self-contained phalanstery to house an ideal community: it was his rediscovery of the third dimension in architecture, the importance of texture, color, relief, light, and shade. Probably it was his experiments with the *brise-soleil*, or sun screen, which he had used on the windows of several office buildings, that turned Le Corbusier's attention to these old resources of architecture, to the play of light and shadow, to all the plastic effects achieved by means of cornices, lintels and columns, mullions and corbels, jutting balconies and recessive window reveals. These effects had been generally abandoned because modern architects were solely concerned with the forms and possibilities of the new technology.

In Unity House and his recent church at Ronchamp, Le Corbusier has embraced these age-old features of traditional building with the enthusiasm of a convert. Certainly, in Unity House it is the three-dimensional qualities of the design that strike the eye happily at every point—the *pilotis*, the flaring entrance louver, the stairs and the platforms they lead to, and the ventilators, all of which turn, under Le Corbusier's hands, into striking pieces of outdoor sculpture. Here Le Corbusier's originality is at its flamboyant best. He has used concrete for all it is worth as a sculptured form, emphasizing and even exaggerating its plastic qualities, to the extent of leaving untouched the evidences of crude, sometimes inept, workmanship. (I do not refer to his allowing the grain of the wood in the molds he used to stay imprinted on the concrete.)

From a sufficient distance, this roughness of raw concrete —"le béton brut"—is admirable. Unfortunately, Le Corbusier has not modulated the effect in places open to a nearer view, and sometimes the coarseness seems carelessness and the strength becomes brutality. Speaking at the dedication of the building, Le Corbusier suggested that these defects were like the crumbled stones in an ancient building, which one accepts as one accepts the wrinkles of an aged face—as a mark of character rather than a defect. He forgot that the wrinkles of age are not what one looks for or loves in a young child or a new building—though they were what every romantic eighteenth-century amateur sought when he erected a Gothic "folly" that faked the effects of time. At any rate, the clarity, the precision, the mechanical slickness of the machine age, all of which Le Corbusier praised so heartily in the nineteen-twenties, have been thrown to the winds.

Yet, up to a point, considered abstractly as a visual experience, the exterior of the building is a success. One reason is Le Corbusier's use of the inset balcony. Such balconies, four feet deep, flank each apartment at either end, and they are separated from it by glass walls. The outer edge of the balconies is enclosed by a concrete honeycomb that serves as a balustrade—and that removes any possibility of dizzy trepidation on the upper floors by the simple expedient of almost completely cutting off the view, even though this flatly nullifies the special virtue of a free-standing building with a magnificent outlook. Since the depth and color of shadows alter with the time of day and the intensity of the sun, the building undergoes esthetic changes that a flat façade does not, and this vitality is accentuated by Le Corbusier's use of primary colors, the Mondrian gamut of red, blue, yellow, to augment the deep shadow of the partitions separating the balconies. To judge by color slides of the building, the original effect of these colors was dazzling; unhappily, the reds and the blues have faded badly in places. Le Corbusier's other innovation in exterior design was to alternate bands of small windows on the bedroom floors with banks of large windows, two stories high, for the living-room floors. (I should explain that in a sense the larger apartments are duplexes; that is, the living rooms are two stories high, though the bedrooms are only one story high.) This not merely gives an interesting alternating rhythm to the openings but makes the building look less formidably high than it is. Another change in the horizontal pattern occurs at the market floors, the seventh and eighth, which are set back. These are marked by vertical concrete members on both sides, creating a pattern of shadows. The north end of the building is also a solid, windowless blank wall. The elevator bank, toward the middle of the building, is identified by a vertical panel, made up of a bank of four-square windows on each floor. Thus the outside of the building not only registers the interior functions but gains esthetically by their architectural expression.

However ineffective the structure may be as a living unit, it serves as an organic architectural expression in which structure and decoration, through the architect's faithfulness to his medium, are one. This is an old story in Frank Lloyd Wright's work, but a significant departure in Le Corbusier's. The only extraneous element in this composition, below the roof, is the fire stairs, on the north end, leading from the market floors, a construction imposed by the municipal code for the benefit of firemen, so that they might reach the upper floors from outside. But Le Corbusier, perhaps tongue in cheek, turned it into another essay in plastic construction, a spool of concrete unwinding downward around an equally plastic core.

Since Unity House stands alone, its setting is important to its esthetic impression, and the approach from the Boulevard Michelet, with the building partly screened by an avenue of trees, some quite old and high, which were wisely preserved, is happier than the approach from the opposite side, across a longer foreground of practically empty space. From the inside, the apartments nearest the ground, which seem almost embowered in the foliage of the trees, are pleasanter than those that have only a distant view, largely screened by the balconies. If my impression is not just a personal reaction, one of the main esthetic reasons for a high building has thus vanished. The architect who showed me Unity House and praised most of its features concurred in this judgment. One thing is sure—that the unique architectural effect of Unity House depends in vast degree upon its isolation; since its intimate features are harsh and contradictory, it is mainly at a distance that it composes into an esthetic unity. But only close at hand is there any vivid interplay between the natural setting and the structure; like the Great Pyramid, it might as well be in the midst of a desert, for all the positive use it makes of the natural environment.

One would hardly guess from the landscaping that this is a region where the peasants, to protect their fields and vineyards from the mistral, use walls of cypress trees, which give the landscape an architectural quality just as positive as Unity House itself. With such green walls, the immediate climate of a Marseille building can be tempered; without them, the outdoors lacks usefulness, on windy days, as well as beauty.

Even the external success of Unity House, then, is a partial one. Though there is a separation of the vehicular and pedestrian entrances to the structure, the very openness of this building on piles makes the parking lot to one side more conspicuous. Le Corbusier "liberated" the land from the building—to use his own romantic expression—by putting Unity House on stilts, but he forgot to liberate it from the motorcar, although, if nature was to be kept inviolate, here was surely the place to build an underground garage. This failure to dispose of the motorcar is capped by the more comical failure to dispose of the family washing. Though Le Corbusier has not hesitated to use a variety of costly technological dodges to reduce sound and provide air-conditioning, laundry is handled in the apartments themselves, with the aid of a mobile washing machine, and, lacking mechanical facilities indoors for drying clothes, the housewives hang the wash on the balconies. On my visit, I counted, on one side of the building, two dozen balconies decorated with the family wash. This somewhat mars the purity of the façade. Le Corbusier's defenders might point out that he had provided ample facilities in the midair shopping center of the building for a large commercial laundry, but that market scheme, to which two floors were devoted, is already almost a ghost city and the laundry machines, lacking a sufficient number of customers, have been taken out.

When one gets to the interior, one's praise for Le Corbusier's plastic achievements must come to an end, and since it is architecture, not sculpture, that is being considered, the value of his achievements on the outside is seriously diminished. The esthetic devices that give monumentality and color to the façade spoil the living space and obstruct the view. Only the living rooms have the qualities of living rooms; though startlingly narrow, they are visually liberated by their high (fifteen-foot) ceilings. The interior corridors that lead from the elevators are long enough to earn the title of street, though except for their lowness, which is accentuated by the use of strong colors and disconcertingly dim lights, they are like any corridor in any apartment house. Here again Le Corbusier has effected a complete reversal of his early esthetic principles by stressing gloom and innerness instead of light and exposure—a departure he has carried a step further in a more appropriate structure, his church at Ronchamp. A long public corridor is the last place in which one should encounter the eerie and the mysterious. Even if one honors Le Corbusier's personal discovery of the value of contrast between extrovert and introvert forms, between the outer and the inner, one can hardly condone its application to a corridor. Architects who follow the letter of Le Corbusier's message here merely by reducing the illumination in public halls will miss the general meaning of this discovery.

The corridors occur only at every second or third floor; this speeds elevator service by cutting the number of stops—an important improvement in high buildings, where waiting for the elevator during a rush hour can become an ordeal. To fit his apartments in with a minimum of space for corridors, Le Corbusier wisely utilized the type of apartment the English call the maisonette, with a narrow private stairs to connect the upper and lower rooms. His one-story bedroom floors run the full width of the building; the two-story living rooms abut on the corridor, and thus are not as long. But while the bedrooms of one apartment occupy the floor above the living room, those of its neighbor opposite occupy the floor below. There are variations on this general plan, to accommodate smaller or larger families. One, which gives access to the apartment by way of the parents' bedroom, is particularly unfortunate.

Yet Le Corbusier's aim, to achieve the greatest flexibility of accommodation, was a sound one. In general, maisonettes in shallow buildings, only two rooms deep, are a positive improvement over the single-floor apartment; hence four- and six-story maisonette buildings have been increasingly adopted by the London County Council in its projects. To lessen the cost of his singular construction, Le Corbusier made Unity House deep, not shallow. Instead of planning to produce the best possible layout for the apartments, he chose the worst possible plan for an apartment in order to squeeze it into his elaborate and costly domino structure. As one admirer of his work put it, the "cellular flats are inserted into the structural frame, rather like the drawers in a filing cabinet, or, to use Le Corbusier's own analogy, *'un casier à bouteilles.'* " As a result, his bedroom floors are sixty-six feet long and thirteen feet wide.

This plan and these dimensions are a reversion to the old New York brownstone, whose owners, stingy with land and greedy for internal space, began building additions in the back yard. But the New York rooms were more generous, with a width of sixteen to eighteen feet, and even the most wretched hall bedroom was more than six feet wide, the width of all Le Corbusier's bedrooms except the parents'. Naturally, the innermost area of Le Corbusier's apartments, roughly a third of their floor space, lacks daylight, view, or direct air. Except for the living rooms, whose ceilings are fifteen feet, the rooms are not only narrow but oppressively low (seven feet). The only escape from this constriction is provided in the children's bedrooms, where one may draw back the thin partition that separates a pair of them, on the theory that even the tenuous privacy of a partition is not needed by day.

All the service areas of the apartments in the building have artificial lighting and artificial ventilation; even the kitchens, which open on the living rooms, need such aids. In the larger apartments, the parents' bedroom has little privacy when anyone occupies the living room, for the bedroom, which is on a mezzanine overlooking the living room, cannot be shut off from the sounds or smells from below. This is worse than an inconvenience if one person should want to read or sleep while others are making music or talking; it is intolerable if a parent is ill. In short, this plan, in its arbitrary dimensions, its lack of privacy, its failure to make the most of its open exposure, is a perfect exhibition of the Procrustean state of mind that has begun to dominate modern architecture. Like the Old Greek innkeeper who chopped off his guests' legs or stretched their frames to fit his beds, the architect of Unity House seeks with violence to accommodate human beings to the inflexible dimensions of his monumental edifice. Nor is the economic cost taken into account; the good features of this building could have been incorporated at a far lower cost in an apartment house a third as high.

Superficially a modern building because of its gigantic size, its concrete structure, and its supposed inclusiveness, Unity House turns out to be no better and no worse than a thousand similar dwellings that the well-to-do built for themselves half a century ago between Fifth Avenue and Lexington. With the audacity of genius, Le Corbusier has succeeded in nullifying almost every advantage he started out with. For here, on an open site, a free-standing building is designed as if a minimum of land were available, as if the building had no view worth bothering with, as if the sun and the air and the outlook could be excluded from a third of the living space without loss. Only those who are willing to sacrifice the internal contents of architecture to the external impression, who are ready to deform life, in order, as Emerson said, to create a death which they call art, can regard Unity House as a model to be praised and copied. But this building is now being imitated widely, both in academic exercises in architectural schools and in actual practice, which says even more about the capacities of our professional mentors than it does about Le Corbusier's magnetic talents.

The case against accepting the living quarters of Unity House as a decisive achievement in modern form is so strong that I hesitate to darken the picture by discussing its shopping center. I do so because of Le Corbusier's belief that he had created a unique sort of dwelling, a compact solution for the whole problem of urbanism, a modern version of that Fourierist phalanstery, isolated and self-contained, whose occupants need not leave the building in order to play, to exercise, to go to school, to visit their doctor or their dentist, or to market. Since playrooms, nurseries, doctors' offices, and even community halls have long been available in such buildings, the only new feature was the midair shopping center. Its failure was inevitable; Le Corbusier overlooked the fact that a population three times the size of Unity House's was needed to support the shops and services he made room for. The shopping center is now, five years after the opening of the building, an abomination of desolation; the unfinished concrete corridors, with their many unoccupied shops, have the sinister emptiness of a Piranesi etching. The chief surviving one is the kind of general store one finds in any village in America. In short, almost two whole floors were sacrificed to an architectural whimsey.

Why Le Corbusier should have regarded this insulated village existence as a contribution to modern living I could not even guess if I did not remember that this was one of my own first adolescent fantasies about improving life in New York. When Ebenezer Howard, whose intuitions in planning were sounder than Le Corbusier's, described a reasonably self-contained modern community, he set the population at thirty-two thousand, twenty times that of Unity House. Le Corbusier's disciples cannot perhaps yet admit that the whole concept of a self-contained skyscraper is an anachronism, but Le Corbusier himself, in his second Maison d'Unité d'Habitation, in Nantes, has at least put the shops at ground level instead of in a less accessible position, a revision that speaks for itself.

What remains of the Unity House idea of a highly organized social unit under one roof is a charming collection of facilities on the roof—play space, a wading pool, a gymnasium, a nursery school, and a backdrop for an open-air theatre—all happily open to the sky, though cut off visually, except for a platform or two, from the surrounding landscape. We have, then, not a better kind of apartment house but a hollow monument, whose best features are apparent only to an outsider, from a distance. And if there were a dozen Unity Houses in a row, standing in the midst of similar tracts of land, even the good features would lose their charm. Consider the new Roehampton Estate, a housing project near Richmond Park, in London, where a phalanx of such phalan-

steries is now marching down a hillside: a multifold mistake,
abjectly imitating a monumental failure.

How is it, then, that Unity House has been so widely accepted and imitated? I don't think there is a satisfactory answer on the basis of merit. To judge by the rash of slab
buildings all over Europe, the irrational and the extravagant,
the morbidly monumental and the empty formalistic are more
in keeping with the tone and temper of this age than buildings that are conceived in humane and sensible terms. Architecture is thus in the same state as literature or painting—
or politics or motorcars. The vices of Unity House have become the virtues of the new monumental package designers,
whose aim is to dazzle the spectator, to publicize the artist, and to sell the product. Their formal shells are most effective when they are most empty. Publicity slogans take the
place of performance.

Many people, including municipal officials, imagine that
Le Corbusier has contributed a startling and decisive solution
of the housing problem and of the whole business of urban
planning. His manifest talents as an artist have seduced them
into overlooking his naïveté as a sociologist and planner. His
main claim to be an innovator in urban planning rests on
his belief that he has found a way to achieve a density of as
much as four hundred people an acre, which is a characteristic of slums, without any cramping or neglect of human needs.
He believes he achieves this by building into the air and so
"liberating" ground that would normally be covered with
buildings. But the space Le Corbusier so releases is visual
open space, not functional open space, which is the space
human beings need for living in.

To provide proper open space for promenades, for gardens,
for adult games and children's playgrounds, one needs a
minimum of an acre of space for every hundred people, which
means that Unity House should have at least sixteen acres of
open space, not the eight acres that the municipality has provided. In short, Le Corbusier's claim to have solved the
problem of urban overcrowding by an architectural stunt is
absurd. Le Corbusier likes to compare the virtues of Unity
House with the failings of a cluttered, one-story, low-income
housing development, with its minimal gardens, its fungoid
bungalows, its excessive roads, but he overlooks Unity
House's serious rivals. By now, all over the world, there are

many examples of good neighborhood planning, with small houses and apartments and with all the conveniences that Le Corbusier has so expensively provided for, at a density of from forty to a hundred people an acre, in surroundings much richer in human amenities.

One of these developments, almost thirty years old, is in Neubühl, a suburb of Zurich. It was the work of a group of architects, two of them now known internationally—Werner Moser and Alfred Roth. After visiting Unity House, I made a point of revisiting Neubühl, which I hadn't seen since 1932. It had dazzled me then, and even on a rainy afternoon it dazzled me again. Instead of its showing signs of decay, there were only signs of improvement. The buildings are ranged in parallel rows at right angles to the access roads and the shores of the Lake of Zurich, and their roofs form a series of steps down a slope; they consist of single-family houses, bachelors' studios, and three-story apartment buildings. At one corner of the estate, there is a group of shops and a bakery, all (unlike the Unity House center) still in operation, but there is no pretense that this small community is or should be self-contained. One reaches the houses by a path on the kitchen side; on the other side is a mass of shrubbery, trees, flower beds, and terraces, a rich texture of ordered green that contrasts with the mostly uncultivated openness about the Marseille skyscraper. These gardens form a completely private and yet altogether open living area, which no one in his senses would trade for a Le Corbusier balcony, thirteen feet by four—all the more because the Neubühl planners provided an unobstructed view of the lake, too, from the second story of the one-family houses.

Within the houses, there is no dark interior space, no narrowness, no lack of privacy in bedrooms, no flimsy partitions, no odd placing of furniture to fit constricted rooms; even the bathroom is open to the sun and provides a view—not the smallest of blessings for starting the day. The only visible improvement the tenants have made on the architects' design is to hang matting, for privacy, over the wire network that surrounds the balconies, which, by the way, are completely open to the sun, not recessed. In what Henry Wright, Sr., used to call the "quality of space," this modest architectural development is a dashing success, while the Marseille slab is a many-dimensioned failure.

So basic is the straightforward design of Neubühl, with its

rich and varied interplay of garden and distant view against
the simple planes of the buildings, that it makes mock of Le
Corbusier's massive efforts to acquire an equivalent esthetic
richness by architectural manipulation alone. To achieve their
beautiful communal form, the architects of Neubühl sacrificed nothing. But in designing Unity House, Le Corbusier betrayed the human contents to produce a monumental esthetic
effect. The result is an egocentric extravagance, as imposing as an Egyptian pyramid, which was meant to give im-
mortality to a corpse, and—humanly speaking—as desolate.
I am again reminded that in the eighteenth century, the
English coined a word for such buildings. They called them
"follies."

*1957*

## SEVEN

# Unesco House: Out, Damned Cliché!

More than three decades ago, Le Corbusier won an international competition for the Palace of the League of Nations. But official opinion was then so frightened of modern architecture that his design was turned down in favor of a more conventional one, which embodied neither the achievements of the past nor the promise of the future. Today, in the heart of Paris, Le Corbusier, in the person of his colleagues and disciples, has achieved belated recognition in the design of Unesco House, the new group of three Unesco buildings fronting on the Place de Fontenoy.

By an ironic slip of history, these buildings have received the official stamp of approval at the moment that Le Corbusier is moving at right angles to the direction he was taking in the twenties. Both his belated triumph and his sudden regression indicate that the modern movement has reached a critical point in its development. Contemporary architecture, mirroring the state of the world itself, is in a state of irresolution and division. One wing, headed by Mies van der Rohe, builds air-conditioned Ice Palaces for virginal Snow Queens; another, headed by Le Corbusier, constructs romantic grottoes where the Tristans and Isoldes of our age may quaff not love potions but nuclear poisons in murky solitude; a third, led by a living American architect who shall be nameless, fabricates visibly acrobatic tents for disabled circus performers.

In view of all the errors committed in designing the United Nations buildings in New York, one hoped that this new headquarters for the educational, scientific, and cultural activities of the U.N. would be full of redeeming features. The designing of the Paris Unesco buildings seemed a providential opportunity for the modern movement to pause and sort out its gains and reckon with its failures—a time to regroup its forces, bring up its baggage train, restore discipline, and tear off all the tattered shoulder patches that had once served for identification and recognition. The moment had come, in short, for the modern architectural leaders, no longer a group of hot rebels, to accept the responsibilities of government.

Was not the time ripe for such a judicious reconsideration? The thirty-year campaign for an architecture based on contemporary technology and interpreted by wholly contemporary designs had resulted in an easy and apparently complete victory. This came not so much through the unqualified merits of the new as through the defects of the old, especially the palpable irrelevance of Gothic, Classic, and Renaissance forms to the daily needs of our age. Under pressure from their students and their prospective clients alike, the architectural schools all over the world had abandoned the old, imitative routines and thrown the past out the window. What opposition now exists to an architecture grounded in contemporary needs comes almost entirely from within—from the New Brutalists of Detroit, Chicago, and London, with their faked mechanical forms and their indifference to human responses; from the Neo-Libertarians of Milan and Rio, who go in massively for whimsey and mistake it for liberty; and from the Old Guard moderns themselves (still confident that they are "avant-garde"), who faithfully repeat the well-tried errors of a generation ago without realizing that they are no longer forgivable as experiments or necessary as identifying trademarks. The slickest opposition to sound contemporary expression comes, though, from the modish little coteries whose leaders, "exterior decorators" rather than architects, like their Parisian colleagues in *la haute couture*, strive desperately to bring out a new "sensation" each season.

Perhaps no one architect, though, is strong enough to restore order and give the younger generation a fresh sense of their destination, as Louis Sullivan and Frank Lloyd Wright did in the eighteen-nineties, as Walter Gropius and Le Corbusier did in the nineteen-twenties. And it would be perilous to rely upon any dominating personality, since it is partly because of the overblown egos of the onetime leaders, too vain to acknowledge their palpable mistakes, that the movement is in such a confused state. Careless plans, tricky elevations, technological exhibitionism, wasteful gadgetry, and deplorable craftsmanship have all paraded as marks of originality —as if it were not far easier to be original and bad than original and good. But the three men who designed these Unesco buildings gave one at least some reason to hope for something better. By now, it could be expected that their collaboration would cancel out the weaknesses of modern architecture and establish the continuity and integrity of modern form by continuing to widen its base. This meant moving from new materials and structural forms to an architecture capable of embodying the historic, the organic, the persistently human. Their mission now, surely, was not to embalm unsuccessful modern forms but to continue to develop all that was functionally sound and to restore in contemporary garb much that had been too hastily and dogmatically thrown out.

Of these three men, Marcel Breuer, originally a Hungarian, began his career in the Bauhaus, but never sluggishly settled down into a formula; Bernard Zehrfuss, a Frenchman, must—if I may judge from his monumental concrete shell, the huge new exhibition hall in Neuilly— be classed as a New Brutalist; and Pier Luigi Nervi, an Italian, is easily the dean of architectural engineers throughout the world, a daring experimenter with concrete shells who retains an essentially classic sense of form that would have delighted his distinguished French predecessor Auguste Perret.

Behind these men stood a panel of eminent architects who approved their plans—Gropius, Lucio Costa, Sven Markelius, and Ernesto Rogers. Here was the team, and here the kind of building, that could have undertaken the revision of stale formulas and the elimination of sterile clichés—changes that were both long overdue. Where but in serving Unesco would one find such a challenge to accept the new task of our time—that of selection and assimilation, after a grand century of experiment? Who could have picked a more likely team of architects or hoped for a better opportunity? Both the purposes of Unesco and the

ample site seemed to encourage a fresh attack on old problems. But the need did not create the desirable response. The
opportunity that the Unesco buildings and the ample site
offered has been largely muffed; it is only by comparison
with buildings of such elephantine mediocrity as the new
School of Medicine, in the Rue des Saints-Pères, that Unesco
House seems a group of worthy modern buildings.

Yet the failure is an instructive one. Perhaps all the mistakes of the modern movement had, for once, to be patient-
ly assembled in one set of buildings to be recognized for
what they are. The result is a Museum of the Antiquities of
Modern Art and Architecture. In this museum, the scholarly
curators have, as if for historical completeness, preserved with
exquisite zeal the mediocre, and the bad, as well as the
excellent, and have placed them all on view at once. As one
would expect of such resourceful artists, there are not a few
admirable features, but there are also many specimens, still
glittering with alleged newness, that should long ago have
been consigned to the rubbish heap of architectural failures.
Of those particular souvenirs of the modern movement, one
may use Chaucer's words: "There's nought so deadde as a
deadde love."

The three Unesco buildings occupy a large, rather irregular
block of seven and a half acres in a still comely district on
the Left Bank, directly across the Place de Fontenoy from
the great École Militaire. The long semicircular front of the
Secretariat Building, which in ground plan is a huge Y, flanks
half of the Place de Fontenoy, a semicircular open space
designed by Jacques-Ange Gabriel in the eighteenth century.
The remaining half of the Place, which, unlike the Unesco
block, is intersected by an avenue, is occupied by ponderous
government offices (the Ministry of the Merchant Marine and
the Ministry of Labor and Social Security) of uniform
height.

When the general plan for this part of Paris was conceived,
the avenue was still the unit of design, and the block was a
continuous wall of houses, by law uniform in height and
appearance, though on occasion, as in the case of the École
Militaire, precise ranks of trees might replace the wall of
buildings, presenting a uniform leafy green façade that under-
lined the rectangular order of the buildings. This geometric
severity and formal symmetry have characterized all the new

quarters of the inner city since the seventeenth century, and the lesser buildings form a modest pedestal for the important public ones, whose domes and towers alone dominate the sky line.

To keep within that order without embarrassing the special needs and functions of our own time offers a difficult problem. But I think that the Unesco architects would have done better for their clients if they had accepted that challenge and translated into adequate modern terms the conditions the municipality laid down. Instead, they have turned the original concept of subordinating routine structures to socially significant ones upside down; they have made the characterless office building, the Secretariat, conspicuous and have converted the deservedly conspicuous public building, the Conference Hall, into a background figure. In making this choice, they have deserted the past without contributing a more valid form to the future.

The biggest Unesco building, the Secretariat, is the southern terminus of what one might call the "modern axis" of Paris, which runs at right angles to the grand axis from the Louvre to the Arc de Triomphe. This new axis begins across the Seine, on the Right Bank, at the Palais de Chaillot, and has for its focal point that audacious steel obelisk the Eiffel Tower. The Palais de Chaillot, in a sort of castrated classic that was still officially acceptable in the thirties, is now, ironically, a museum of modern art, whose collections were once more happily shown in the old Palais du Luxembourg. Already its architecture, looking far more seedy and moldy than the honest classic of the seventeenth century, casts a premonitory shadow that suggests what the Unesco buildings may look like a generation hence.

From the seventh, and top, floor of the Secretariat, this axis is as clear and elegant as it would be in a Beaux-Arts drawing, though only someone who can pass through walls and walk on water could follow it on foot. In compliance with a now obsolete eighteenth-century formalism, the main façade of the Secretariat—the two prongs of the Y, which curve to form an arc—follows the curve of the Place de Fontenoy. This building contains no less than seven hundred offices. The stem of the Y extends deep into the Unesco site, and near the end of it a passageway turns abruptly southwest, almost at right angles, to join the Secretariat with the Conference Building, which in ground plan suggests a keystone. Off to the east end of the site is the third, and by far the smallest, of the three edifices, the Delegations Building, which is a perfect square in ground plan and which stands by itself. The point at which the three wings of the Y-shaped Secretariat meet forms the principal entrance, on the Place de Fontenoy side.

This scheme neither conforms to the old block pattern of Paris nor establishes a better order based on free-standing buildings; rather, it has the effect of turning the site into an esthetic void, filled chiefly with unrelated, if physically connected, structures and scattered objects of art, which are disposed almost at random about the open spaces. Visually, the curving glass façades of the Secretariat hog the show and spoil the possibilities of the rest of the site. They demand attention without evoking admiration. Most of the open space corresponds to the scraps left by a cookie cutter when the cookies are lifted out. Strangely, the only parts of this complex that are properly related and subordinated are the series of car parks. Instead of providing one large area, the designers have intelligently distributed the automobiles in three smaller zones. This is in happy contrast to the usual sprawling Sahara of parked cars one finds in our own country.

Such an over-all layout would be successful only if the main building overwhelmingly captured and captivated the eye. But since the one structure that might have achieved this, the Conference Building, is hidden away in a corner, the whole scheme must stand or fall on the success of the Secretariat. That structure lacks the lordly emphasis of height that makes a few other office buildings—such as the Daily News Building and the Seagram Tower—effective, and, likewise, the sculptural form and the rich texture that made some of the earliest office buildings, like the Monadnock and the Schiller Buildings, in Chicago, and the Wainwright Building, in St. Louis, so handsome and effective. Instead, it is a repetitive void of glass, outlined in concrete and aluminum frames.

In a structure as small as the Delegations Building, the repetitive anonymity of the Secretariat's office façades can be accepted, all the more because the trees and open spaces supply what the design does not. But the unbroken sweep of the Secretariat provides no interesting play of light and shade, no change of form, no modulation except what is offered by the *brise-soleils* or by the accidental changes of surface produced by its raised or lowered Venetian blinds. The result constitutes a sad if wholly unconscious caricature of the bureaucratic process.

By what blind compulsion did the architects of these buildings, and their client, the United Nations, repeat, with lamentable faithfulness, the basic error of the U.N. complex in New York—the mistake of letting the office building dominate the whole composition and virtually conceal the Conference Building? Perhaps our era of paperwork and processing, of manifolding and rubber-stamping and filing, constrains even the liveliest of creative minds from considering any departures from standard administrative practice. The Secretariat carries into architecture the fatal limitations of the bureaucratic mind. If architecture is essentially the creation of space, as Bruno Zevi has eloquently pleaded in his recent book on this theme, then plainly the designers of the Unesco complex were uninterested in architecture, for, except in their treatment of the parking lots, they muffed all the many opportunities presented them to give spatial order and unity to this whole composition.

What the artists have triumphantly done is to assemble in one group of structures all the clichés of not only the last thirty years but the last century. Here we have the metal skeleton and glass wall (Paxton, 1851), the all-glass office building (Reliance Building, Chicago, 1891, and Mies van der Rohe, 1922), the *bâtiment en pilotis* (Le Corbusier's Swiss Pavilion and Maison de l'Unité d'Habitation), the *brise-soleil* (Le Corbusier and Niemeyer, Brazil, 1935). But in their totality they add up to zero, somewhat like the Stuttgart Exhibition Siedlung of the twenties, for the art of site planning and architectural composition, which alone could have brought them to life, seems wholly lacking. As experiments, all these new forms originally were admirable, for they enlarged the working vocabulary of the modern architect and opened possibilities that had hardly existed in a purely masonry architecture. The only thing wrong with automatically repeating these forms today is that they are no longer experiments. Some of them have failed and should be discarded; others must be used circumspectly, with a scrupulous attention to human requirements, never for the sake of merely *looking* "modern." These forms were conceived in terms of function, but they have now been reduced to tricks of decoration, or to symbolism without functional justification.

The most glaring misapplication of modern technical facilities is the indiscriminate use in the Secretariat of the all-glass wall. Except under the strictest discipline, this wall has proved to be an architectural nonentity, often an aberration, and it would have been relegated to a minor place long ago if architects had not foolishly clung to it as an easily identifiable emblem of progressive form. Unfortunately, practical men of affairs have sanctioned this hothouse mode of construction, functional only for forcing plants, because—alas! —glass is cheap, and a glass wall, if first costs alone are considered, is the simplest if not the least expensive way of sheathing a building sufficiently to make it seem habitable. This initial facility takes no account of later bills for heating and cooling, for cleaning and lighting, for extra insulation. As for habitability, only the north façade of a building can tolerate a maximum area of glass, as Breuer himself so adroitly used it in the offices of the Beehive department store, in Rotterdam. Even then, an excess of glass must be paid for in higher heating bills in the winter. But full exposure indoors to the sun, even in the latitude of Paris, comes under the head of cruel and unusual punishment. If one wants to keep cool in summer behind a yawning area of glass, one must forfeit the virtues of a window, including the pleasure of opening it and seeing through it; if one wants light, one must forfeit most of the virtues of a wall— privacy, seclusion, contrast, and comfort. Walls that are windows and windows that are walls cannot fulfill one function without spoiling the other. The careful disregard of this simple theorem has become almost the equivalent of a diploma in modern design.

Curiously, the architects of the Secretariat had at least a glimmer of this antipathetic relationship, for they provided sliding glass panels in the windows, which permit the air to flow freely and the full sunlight and its bacteria-killing ultraviolet rays to enter. (Glass obstructs these rays.) Not only that, but they erected vertical fins and horizontal overhangs —doing duty for the old-fashioned cornice—that extend beyond the glass walls and break the force of the sun when it becomes too hot. Beyond these buffers they hung horizontal bands, perhaps three feet high, composed of a new kind of glass that is supposed to diminish the heat rays and yet permit ultraviolet rays to pass through. In other words, the building boasts sunglasses, which have the sort of blackish

tint you might give a glass of water by adding a spoonful
of ink. Unhappily, they and their metal attachments give a
blurred look to the façades that face the sun. (The north side
of the building, which faces the Place de Fontenoy, naturally needs no sunshades and has windows that are set in more
conventional stone frames.)

But even these sheltering devices are insufficient in the
morning or late afternoon, when the sun is not far above
the horizon. On hot, sunny days, the offices, by all accounts,
are decidedly uncomfortable. In America, the quack remedy for this mode of planning would be a costly system of
air-conditioning backed up by Venetian blinds. But in the Secretariat only the rooms at ground level and in the basement
are air-conditioned, so in some offices both Venetian blinds
*and* curtains have been added to ensure a modicum of
comfort. In short, the architects have had to fabricate five
coverings—two of glass, one of concrete and travertine, one
of plastic or metal slats, one of textiles—most of which need
to be cleaned frequently. What is worse, this tortuous scheme
has esthetic shortcomings as well as practical defects. Apart
from their fussy structural appendages, the ceiling-to-floor
windows reveal, to the viewer outside, the usual litter of any
office—the wastebaskets, the portfolios, the legs of the tables
and of the stenographers. Glass below the level of a table
serves no purpose as a medium for natural illumination,
unless Unesco officials, like little boys with the comics, like
to lie on the floor to read their reports. By clinging to the
now badly cracked cliché of the all-glass wall, the architects have come no further along than the Victorian parlor,
with its multiplicity of architectural petticoats—shutters, lace
curtains, shades, and drapes. The technical means of com-
pounding these errors are as contemporary as nuclear weap-
ons, but the result itself is empty of either practical or
esthetic justification. Such purposeless architecture is perhaps
a fitting prelude for even more purposeless collective extermination.

For seasonal changes and daily use, traditional masonry
buildings are often superior to glassed-in enclosures. This
perhaps explains why not a few modern architects coyly prefer to live in old-fashioned buildings instead of the ones
they delight to foist on their clients. Despite these patent
disadvantages, buildings of steel and aluminum using a maximum amount of glass sheathing, easy to prefabricate, to

build quickly, to tear down precipitately, have become the hallmarks of modern form, in Paris, Geneva, Genoa, and Athens, in Chicago, Caracas, and Mexico City, and these ill-conceived structures vie with the automobile in making life in cities disagreeable, inefficient, and oppressive.

Glass is the one material that the modern mind has not apparently seen through. Hence the architecture of our times dangles dangerously between two contradictory extremes—the hothouse of glass and the windowless cave of concrete: the first fit only for growing plants, the second only to house a nuclear reactor or the cowering victims that await a nuclear holocaust. Neither is acceptable for permanent human habitation, and failure to play off one against the other in traditional fashion in the same structure results in an absence of contrast between light and shade, between innerness and outerness, between enclosure and openness, that is too often esthetically deadly. The resulting flatness and dullness then incite the architect to meaningless caprice, as a host might seek to save a dull party by practicing parlor magic or standing on his head.

In short, the freedom to use new constructional methods and new materials, which should give an immense range of choice to the architect, has instead produced a blind conformity to stock patterns, erected everywhere without regard for the site, the climate, the orientation, the outlook, the practical functions, or the desperate human embarrassment that results from ignoring these matters. Here, as in so many other phases of our life, we have turned a permission into a compulsion.

Among the other stale tags of once-modern modernism on exhibit in the Unesco complex are the *pilotis* that support the Secretariat. In this form of construction, the many slim vertical columns that form a steel or concrete cage give way at the ground floor to a limited number of heavy columns, which, like the strong man at the bottom in a balancing act, lift the whole structure above the ground. Le Corbusier calls the use of *pilotis* a "liberation" of buildings from the earth, and, indeed, buildings so constructed do seem, from some angles, to float in the air, confronting the viewer not with a solid wall but with glimpses, between the *pilotis*, of verdure and vistas beyond. But since the architects of the Secretariat have almost completely enclosed this "liberated" space with glass walls, the esthetic justification for using *pi-*

*lotis* does not hold. Admittedly, within the building the *pilotis* form a striking corridor, giving almost the effect in perspective of a new-fangled triumphal arch as one walks down the middle. But while these gigantic forms permit reception desks and various kinds of magazine-and-postcard stalls to be freely disposed about the ground floor, they also march into the reference library and clutter up its all too narrow quarters. It appears, then, that the principal value of *pilotis* in the Secretariat is to "liberate" space at the ends of the building to provide room for extra motorcar parking.

As for the Y plan of the building, the very fact that its curved façade fronts every point of the compass makes it forfeit the special virtue free-standing buildings might boast —that of being effectively oriented and arranged for comfort, and for easy circulation. The Y plan makes the Secretariat as hard to get one's bearings in as the Pentagon, so that, with good reason, the receptionists provide each visitor with a slip showing the layout of the whole group of buildings and the floor plan of the main building, on which the position of the room he is bound for is carefully checked. Each wing of the Secretariat has been assigned an identifying color of its own, which is repeated on a plaque beside the door of every room, but the interiors might be a little less cold and a little easier to identify if the doors, or their trim, or the walls of the corridors also bore the identifying color.

Unfortunately, the very form and size of the Secretariat have induced a uniform mass treatment of its parts, and the need for countering the atmosphere of a large-scale bureaucratic organization by interpolating small-scale units in which easy association and social intercourse can take place has been ignored. Here again the oversights and missed opportunities in the Secretariat in New York were forgotten. Take the restaurant and the cafeteria on the top floor, one of the few points at which the almost uniform window pattern is happily broken. These rooms are bright and pleasant, but they are dedicated to mass feeding (again a parallel with the Pentagon), which is perhaps why my French friends in Unesco took me to an admirable restaurant in the neighboring quarter, instead of letting me feast solely on the view from the Secretariat. My guide boasted that the cafeteria is the most modern in Europe, and this probably means that it is equipped with electric stoves, which no self-respecting chef will use, and with steam tables, to enable quantities of food to be cooked long enough ahead of time to become stale and tasteless. (That is what "modern" usually means.) But even in America there is rebellion against mass feeding, and in some of our big offices rooms have been made over—with refrigerator and stove, and sometimes radio or television—to enable the lower echelons to eat their own food under more casual and sociable conditions, at a less pressing noon-hour tempo. A score of such kitchenettes, scattered over a building as big as the Secretariat, would have released the top floor for other purposes, such as the social functions of the upper echelons or the growing demands of the library, already crowded and constricted in its present *piloti*-infested quarters downstairs. Unless the small unit and the intimate scale are respected at every turn, world organization might become another name for totalitarian automatism, which would betray all its noble hopes.

Perhaps the most unkind thing one could say about the Secretariat is that the architects, with their unrevised clichés and stereotypes, have succeeded in making it look like any other office building in any other place. They have glorified all too faithfully the bureaucratic look. The great human enterprise on which Unesco has embarked is not reflected in this structure and site layout, and receives little aid from its manner of execution.

The ultimate effect of casting about for visible abatement of the bureaucratic look would probably have been to create a more interesting façade—one with the liveliness that has been achieved, precisely by a careful regard for social relationships, in Harvard's new Quincy House. All in all, both the central concept of the Unesco building and the site plan that derives from it hardly deserve a passing mark, even after the most lenient examination. The Conference Building, on the other hand, deserves scrutiny and a large measure of commendation—all the more because it suggests, in addition to its own architectural merits, what could have been a sounder setting and a handsomer design for the whole Unesco group.

*1960*

# EIGHT

# Unesco House: The Hidden Treasure

The Secretariat, the main building of Unesco House, does not, alas, rank high as either an esthetic or a practical achievement. But, quite apart from its other shortcomings, it performs the absurd office of concealing the Conference Building, the one structure of great architectural distinction in the group of three, which has been strangely stuck away in a far corner of the site.

The two main buildings are as unrelated in conception and design as they are in placement. The Conference Building is as finely molded as a scallop shell; the Secretariat is a building almost as anomalous and transparent as a jellyfish. The Conference Building, properly conceived and placed, might have been the core of a great design, but the architects have made it a mere appendage of the Secretariat. By tying these two buildings together with a low, broad, nondescript passage, they have deprived the more interesting one of the only thing that would have enhanced its distinction—an adequate approach. Flanking this umbilical corridor is a so-called plaza —an open space that accounts for one-third of the seven and a half acres in the site. Despite a couple of unrelated free-standing walls, which conceal nothing and reveal little (except some colored tile abstractions, a Wall of the Moon and a Wall of the Sun, by Miró), a large recumbent female by Henry

87

Moore, and a rounded carpet of grass, surrounded by sand, the "plaza" is an esthetic void. The Moore sculpture is effectively cancelled out by an all too vigorous piece of abstract "sculpture" designated as an entrance canopy, though the real entrances to the buildings are in other places and the canopy has no reason for existence. No one would ever visit this area except in a guided group on an educational tour, since if he were found there alone, without credentials, he would be as open to police suspicion as a pedestrian in Los Angeles.

Even more eloquent works of art than those on display could not register here. The chief positive feature of this open area is the long, oblong car park that adjoins one façade of the Secretariat, for its walls and hedges and double rank of mustard-colored flagpoles mute the usually dreary effect of massed cars. The ultimate fate of this open area is easy to foresee. In a few years, the whole thing will become a car park. Unlike the Place Vendôme, now inundated and effaced by the automobile, it hardly deserves a better fate.

Happily, in the Conference Building itself the architects of the Unesco project have something fresh to say, and they say it boldly and on the whole successfully, if the building is considered as an independent, unrelated object. This favorable judgment, I hasten to add, does not apply to the huge Picasso mural in the main concourse, for that has the effect of an exhumed corpse, not even fit for medical dissection. This painting marks the spiritual destitution of an artist whose extraordinary gifts as a draftsman might have put him safely, after his "Guernica," among the great ones, had he not continued to cultivate a modish outer emptiness that matched the inner emptiness of our war-shattered and nihilistic generation. This mural gives me the impression of a sniggering adolescent scrawl on an inviting wall, though a critic writing a long encomium in *Civiltà delle Macchine* has reverently interpreted it as Unesco's modern version of the Sistine Chapel. But the Conference Building is nevertheless strong enough to at least counteract a spiritually mildewed Picasso, even if it cannot, by its own achievement, overcome the defects of organization and design in the whole Paris Unesco complex of buildings.

I have no information as to how the work was apportioned between the three master architects—Marcel Breuer, Bernard

Zehrfuss, and Pier Luigi Nervi—but the Conference Building bears the unmistakable imprint of Nervi, for he has been a most imaginative and daring exploiter of the new methods of thin concrete-shell construction, which have been employed in fabricating it. In form the building is so different from traditional compositions that no architectural vocabulary exists to describe it. In plan, it is rather like a keystone, with parallel ends unequal in length and two splaying sides. There is a street entrance at one side and, at the other, the wide corridor that links it to the Secretariat. The two ends of the building are the highest points, for the top dips toward the middle of the structure to form what is technically known as a butterfly roof—an old favorite of Breuer's, once used on an exhibition cottage for the Museum of Modern Art. The end walls are vertically fluted, or perhaps "accordion-pleated" would give a closer image. The fluting forms a series of narrow vertical triangles—one sitting on its base, the next one sitting on its apex, and so on. The deep bays that are created by this device afford marked contrasts of light and shadow. In these fluted walls there are no windows to diminish the sculptural quality of this concrete shell; what is more, the pattern of fluting carries through not merely from the walls to the roof, which is sheathed in bronze, but from the outside to the interior. In short, the building is all of a piece.

Here is the precise opposite of the transparent glass surfaces of the Secretariat. This molded mass brings back the play of light and dark that has almost been lost to modern architecture through its preoccupation with slick, unbroken surfaces and curtain walls. In no imitative way, this shell suggests the lid of a stone Egyptian sarcophagus, the same within and without, monolithic but not looking ponderous or oppressive. No small part of the success of this design results from the flawless handling of the concrete, which harmonizes, in both color and texture, with the travertine stone that forms the walls on the long sides, in which there are window openings. The incised horizontal lines that run across the concrete walls suggest stone without imitating it, and this final refinement reminds the observer how good concrete can be in the hands of a master builder commanding master workers.

A weak point in the shell is the street face of the building, and the weakness derives partly from the butterfly roof,

which sags with a kind of inverted emphasis precisely where
the entrance from the street should suggest the opposite
movement of elevation. The axis of the main corridor, which
is in a sense a continuation of the corridor leading from
the Secretariat, lies just a little to one side of the dip in the
roof, and this one-sidedness is further emphasized by the
fact that all the openings are there, too, while the other
side is a solid wall of travertine. A single row of massive
pylons, like the ones upon which the Secretariat rests,
runs along this axis.

The angle created by the roof increased the architects'
difficulty in finding a congruent shape for the windows, and
they did not succeed; the windows are set in heavy, clumsy
ribs, which create arbitrary rectangles of unequal size that
have no relation to the interior needs or to the odd shape
of the walls. These windows are a continuation of the glass
panel above the entrance—a panel that reaches the ceiling and thus discloses to the visitor on the outside the great
axial corridor. Unfortunately, this fine effect has been esthetically diminished by a picayune black boxlike entrance that
protrudes from the façade. This gives the building the
air of an establishment dedicated to *pompes funèbres*. The
architects have turned this lapse of taste into a grim practical joke by placing a huge black Alexander Calder mobile
in the open space a bit to the left of the doorway, where
it dominates the approach like a sentinel crane, whose wings
add a final touch of the undertaker's parlor to the coffinlike
entrance. Surely it is a sign of academic pomposity to take
the work of such an artist, charming because of its childlike
pleasure in waving arms and moving shadows, and endow it
with a serious function. A Calder mobile, as a lady I admire has observed, would be the best of companions if one
were in a hospital bed, too weak to read, too sensitive to lis-
ten to the radio; a complex mobile, hanging from the ceiling
and casting endless shadows on the walls, would be as beguil-
ing as a kaleidoscope. But in its present setting, this bit
of solemn frivolity—or frivolous solemnity—reflects upon the
intelligence and esthetic discretion of those who commissioned
it. Empty of content, unrelated to either the structure or the
purpose of the building, this mobile is another dusty period
piece (circa 1935). In their choice of non-related objects
of modern art, the designers have equalled the non-related-
ness of their buildings, and have insured the eminence of

Unesco House as a Museum of Antiquated Modernities.

The Conference Building is, in essentials, a work of organic architecture, and it therefore does not require extra effort by the interior decorator, the muralist, or the sculptor to transform it into a work of art. If it were not for the overbearing effect of the V-shaped *pilotis* along the axis, this monumental shell might have been enriched by a single piece of sculpture. Such a construction might have provided an esthetic focus for the concourse, and might even have served as a useful point of orientation for meeting, like the information booth in Grand Central. But architecture as positive as this would be weakened or actually defeated by minor works of art, as the interior of the Conference Building is weakened by Picasso's lamentably infantile mural.

Happily, the external form of this building is justified by the sober splendor of the two main conference halls, at the sides of the high and spacious axial concourse. The smaller hall, with windows on one side and a light-toned wooden panel of translators' booths on the other, is the more genial, but the big hall, which is on a windowless side of the building —it has a spectators' balcony in the rear as well as the usual desks for participators in the conference—produces, through the play of lights on the wall behind the rostrum and on the ceiling, an even more striking effect. In both rooms, the noble proportions and the severe but complex geometry of the fluted shell—there are no obstructive columns in the auditoriums—create an interior of great dignity. There are six other conference halls, of various sizes and shapes, including a circular one in the mezzanine and three in the basement, and this assortment of sizes gives a needed flexibility of accommodation for large and small groups, freed from the necessity of apparatus for simultaneous translation used in the big halls.

As for the concourse, its monumental dimensions are well justified by the need for visual change and relaxation after participation in a conference. Its very amplitude lends itself to striking architectural features, such as the overdramatized stairs that lead to a mezzanine of limited area. What is lacking in the public space—apart from one recess in the connecting corridor leading to the Secretariat—is little nooks and recesses for conversation in small groups or for private reflection. This might easily have been handled by screens and similar mobile barriers—an omission that is all the odder be-

cause the architects have thoughtfully provided the space
with sundry well-shaped wicker chairs, which, incidentally,
are superior on every count to most more studiously "modern" designs in steel and aluminum. Then, too, let me com-
mend the bold, clear labelling of the rooms and offices, the
convenient disposition of the cloakrooms and other services
—in fine, a sense of clarity and order that carries through the
whole structure, right down to the basement floor, which is
on the level of a sunken garden outside and which is connected to a series of lower-level rooms in the Secretariat.

One more feature remains to be described, if not account-
ed for—the Japanese garden, designed by Isamu Noguchi.
This is placed in a bit of leftover space between the Secretariat and the small Delegates Building, which is in one corner of the Unesco site, but it is cut off by the Secretariat
from a small though useful sun terrace, where the staff gather
for midday relaxation. Here is a variation of the traditional
Japanese garden, with all the usual features—odd stones, running water, stunted trees and stunted mountains—transposed
into bolder modern forms, and using strong contrasting colors. These colors and the over-all pattern register best not
from the ground but from the windows above, where they
look like a colorful collage in relief. To a Western eye, insen-
sitive (without instruction) to Japanese symbolism, the
flock of weathered stones produces the effect of an abandoned
ancient cemetery, a Stonehenge in miniature. But for all its
romantic ingenuity, there is no getting away from the looming glass façade of the Secretariat, so the garden seems like a
curio snatched by a tourist on his travels, not an integral
part of this complex of Unesco buildings.

In short, the garden is a mere showpiece, or, even worse,
a conversation piece—not a place to be used by either the
public or the members of the Secretariat. Plainly, this was
not the sort of task in which Noguchi's high talents as an
artist could show themselves at their best. Even if this garden
were not too heavily charged with ancient, narrowly national
idiosyncrasies to represent an emerging new universal order
in both art and life, it would have been nullified by its hostile
surroundings. On the whole, I prefer the sunken greensward
with white stepping stones that serves as a rug beside the
Conference Hall; it has a purity that says "Peace" more clearly
than the symbolic headstone denoting Peace from which the
water flows in Noguchi's garden.

I have said enough about the Conference Building to indicate my belief in its architectural importance. But I do not know why the architects—or was it, more likely, their clients?—had so little appreciation of its social functions, its public interests, or its esthetic potentialities. Only by forgetting all these aspects, especially the last, could they have decided to shove it into a far corner of the Unesco site. From both an architectural and a human standpoint, the Conference Building should have been given centrality, or at least dominance. Despite municipal regulations, which require any building that faces the Place de Fontenoy to follow the arc of the Place and to approximate the height of the neighboring structures, the architects of the Unesco buildings, who put the Secretariat on that part of the site, might have found a way to focus attention on their one positive structure. To achieve this, they might have been forced to pierce the street front on the Place de Fontenoy, in order to open up an adequate approach to the more public parts of Unesco House, and they surely would have had to change the whole spatial composition of the Secretariat, making it modest and reticent, like a garden wall, rather than emphatic and ostentatiously vitreous. The reward would have been a unified and coherent combination of buildings, trees, grass, gardens, one form playing into another, that could lay some claim to be a work of organic architecture and that would serve as more than a showpiece. But since the architects made the Secretariat dominant, the very shape and sweep of that building have destroyed the coherence of the site. The result is three completely unrelated structures, surrounded by parking lots and unusable—visually unrelated—open spaces.

In judging a work of architecture, one must necessarily pass criticism on the architects, but it is hardly fair to end there. In this case, in which the major errors of the United Nations buildings in New York were committed for a second time by the same agency, one must also criticize, and perhaps even more severely, the clients—the officials who wrote the program for these buildings. Did they learn nothing from the errors in the design of the New York headquarters? Have they learned nothing in the past fifteen years about the profound appeal that this great organization makes to a multitude of people in every part of the world, and how necessary it is to carry their own educational function further, if they are to accomplish in the end all that the United Nations must do to promote a new self-respect among the constituent nations and cultures?

This appeal is not to be satisfied through organizing guided tours of earnest sightseers through its barren halls, punctuated by explanatory lectures on its often sterile and far from intelligible works of art. If the guiding spirits of Unesco had conceived Unesco House as a public meeting place for the cultures of the world, they would not have permitted the Secretariat and its dusty plaza to be the main goal of the many visitors who converge on these buildings, hoping for visible manifestation of the spirit that is needed to bring harmonious order to a divided and troubled world. Even granted the limited funds at their disposal, those guiding spirits might at least have insisted upon an Exhibition Hall of the cultures of the world, East and West, primitive and "civilized," as a necessary public feature of the whole enterprise. In such a hall United Nations activities could be placed on view from week to week and month to month, translated into graphic and pictorial form, and the member nations, down to the humblest and obscurest tribe, could be invited to show to the rest of mankind their past cultural achievements and to project their present goals. Even the active officers of the Secretariat need to be visually reminded of one another's work and of the common sphere in which they operate.

There was a suggestive sample of such a show in the Conference Building when I visited it—some splendid photomurals showing the great Egyptian monuments that Unesco has been trying to salvage before the dammed waters of the Nile cover them over. A continuous procession of such exhibits, with photographs, posters, models, exemplary works of art, would do far more to promote cultural understanding than the perfunctory, often sublimely meaningless, murals and sculptures that are permanently on display. But the Conference Building is closed to visitors when it is in session, and no outsider is allowed anywhere without a permit unless he is on a guided tour, so even the small exhibition space that is available has no relation to public interests. If the Conference Building had been conceived as the public focus of all the Unesco's great enterprises, it would not have been diminished by the looming walls of the Secretariat and relegated to the rear of the site.

The architectural failure of these buildings, then, reflects an even greater failure of imagination on the part of those who commissioned them and who allowed their funds to be spent lavishly on technological exhibitionism rather than cultural and educational needs.

If Unesco is to serve mankind well, what it needs is not guided tours of the less functional part of its bureaucratic structure but guided tours of the cultures of the world, dramatizing all those historical movements and technological achievements and ideal pursuits that are leading to what one anthropologist, the late Father Teilhard de Chardin, called the "planetization of man." It is this, and not the bureaucratic idea, that needed glorification, or, rather, honest emphasis without glorification, in Unesco House. Matthew Nowicki once said, "To have great architecture one must have a great client." Here *was* a great client, yet in the basic concept of these buildings I see no evidence of that greatness, but only a busy superficiality and a trite modishness that hardly do justice to the mission of the United Nations, to the many able and dedicated spirits that work within this organization, or to the cultural needs of our threatened planet, seething with catastrophic hatreds and facing hateful catastrophes.

*1960*

# NINE

# From Crotchet Castle to Arthur's Seat

On a summer visit to Britain, I spent ten days in a roughly triangular journey that took me from London through Birmingham into North Wales, then by way of Manchester to Edinburgh. I came back through Durham, whose cathedral, embedded—like the fortress it was—upon a rock, is as fine an example of grand architectural form married to its site as can be found anywhere. On this journey, my architectural discoveries were all quite incidental and unplanned, though occasionally my hosts took a hand in them. By good luck, it turned out that these discoveries cast oblique illuminations over many of the major architectural and planning problems of our time.

Going to and from Wales by the routes I took, one passes through the classic wastelands of the early industrial period, with their scorched-earth landscape, their slag heaps and coal tips (so mountainous that they seem geological formations, not man-made accumulations), their begrimed rows of workers' houses, set in a clutter of factories—the whole scene exhibiting diagrammatically all the typical mistakes of the hasty beginnings of industrialism. After years of helpless acquiescence, efforts are now being made to absorb these mountains of debris into the urban landscape; the efforts range from levelling the heaps with steam shovel and bulldozer to coaxing grass and even trees to grow on their inhospitable slopes, as Mr. Michael Graham, C.M.G., a devoted son of Lancashire, has been lately doing, with children and riding horses as assistants. But the process of accumulating soil and humus is a slow one. One of my brief halting places was Eccles, near Manchester, and the home of the delicious Eccles cake, which, like the Bath bun, is at its best in its native habitat. Wandering about one of Eccles' Victorian suburban estates, I was struck by the fact that the ruling classes, even when they commanded plenty of land and money, had not known how to use these resources to produce a pleasant environment for themselves any more than they had for their workers; at best, they had made an art of ugliness and a virtue of the grime they shared with their poorer neighbors.

But here comes the architectural paradox. This blasted environment has produced over the generations no small number of people whose moral and intellectual qualities have been of a superior order. For it was in this kind of setting that the Rochdale weavers founded the great Consumers' Cooperative movement, by applying Christian principles to marketing, and built up a huge, ramifying organization that set a pattern for later chain-store economies under capitalist management. Here, too, the weavers of Manchester upheld the cause of the North during our Civil War, though they themselves were starving for lack of Southern cotton to weave. One of the oldest problems in human development, the relation of moral qualities to esthetic forms, of goodness to beauty, hits one between the eyes here—far harder than it hit Plato, in an environment much richer in handsome bodies and well-formed buildings. The moral order and the esthetic order should not be congenitally incompatible, for they presumably have the same parents; but, like jealous offspring, they are often contentious and unresponsive to each other, and in the old industrial conurbations of England— "conurbation" is now a favorite English word for the endless scrambled urban sprawl—this aloofness sometimes comes close to downright hostility.

As often happens, nature saves the day, for a sudden splash of color will now and then redeem this urban wasteland, especially the color of purple lupin, growing wild along the railroad cuts, as the goldenrod grows in our own country. The lupin followed me all over England, brightening the

most depressing railside views, but my awareness of the
rhododendrons was even stronger. If their splendor in June
has been sufficiently appreciated and described, I have
not stumbled upon the written passage that says so. In
England, rhododendrons seem to thrive everywhere, but they
are at their overpowering best, and in all their possible va-
rieties, in a place near the country house where I stayed in
Wales. The place is Portmeirion, an artful and playful little
modern village, designed as a whole and all of a piece, on
a peninsula close to the sea; and the rhododendrons alone
justify a pilgrimage to it, though there is more to be seen
in this lively landscape than their great bushes and trees, and
the equally lush camellias, azaleas, and hydrangeas. This is
still the country of Thomas Love Peacock, and perhaps the
way to describe Portmeirion is to say that it is Peacock's
Crotchet Castle come to life, with its contending dinner-ta-
ble opinions taking concrete architectural form in an amusing
array of politely incompatible, argumentative, but elegantly
phrased buildings. These buildings are conceived as embellishments to a small seaside hotel resort, started only a generation ago, along with a shop selling Welsh arts and crafts
and a tearoom to take care of the casual visitor, all admirably secluded, with admittance through a guarded entrance,
so that extra loads of trippers who might turn the place into
a shambles can be excluded when traffic becomes too heavy;
indeed, the whole place was once temporarily turned into a
private preserve, for a visit by the Royal Family.

Portmeirion is a fantastic collection of architectural relics
and impish modern fantasies. The entire village is the work
of the Welsh architect Clough Williams-Ellis, whose book
*England and the Octopus,* more than thirty years ago, was the
opening gun in a fresh campaign to overcome the devastating ugliness that was spreading again in the motor age, as
it had spread in the earlier railroad age, over the small historic towns and still verdant rural areas of Britain. Williams-
Ellis was resuming and following through the pioneering
work done by William Morris two generations before;
and as a result of a sharpened public conscience about
both the natural landscape and historic buildings, a whole
series of public trusts and national foundations are now
addressing themselves to this task, taking over ancient country inns and running them well, opening historic country
houses and castles to public inspection, preserving ancient

monuments and works of art—in short, reversing the policy of contemptuous and ruthless destruction that the old ironmasters and mill-owners regarded as a happy emblem of progress. At long last, even wild areas that had been deemed fit only for mining, quarrying, or for exploiting hydraulic power have been turned into national parks. So sensitive has England become over the quality of its landscape that the Electricity Board does not site a row of pylons to carry its high-tension wires without calling in its eminent architectural consultant, Sir William Holford.

In all these efforts, Mr. Williams-Ellis has had a hand; indeed, he acquired and held a large part of the magnificent Welsh landscape that is dominated by the peaks of Snowdon until Parliament followed his lead by turning the area into a national park. As an architect, he is equally at home in the ancient, traditional world of the stark Welsh countryside and the once brave new world of "modern architecture." But he realized earlier than most of his architectural contemporaries how constrictive and desiccated modern forms can become when the architect pays more attention to the mechanical formula or the exploitation of some newly fabricated material than to the visible human results. In a sense, Portmeirion is a gay, deliberately irresponsible reaction against the dull sterilities of so much that passes as modern architecture today. If Williams-Ellis' work is more traditional in its echoes of old forms than the nursery-book novelties of Le Corbusier's chapel in the French town of Ronchamp, it is nevertheless prompted by a similar impulse, which does credit to both architects: to reclaim for architecture the freedom of invention—and the possibility of pleasurable fantasy—it had too abjectly surrendered to the cult of the machine.

Portmeirion lies, so to say, at the end of the road to Xanadu, and, appropriately, the architect has lately decreed —and designed—a "stately pleasure dome" whose one purpose is to delight the beholder by serving as the architectural crown to the hillside on which the little houses and gardens and shops are scattered, overlooking a wide tidal estuary. "The whole place," in the architect's words, "is unashamedly romantic" in its terraced gardens, its cobbled square, its slim, Italianate bell tower, and its constant effort to give human emphasis, by leaping walls and pinnacles, to the natural rhythm of the landscape. Romanticism itself was a revolt against the exactitude and repetitiveness of the eighteenth-

and early-nineteenth-century classicists, who favored flat sites, and who could do nothing with picturesque landscapes except turn away from them. Here the romantic and the picturesque come back again, in baroque rather than Gothic form—with tongue in cheek. The architect is almost willing to shock the more prudish spectators by dancing on their principles, provided they are—even if against their will—amused. But the fact that he does not take his playfulness too prayerfully prevents his architecture from having the integrity of a serious style, even such a make-believe style as the neo-Gothic. I suspect that, from a purely esthetic standpoint, Portmeirion was at its best some moment before the Second World War, ere he had gilded the lily. By now it has sacrificed a little of its formal coherence to its function as an architectural museum, where a superb Jacobean plaster ceiling in the "town hall"—there is no town and no government!—vies for attention with Victorian Gothic façades from demolished structures elsewhere. Williams-Ellis has accurately described the place as a "home for fallen buildings," for his shrewd antiquarian eye and happy fantasy have given a respectable status and a new life to memorable fragments of structures that had "lost their virtue" and might have vanished without a trace in some architectural Potter's Field.

Portmeirion is a "folly" in the eighteenth-century architectural manner; indeed, a folly piled upon folly, as in an uninhibited dream. But the total effect is relaxing and often enchanting, now more than ever, since the buildings contrast happily with the rigid irrationalities and the calculated follies of our so-called Nuclear Age. The playful absurdities of this architecture, always delicate and human in touch, are a happy relief from the grim absurdities of our thermonuclear strategists, who are blandly planning to turn our whole planet into a heap of radioactive rubble. Though I prefer Williams-Ellis' work in his more sober moments of landscaping and building—which I will come to in a moment—I enjoy the spirit of nimble improvisation he has shown here. The nineteenth-century owners of this site were responsible for the great plantation of rhododendrons for which the place is famous, but this weird forest of them is very much in the Williams-Ellis vein, as if by anticipation. The landscape of North Wales was new to me, and its bare hills, its dark outcropping of slate and granite, its stone walls and stone farm buildings, its compact villages, also of stone, whose minute squares and open spaces relieve an otherwise oppressive sobriety and grimness, brought more than a tremor of delight to me; and the roadsides, with their stone fences to keep in the sheep, are edged with spiky pennywort and magnificent dark-green nettles, almost twice as high as our own breed. My visual experience was sharpened by my eating, on the first night, green nettle soup and Welsh saddle of lamb, both delicate and delicious regional dishes. The rearing barebacked mountains of Wales, which finally plunge into the sea, must be counted among the most noble landscapes in the world; they have the starkness and almost the capacity to lift one to a super-mundane level that the landscape of Delphi has; indeed, one might even call Snowdon Wales' Parnassus, which would be proper only in a country that still does homage to its bards and orators, where every countryman still speaks in a soft singsong, as if verse were more natural than prose. In their usual callous manner, the Nuclear Gods have chosen this almost untouched part of wild Wales as the site, only a dozen miles from Portmeirion, of one of the great temples in which their priests will perform their dangerous even though seemingly innocent cosmic rites—a power plant that forms a vast, desolate pile, already half finished, which not even the talents of Sir Basil Spence, its architect, will be able to make acceptable to the eye.

To efface that image of desolation, one turns again to Portmeirion for communion with an older pantheon of earth gods in the rhododendron grove. The rhododendron bushes here often attain the height of trees, and in June they are bursting with multicolored clusters of blossoms. Here one stumbles along narrow paths, through almost impenetrable thickets and dark tunnels filled with purple light, tripping over twisted roots, battling with writhing stems, until the tangle suddenly ends on a cliff that discloses the sea. Nature has taken over this human plantation and turned it into a magnificent display of the savage energy of life itself, with its continued growth and efflorescence—perhaps our last hopeful symbol of deliverance from the death-oriented institutions, the suicidal strategies, and the dehumanized routines of our age.

I cannot leave Wales without a word about another work of Clough Williams-Ellis—the David Lloyd George memorial, a work that shows to the fullest his robust talents in both architecture and landscape design. This monument is at the edge of the tiny village of Llanystumdwy, where that fiery and slippery little man once lived. The present generation, even in England, hardly knows him; it has forgotten his leadership, with the younger Winston Churchill, in social legislation back in the nineteen-tens, and the crisis during the First World War, when the wily politician almost achieved the stature of a statesman. But despite recent efforts to denigrate Lloyd George's personality, headed—in classic Freudian fashion—by his own son, Lloyd George is still a hero to the Welsh, and the monument that Williams-Ellis has designed does justice to the emotion he still excites in Welsh bosoms, without raising any uncomfortable questions about his heroic stature by way of sculptured effigy or extensive laudatory description. Fortunately, the architect was entrusted with the choosing of the site. Instead of a conspicuous place in the village, he took a small ledge at the top of a wooded escarpment, a place to which Lloyd George often retired, to brood over the little Dwyfawr, a ribbon of water that unwinds below, separating the steep slope from the pleasant farmland that stretches across the valley beyond. The monument is cut off from the nearby highway by a beech hedge, and the whole hillside is canopied with trees. The outer rim of the monument is oval, in the form of a low stone wall. The stone "entrance" (an entrance for the eye alone) rises above the wall to a central gabled peak, with curving sides and two openings—an iron grille outlining a funerary urn beneath a round arch, and an oval opening above, with Lloyd George's initials in a scroll of iron. From the path that circles the hillside site of the monument, always close but always separated, one beholds Lloyd George's grave beyond the entrance, in the center of an oval lawn, which is surrounded by the stone wall. Within that grassy plot is a flat oval of smooth round stones, the shape of fat cigars, converging toward the center of the grave. The main feature of this oval is the very stone on which Lloyd George used to sit and meditate.

The point of the design is that the pilgrim who visits this grave can pass around it, while getting a full view of the interior of the enclosure, without being tempted to trespass. In fact, no sign is needed to warn him against intruding, since the spiral walk was contrived to keep him far enough above or below the grave to prevent access. Apart from the simple inscription and the serene enclosure, nothing disturbs the landscape that Lloyd George saw, and only a small sign by the roadside reminds the tripper that this is consecrated ground. To the honor of the tourist, there was, when I visited it, not a sign of his presence in so much as an empty cigarette pack or a scrap of paper.

The restraint of this monument only emphasizes the perfect combination of pure form, delicate textural contrasts, and sensitive siting. And the whole impression is singularly in character, for this is the scene the hero's eyes beheld, this is the Wordsworthian "old gray stone" on which he sat, and even the fact that he sat there says something about his quality as a human being. Each visitor who brings his private image of Lloyd George to the grave will find a setting ready for it, and when time or indifference effaces all the images, something that Lloyd George's life evoked in the mind of the architect will nevertheless remain visible—and valuable. This is a classic memorial, not because it piously imitates some ancient work of excellence but because it has the same sense of reverence for the setting, the same sense of the human scale, and the same delicacy of feeling that a Greek tombstone of the fourth century had. Would that we in America had a comparably forthright and eloquent memorial to Lincoln!

To descend from the high level of this austere landscape to the dreary miles of seaside huts and trailers that line the northern shores of Wales, from Colwyn Bay eastward, is the sad fate of the railroad traveller who is headed for Manchester. I had last seen that city in 1946, when it gaped with wartime desolation. By now there has been much rebuilding—less disorderly and congested than Birmingham's, but not yet very impressive—in the center of the town, and in more than one other area the carefully planned replacement of obsolete buildings and antiquated urban layouts by more modern designs, timed to avoid the brutal wholesale clearances dear to American planners, has been going on. This is largely due to the admirable plans made during the Second World War by the Town Surveyor, Mr. Rowland Nicholas, one of the first planners to conceive planning operations in a series of stages, over a period of a generation or even a half century, thus combining the virtues of a large and bold over-all scheme with those of piecemeal planning, amenable to correction and modification in case of unforeseeable emergencies or often equally unforeseeable mistakes and opportunities. My chief architectural find in Manchester, which I was visiting on my way to Edinburgh, was a purely historic discovery—a glass-covered shopping arcade of Victorian vintage in the very midst of the bombed central area. For all its frailty, it had survived, to testify to the Early Victorian enthusiasm for iron and glass, long before those materials were debased into a showy popular substitute for a more organic and functional concept of modern architecture. The nineteenth century's pride in its new techniques and new materials was justifiable, for iron and steel and glass had immensely widened the range of constructional possibilities. But that architects today should have learned nothing about the abuse and misuse of these materials after a century of experiment is a reproach to our architectural schools and to the common sense of those who set the present fashions.

Edinburgh is one of the few large cities in the British Isles that escaped the uncivil attentions of the German bombers, perhaps for the obscure reasons that permitted Oxford to escape, too. As the Edinburgh Festival has now caused many visitors to know, the Old Town presents one of the most striking urban sky lines in the world, with its historic core built on a volcanic rock that juts upward to a climax in the ancient castle, and its craggy buildings stretching down the length of the Royal Mile toward the ancient Holyrood Abbey, where two kings of Scotland were crowned. The tall tenements along this rocky ridge vie with the church steeples and the castle walls in producing a romantic profile, sombre but exciting. Here is the picture-book medieval city, though most of it was built after the sixteenth century, and though at the bottom of the huge rock two railway stations and a wilderness of tracks and marshalling yards insulate Castle Hill from the park that forms the near side of Princes Street —the great shopping mall of the city. Beyond and around Princes Street stretches the New Town, begun in the eighteenth century, and in itself a classic example, on a par with Bath and Bloomsbury, of the bold upper-class concept of a fine residential quarter, with its terraces, circles, ovals, and squares, with its parks surrounded by iron fences and open only to nearby residents entitled to enter by a gate key. Given the social circumstances that produced these great row houses, given especially an ample retinue of servants, there are few better urban quarters anywhere—though if one pushes behind the imposing façades, one finds drably unfinished rear walls, with mean back yards, and meaner small houses and stables provided for the "lower orders."

Since the thirties an even newer New Town has come into existence, on the outskirts of the city, marked architecturally by a preposterous hybrid, the Scotch bungalow, done in stone, overexposed to the raw winds and the ground cold—the sort of compromise between East and West a homesick Scots civil servant might have brought back from India. This low building, defiant of both tradition and climate, is perhaps belated overcompensation for the tall tenements that dominated the Old Town, tenements that forced housewives to walk up eight or ten stories, lugging their coal, their water and food, or their babies to their one-room flats. Edinburgh reminds one that the skyscraper is no American invention, for eight- and ten-story flats were built here as early as the seventeenth century, and legend tells of a much higher one that finally tumbled down. In its own right, Edinburgh is a sort of open-air museum of European architecture and town planning, from the Middle Ages onward, and till lately, when the University undertook to build new quarters, only one thing was missing—a decent modern building, or, rather, any modern building at all, since Charles Mackintosh, Scotland's bold pioneer contemporary of Louis Sullivan, did most of his work in Glasgow. The sole exceptions I can recall are the traditional but unstylized stone buildings done by Patrick Geddes and Frank Mears for the Edinburgh zoo. This is still, happily, a city of walking distances, easy for the visitor to take in. Almost anything of architectural or historic interest can be encountered within the compass of a mile, between the castle and Holyrood Abbey, or between the University and the farther side of the New Town. The Firth of Forth Bridge, one of the world's few masterpieces in cantilever construction—the Eads Bridge at St. Louis is the other—requires, it is true, a longer journey from the Old Town. Even much of industrial Edinburgh, to say nothing of the poverty-pocked neighborhoods that accompany it, is embraced by this mile-square city, which must hold around two hundred and fifty thousand people, for the great breweries of the town are scattered through this area—often handsome stone buildings, with striking conical towers where the hops are dried. The city of some five hundred thousand people that began to spread beyond these limits with the introduction of the trolley car, at the end of the nineteenth century, has nothing to offer that the smaller city did not possess, not even green open spaces, for one of the glories of Edinburgh proper is that, thanks to the surrounding hills, and above all Arthur's Seat, it has maintained large parts of the green matrix essential to the health and beauty and balance of any city.

Edinburgh, in short, is a city to preserve, and one of the first steps necessary is to prevent the surrounding countryside from being eaten up by any more of the random residential extensions that are going on. It is not, of course, necessary or even possible to stop the process of growth, but the mode of growth must be altered. Instead, a series of properly planned smaller towns, with their own business and industrial facilities, could be built around Edinburgh, near enough to participate in the advantages of a big city without adding to its congestion and without destroying those advantages, which give the central urban area its distinction. The overcrowded city of Glasgow, even more addicted to tall tenements than Edinburgh, rejected this organic method of growth as impossible when it was proposed fifteen years ago, but that municipality has lately reversed its past judgment and is settling its excess population and industrial plants in a series of neighboring New Towns, far more commodious in design. The most interesting of these is Cumbernauld, now in process of building. The alternative method of unregulated automatic growth, in the hands of the real-estate speculator, the highway engineer, and the industrial organizer, will act to destroy both urban and rural values, just as it has already done with savage swiftness in so many American cities, and is doing, to the accompaniment of even more grievous loss, in once exemplary English towns like Oxford and Bath. No city can prevent decay at its core if it encourages disintegration and corrosion by random building on its loosely sprawling periphery.

An internal question of great moment has lately come to a head in Edinburgh, and that is: How much of the historic quarters should be preserved when new needs, new purposes, demand fresh forms, suitable to our own age? This question became a public issue when the University published its plans for a group of high-rise buildings at one end of George Square, one of the occasional eighteenth-century squares with which the Old Town eased its foul overcrowding and fostered a residential growth more favorable to university life. Strong protests were voiced by people who wanted no changes in the look of the square, which still boasts the modest, sober row of three-story stone houses in one of which Walter Scott lived. This question of what to save arises in many other cities today; it came up not long ago in London when the design of the huge United States Embassy in Grosvenor Square was made public, and in several American cities, among them Baltimore, Philadelphia, Boston, and Savannah, it has raised a problem that has hardly been satisfactorily stated, much less solved.

Wherever there is a demand for the continuing original, residential use of town squares, there is good reason to retain the original form. (In the larger squares, such as Rittenhouse Square in Philadelphia, where the sides are too far apart to make possible a visual unity, the original residences could have been doubled in height, and so might have fended off the skyscraper apartments and hotels that have replaced them and have thus both congested the square and jumbled its form.) In the case of George Square, the University, which owns the buildings on it, has piously kept intact the side of the square on which Scott's house stands but has planned a series of tall buildings at one end. This is one of those compromise solutions that decently satisfy neither party. Actually, a more radical solution was necessary. There is plenty of public open space in the immediate neighborhood, in a handsome green called The Meadows. Hence the University's need for new quarters should have led to turning both the old building lots and the square itself into a unified University Precinct, with the blessing and overt aid of the municipality. This precinct might have contained virtually as much open space as the original square, but it could have been designed, like Harvard Yard, in our Cambridge, to provide inner greens and malls, with all the wheeled traffic kept on the perimeter. This would have permitted the buildings to be grouped in a far better fashion, functionally and esthetically, than is possible in the old-fashioned pattern of being lined up along a corridor street. Here, plainly, is a case in which a valued past should not have stood in the way of a more valuable future.

While all this fuss was being made about George Square, a commonplace specimen of architecture compared to what exists in the eighteenth-century New Town, especially that aristocratic quarter behind Princes Street, some of the finest aspects of James Craig's planning of that town have now been marred by the invasion of business into this handsome residential area. The granite dignity of the buildings has here and there begun to give way to gaping glass fronts and loud signs. This is a strikingly inept adaptation to modern needs, for though these magnificent houses can no longer easily be kept up by private families, they are well suited to being turned into apartment houses and hotels, and with the great influx of tourists into Edinburgh, and the extreme dearth of hotel accommodation, it is absurd to permit this quarter to be used for any other purpose, except perhaps, as now, on certain side streets. The latter, indeed, connecting Princes Street with the great squares, might without serious loss—in fact, with considerable gain—be converted into a more modern kind of business quarter. If the pressure for shopping accommodations on Princes Street grows, one might even envisage one or more pedestrian shopping malls, with facilities for motor parking, directly behind the present line of shops and commercial buildings.

Adroit planning and intelligent financial support by lending institutions might conserve this whole area for the delight and convenience of both the resident and the tourist, and the very act of conservation would add immensely to the value of the new business quarters in the adjacent streets. Unless such positive measures are soon taken, one of the most beautiful and commodious of residential quarters will quickly be gutted, for no purpose that could not have been better accomplished by putting business in Edinburgh where it belongs.

The term for this adroit kind of planning and rehabilitation, "conservative surgery," was coined by Patrick Geddes, one of the founders of the modern city-planning movement, whose Outlook Tower and apartment house lie just below the Castle, on Castle Hill: its purpose is to remove decay and encourage healthy growth without extirpating necessary organs. At present, in most cities, the field is unfortunately divided between two equally mischievous schools—the conservative "touch-me-nots," who would wait till gangrene sets in before being ready to consent to an operation, and the knife-happy surgeons, who, like Mr. Surgeon Cuticle in Melville's *White-Jacket,* are so eager to practice their art that they do not distinguished between healthy tissue and diseased but remove both and let the patient die. Edinburgh, like many other historic spots, is too rich in both ancient memories and present vitalities to be in the hands of either school.

*1962*

## TEN

# London—to the Skies!

Recently London has been hit by a building boom—I almost said, with greater accuracy, a building bomb. It is like what has been going on in New York, and since London has a far greater core of fine buildings and historic areas that both recall the past and esthetically grace the present, the effect threatens to be even more devastating than, say, the ruin of Park Avenue. The present edification and elevation of London's new business bureaucracy in a multitude of new skyscrapers are enough in themselves to upset the precarious inner balance that London, despite its continued expansion, achieved within the last half century. But, in addition, the motorcar, floating in on a wave of prosperity, has clogged the highways and byways of the city. This congestion has brought with it the conventional train of expert pseudo-remedies, from parking meters to the chipping away of space in squares and parks, above all, in Hyde Park. But all that—besides reducing the acreage of precious recreational areas, transforming building lots into parking lots, and inviting still more traffic—simply insures that movement will eventually come to a standstill unless the combined remedies bring about a total evacuation of the central core of the city. (By now, two-thirds of downtown Los Angeles, the classic case of motorized paralysis, consists of freeways, garages, and parking lots. This is a powerful example of the old proverbs "Haste makes waste" and "Waste makes want.")

Even the public-transport system of London, perhaps the best in the world, cannot cope with the inundation created by these high buildings and the increasing traffic of private cars from suburban acres on the far side of the Green Belt. The Green Belt is a semirural area, protected legally as a public reservation of open space, that engirdles London. This private traffic, by its slowing down of bus speeds, has caused a diminution of bus riders, who are driven to take the Underground; and the Underground, its directors tell me, can serve no more people at the peak hours with the existing facilities. To increase the density of occupation in the central areas of London in the face of these conditions is municipal madness, the only adequate term for the building and traffic policies of most of the great metropolises today— Paris and Rome and London as well as Boston and Detroit and New York. San Francisco and Philadelphia, after doing vast municipal damage in the name of "improved" traffic circulation, have the distinction of being the first to awaken to the real needs of the city by turning back once more to public rapid-transit systems—stupidly abandoned in the name of progress during the last two decades.

The picture is, for the American observer, a dismally familiar one. But what is most discouraging is to find that London, the most decentralized and individualized of all great cities, the one most capable of maintaining the human scale, is flinging away both experience and common sense in a spate of ill-sited high-rise building. Under the impression that they are serving the cause of progress, the English have thought it worthwhile to repeat all our characteristic urban mistakes of the last twenty years, possibly for no better reason than the unreason that prompts *us* to go on making them. In addition, the quick-profit motive enters into the present concentration on high buildings in London, exactly as it does here, and it is just as damaging from the standpoint of public welfare. So in looking closer at London, one gets only a more detached view of our own urban devastation.

At first glance, this tide of new buildings seems a belated but welcome replacement, in the idiom of our own day, of those endless acres of buildings that were wiped out by the Blitz and the rocket bombs between 1940 and 1945. In 1946, when I first visited London after the war, almost every neighborhood showed gaping cellars, battered walls, vacant lots. While even the most heavily bombed areas were incredibly tidy and trim, considering all the national energy that had gone into the war, the effect was that of a respectable family which, having lost its fortune, had been compelled to sell off much of its best furniture but still cleaned and polished lovingly what remained, though some of it was beginning to fall apart. Parliament Square, with boxes of red geraniums again decorating the buildings on the Whitehall side, was still handsome, and the view framed by Waterloo Place, over St. James's Park, with its delicate silhouette of turrets and treetops, was still one of the most inviting of urban vistas, though more a product of happy chance and restrained building practices than of any deliberate town-planning art. One remembers that vista all the more poignantly because, unless the present activities are abated, this view, and many others equally characteristic of London at its best, will soon be obliterated.

By 1953, the year of Queen Elizabeth II's coronation, the gray fog of fatigue and dearth had blown away, to disclose a city not radically changed from that of 1946, but smiling with flowers and fresh paint and an inward vision of better things to come. The heroic South Bank Exhibition of 1951 had restored the Britons' confidence in their future by justifying their pride in their past. The most conspicuous bit of new building on any scale anywhere in London—and still among the best—was the Lansbury housing estate, in the East End, designed as part of the 1951 Exhibition. But the city already looked brighter than its grimy prewar self, what with the "coronation-blue" lamp-posts, the procession of delicate arches that spanned the drive between the Admiralty Arch in Whitehall and Buckingham Palace. Happily, too, the repainting of the stucco fronts all over Victorian London in light colors avoided the murky oxbloods and mustard creams that had once characterized endless rows in Pimlico, Belgravia, and South Kensington. The area around St. Paul's was still an appalling waste of rubble, and the most conspicuous result of the slow-motion rehabilitation of buildings in the City was the unearthing of a Mithraic temple on a site excavated for a foundation beside the old Roman wall. Even as late as 1957, the chief new office buildings formed a palisade of uniform height on the South Bank, near Westminster Bridge, and the principal form of construction was still the one desperately needed to make up for wartime losses—that is, housing. All over London, from Roehampton, on the borders of Richmond Park, to the devastated areas of the East End, public-housing estates good, bad, and indifferent, were under construction.

But the picture has suddenly changed. The new Tory government stopped encouraging the growth of New Towns (more or less self-sufficient urban communities, with their own industrial bases) that were literally planned from the ground up, to relieve the overcrowding of London. What was worse, it made no plans of its own to prevent the historic core of London from being turned into a highly specialized financiers' New Town, whose success would be based on recklessly increasing London's density of both business and residential occupation. As a result, the whole sky line of London has begun to heave and billow upward with tall buildings, as if so many volcanoes were bursting through great fissures. The London County Council has led this movement by sponsoring municipally owned high-rise flats from once-suburban Roehampton to the East End's Golden Lane, from Pimlico to Paddington, but private interests were not slow in following suit once the lid was off and business opportunities for gain took precedence of public needs.

Up to this point, London had been a spread-out city of low buildings, two and three stories high in the oldest parts and the outer boroughs, four or five in the newest, not more than six in the most crowded business areas. On that broad base of brick and stucco, the most notable buildings, done mainly in Portland stone, stood out as spires, towers, or domes, above the low roofs—St. Paul's; the Monument and the Tower; the Senate Building of the University of London, in Bloomsbury; the Tower of London and the other towers of the outstanding parish churches (not all by Wren or Hawksmoor); the Houses of Parliament and Big Ben; the cluster of museums in South Kensington; the fine dome of Albert Hall. This was historic London, a London that even in the days when capitalism was hard-fisted and ruthless in all its human dealings kept business in esthetic subordination to its monuments for religion, culture, and politics. From the Thames below Westminster, the chiaroscuro of Portland stone, with its contrasting washed and sooty surfaces, still magnifies the splendor of London's historic succession of public buildings and lifts them out of the commonplace mass.

Now that the old restrictions on building heights have been taken off, fifteen-, twenty-five-, even thirty-story buildings have risen all over London, though the eruption has been less conspicuous in the ancient commercial City, where a conservative mediocrity prevails, than in the mixed areas of the central boroughs, where new accretions of capital derived from oil, airlines, and chain stores have been more adventurous, not to say giddy. Thus, close by Oxford Circus, where the rush-hour traffic produces long queues for the Underground, making its station there the most heavily used one in London, a tall department store is under construction, which will add its regiment of clerks and customers to the crawling, lengthening evening queue. Near Trafalgar Square, another point of congestion, a whole nest of tall buildings is going up, for the further stagnation of traffic. The practical effect will be undesirable, and the esthetic results will in some cases be deplorable. An occasional skyscraper tower, when it is well placed, as is the Shell-Mex Building, on the South Bank, may both serve its special purposes and characterize the twentieth-century mode of life, as the uniform block front did that of the eighteenth century. Height makes a single building prominent and seemingly important, even if it possesses no real architectural distinction. But when one high-rise building is surrounded by many similar structures, height alone loses this special distinction: esthetically, the buildings cancel each other out and produce a heaving mediocre mass that flattens out visually any better structures that may remain below.

Even when standing alone, such overbearing buildings should not be permitted to violate certain districts in London that are historically unique—areas like the great political and religious complex of which the Houses of Parliament and Westminster Abbey are the focus. Here the erection of London's tallest skyscraper, the thirty-four-story Vickers tower, on the Embankment west of the Houses of Parliament, dwarfs the fine towers of Barry's and Pugin's great building, as if to proclaim that finance, not politics, controls the destinies of the Commonwealth. Perhaps that is true, but it should not be so painfully conspicuous.

Westminster is, in fact, already overloaded with business buildings, and every effort should be made to preserve or rebuild its residential area, as well as the adjacent domestic quarters of Pimlico and Chelsea, and keep them free from speculative invasion, so that large numbers of its office workers—to say nothing of Members of Parliament—may live in this area and so take a considerable load off its overburdened transportation system by walking, or riding local buses, to work. The London County Council, which permitted this officious skyscraper to be mis-sited so near this historic core, already realizes, I believe, that this was a gross blunder in town planning, for it has now stymied the efforts of an American corporation, which has acquired twenty-four acres of land in Pimlico, to plant a whole group of high-rise structures there.

There has been much debate about the architectural design of these new skyscrapers, but it has been chiefly over superficialities, such as the treatment of glass and steel, and not over more basic problems, such as the most efficient and humanely rewarding form of office buildings and the proper grouping of such structures within a given quarter of the city. On this matter, the complex built by Marks and Spencer on Baker Street, with three shallow slabs at right angles to the street, spaced on a base that covers the whole site, seemed to me an admirable innovation that avoided both dingy inner courts and all-day fluorescent lighting.

If London architects, like their New York colleagues, have not been sufficiently critical of these new developments, it is probably because their understandable desire to try their hands at large-scale design, using new methods of construction and new materials, has overcome their good sense and made them forget the ultimate result of such building on the character of London. But the fact is that the present investment in tall buildings is primarily a financial phenomenon; architecture is secondary and civic design noticeably absent. The financial motive, unembarrassed by social concerns, brashly subsidizing esthetic "originality" as a branch of advertisement, dominates the whole conception, as it has dominated the cluttering of Park Avenue, Third Avenue, and Vanderbilt Avenue. The building of huge office units is often a device for diminishing the income tax by pouring money into a structure that can be quickly sold off at a profit. Such profit is reckoned as capital gains. In England, even under the Labour Government, there has never been even as moderate a capital-gains tax as exists in this country. Undeterred by any such brake on speculative investment or advertisement, skyscrapers zoom upward in both residential and business districts.

Before Londoners wake up to what has been happening, a great deal of damage will have been done. A generation ago, the Danish architect Steen Eiler Rasmussen could write a whole book in praise of London, which he characterized as "The Unique City," the only metropolis conceived on the human scale, its brick and stone interwoven with constant patches of green in its parks and squares, and with endless acres of concealed back-yard gardens behind its drab little outer-borough houses.

This great city, spreading over a nest of historic villages and country towns, was composed of many minor cities. Some of these ancient boroughs, which had been almost obliterated in the tides of nineteenth-century building, were actually restored as active political entities, with responsible borough councils, at the end of the last century. When Bernard Shaw, in *Pygmalion*, pointed out that Hoxton's pronunciation was as identifiable as South Kensington's, he pointed implicitly to a hundred other identifying marks, place names, architectural styles, open spaces, that would enable a blindfolded lover of London, set down almost anywhere in the metropolis, to name the borough.

Today that unique metropolis is in danger of turning into a mass of undistinguished, if not uniform, high buildings, encircled and penetrated by ever wider lanes of motor traffic, where a constant surge of motorcars and lorries will wipe out the last traces of those human qualities that had been protected by the very intricacy and deviousness of London's old web of streets, alleys, mews, and cul-de-sacs. There will be gains in hygiene and comfort from some of these changes, but they would be equally available if the human scale were preserved.

The misdirection of London's present building boom is all the more vexing because there are vast areas—largely unbombed but blighted and obsolete beyond piecemeal repair —that *need* to be rebuilt, not on a denser pattern but on a better one. The new order of design should not rest on the old framework of corridor streets with the buildings fronting the traffic stream, or on the uniform building lot, the uniform house front, the uniform roof line for the whole row. These mark a now obsolete type of plan and a now moribund class structure. The insulated-from-traffic precinct, or superblock, rather than the street and the avenue, should be the unit of design, and there should be scope for a far livelier mode of architecture, with an interplay of openness and enclosure, of low structures and high ones. The guiding principle for such a rebuilding is the establishment of desirable densities of human occupation for residential, commercial, industrial, cultural, and mixed areas. Then either high or low buildings can be built, as function and taste may dictate, but the open spaces must grow in direct ratio to the number of permanent residents of the district. Thus no one, even in a business quarter, will be tempted to overcrowd his site by increasing the bulk of his building. In principle, the London County Council has established such a rule, but the densities of its own housing are often far too high, and that very fact has weakened its position in dealing firmly with the commercial overexploitation of land. Such weakness, incidentally —along with a willingness to tolerate sky-high land values that will provide a higher municipal income from taxes— has made nonsense of zoning regulations in America: all the worse because the increased taxes, plus more public money, are drained off in extravagant engineering measures to relieve traffic congestion. The areas that need the most stringent control get the least, since high densities lift land values, and high land values, in turn, demand ever-higher densities. By the same token, low-density areas, which should encourage a freer order of design, are often officiously overregulated to the point of regimentation or, on the pretext that they have become irreparable slums, are turned into high-rise "urban renewal" projects, to the profit of speculative builders and their clients and colleagues.

None of this regulation, of course, deals with the congestion fostered by the private motorcar. Until recently, British planners, ignoring American experience, took it for granted that the major part of the population would not be able to afford automobiles. Even in the New Towns that were built after 1946, a minimal number of garages were at first provided. During the last decade, in England as everywhere else in Europe, the motorcar, like the television set, has become a beloved symbol of economic progress, representing both a higher standard of living and a higher social status, promising to one and all—however deceitfully—such a command over time and space as no other age has ever enjoyed. Today even the working classes of England, though far from affluent, aspire to a car. Meanwhile, the rapid growth of suburban areas has increased the pressure to provide more accommodation for private cars within London and to multiply the major traffic arteries, especially by creating long-distance expressways like the M-1, which connects the city with the Midlands.

The old song "I don't know where I'm going but I'm on my way" is the current theme of British road planning as well as high-rise building. A few of us in America *do* know where England is going, and wonder why it should follow so assiduously all our misconceived procedures, now that they have turned out so sour: that is, so costly, so inefficient, so wasteful in space and time.

Even those who delight in speed should by now realize that the greatest obstacle to it is a transportation system which throws such a load of vehicles on even the most generously designed expressways and freeways that it reduces the flow at peak hours to the tedious Saturday-Sunday crawl at the points of exit from and return to the city. In defiance of these drab urban realities, certified by the sad experience of American cities, Britain has lately brought forth a new society dedicated to the perverse object of wiping out the nation's railway system and bringing both people and goods into London by bus and truck. Apparently only the congenitally blind and the halt fully qualify as traffic experts.

If motor transportaton is to be the liberation and pleasure it should be, we should plan every part of a whole region, from the relatively close-built central neighborhood to the most sparsely settled rural area, so as to reduce the number of unnecessary journeys, to transfer as much long-distance freight as possible from roads to railroads and canals, and to lessen the length of daily journeys to work by multiplying the industrial and business subcenters within a metropolitan and regional area. (The transportation system of London has been kept from total breakdown up to now chiefly because more than forty per cent of its population works within the boroughs where it lives.) The first step in meeting this situation, with its congestion within and its planless sprawl without, is to distribute population and production into smaller, decentralized urban units—either existing boroughs or small towns or additional New Towns. This is the last notion that highway experts seem capable of entertaining, perhaps for the simple reason that it would diminish their vast opportunities for extravagantly misusing the technological resources they command.

No city can solve its transportation problem if it neglects the greatest self-propelling vehicle of all: the pedestrian. A hundred thousand pedestrians can cover half a mile in a fraction of the time that sixty-six thousand motor vehicles, each carrying one and a half persons—our average American occupancy—can carry them. And at the end of their walk, they would, even if they all suddenly decided to sit down, require a similarly minute fraction of the motorcar's wasteful parking space. London, happily, still makes use of pedestrians, as one may discover during the evening rush hour along St. James's Park on the way to Victoria Station. And, finally, the planners of the London County Council have realized the advisability of a more viable means of handling traffic than a scheme to replace the city itself with multiple expressways, for they have sponsored experimentally an entirely new kind of mixed development, called the Barbican Plan, in the City of London.

The Barbican complex, just east of Smithfield Market, is now in the process of building. This is a congeries of office buildings and upper-income-group apartment houses, forming a district and partly enclosed precinct, within easy walking distance not only of its own offices but of the City. Similar groups of office buildings, with what the British call luxury flats, are now going up in the neighborhood of St. Paul's. The aim is admirable, but the means are inadequate, since the upper-income groups so served make up but a tiny part of the working population that pours daily into the City. The high cost of land in this district will, I am afraid, make the Barbican scheme too congested, and the decision of the traffic authorities of the London County Council to plow a major road right beside the Barbican quarter may, because of the incessant noise it will bring, offset the attractions this development will have as a permanent weekday residence. But it would be a pity if this effort came to grief, for the idea of building mixed neighborhoods, able to sustain more than one urban function and demanding far less vehicular transportation for those who work there, is one of the ways a stable traffic pattern, which will make proper use of the automobile, will be achieved, without sacrificing all the special amenities of a city to the single method of motor transportation.

Fortunately, the picture of the rebuilding of London is by no means as murky as my stress on the worst features makes it seem. The most hopeless of all London's blighted areas before the war—the East End, from Finsbury to the dock-and-warehouse area of the great port itself—has become an astonishing achievement in large-scale rehabilitation. The core of this development is the Borough of Stepney, one of the most heavily bombed areas in the whole metropolis, and here the rebuilding, instead of retaining its particular mixture of functions, has properly sorted out the heavy industries and removed some of them from the domestic areas they befouled with their dirt and their noise or menaced with their dangerous trucking. The 1951 exemplar of good building, the Lansbury estate, has been imitated and in some ways carried further in other estates in this borough, producing a minimum of tall flats and a large proportion of row houses (with gardens) and "maisonettes"—that is, four-story flats in which each family occupies two floors, an arrangement that combines economically the more satisfactory features of the private house and the apartment house. This reconstruction has been of such magnitude that the L.C.C. planners have been able to girdle the area with a continuous strip of parks, which need only further planting and time for maturation to make the quarter a highly livable one, on a scale that was unthinkable in the nineteenth century, when Victoria Park, the district's chief recreation space, was developed.

Only a small portion of the decent older buildings has been put back into shape, but the planners have gone to great pains to restore the few historic ones that deserved preservation and could be rehabilitated. They have rescued a fine church, classic in detail and almost Gothic in silhouette, attributed to Hawksmoor, and an old people's home, long obliterated by the slums around it, done by Christopher Wren. This borough is also the site of Queen Mary College, one of the group of new colleges that the University of London has begun to distribute around the city (as our own City College in New York has established semi-autonomous units in all our boroughs), so the area will in time have even more of the special advantages of a well-balanced city.

This is effective urban design of a high order—all the more striking because it has taken place in what was, until the Second World War, one of the most sordid and dejected areas of London, full of fine Cockney traditions but streaked with raw poverty, misery, vice, and crime. Perhaps this is an example of Emerson's law of compensation—the part of residential London that suffered most from the bombs has undergone the greatest renovation. Luckily, the very hugeness of London gives it a certain resilience in absorbing, if not always correcting, its mistakes. Since it survived the German bombs, it may also survive its new building boom—especially if the current financial stringency lasts long enough to slow down the destructive anti-urban forces that are artfully disguised as modern architecture and modern traffic planning.

*1961*

# ELEVEN

# Lady Godiva's Town

Everyone has heard about Coventry, if only because in the Middle Ages it originated the ultimate form of the strip tease in the naked lady on horseback from whom all citizens turned their eyes except Peeping Tom, who in punishment was stricken blind. The legend is still so alive that the new hotel in the shopping center is called the Leofric, after the chaste Godiva's husband, the feudal lord of the town. In their time, the chief industry of the municipality was a Benedictine monastery; not until the end of the Middle Ages did Coventry become a manufacturing center for broadcloth, silk ribbons, and watches. At the end of the seventeenth century, when its bigger present rivals, Birmingham and Manchester, were little more than mean villages, Coventry was still a comely city; the much-travelled Celia Fiennes, an admirable contemporary observer of cities, noted in her travel journal that there "are severall good walks about the town, a large parke above the town which most people walk in." But if the blight of nineteenth-century industrialism destroyed most of Coventry's beauty, the Blitz of November, 1940, effaced much of that blight. Today the chief reason for going there is to inspect its famous shopping center, which has risen out of the ruins, and to behold its unconventional new cathedral, which should be consecrated in the spring of 1962.

Here one can see what a thriving industrial town, noted now for its motor, aircraft, machine-tool, and electric industries, can do toward making itself over into a handsome, many-sided, culturally rich modern city.

My first stop was at the cathedral, and I had the good luck to see it in the company of Sir Basil Spence, its architect, who won a competition for the task from two hundred and nineteen rivals. Historically, this is the correct way to begin a visit to Coventry, for it was the ancient monastery and cathedral that brought the market and the industry to Coventry, and many people will be coming to Coventry now just to admire the way a modern architect, using only modern means imaginatively but humbly, can bring into being a structure that does justice to a traditional institution while visibly uniting it with the fresh life of our time.

I beheld the cathedral under the worst weather conditions possible, on a dark, drizzly morning, when the mottled native pink sandstone of the walls was turned to a uniform charcoal brown by the rain, and when the cathedral was still under construction, disfigured by the usual scaffoldings and the raw surfaces one must expect in an unfinished building. But it was impressive in its almost flat, rectangular, boxlike simplicity, so unlike the soaring Gothic edifice it replaces, and impressive for the very reason that made the original sketches for this structure rather disappointing: it does not attempt to "look like" a picture-book cathedral, and it does not—the usual alternative—try to pass itself off as a striking exhibition building by the kind of visual acrobatics that centers the attention, with unfortunate symbolic accuracy, upon the technological adroitness of our age rather than upon our religious unction. The side walls are a succession of vertical stone panels alternating with narrow windows that likewise reach from floor to roof, and all arranged so that the panels and windows are at right angles to one another. Thus the ground plan of the nave forms a sort of sawtooth pattern whose purpose is to focus the incoming light upon the altar. Another divergence from the Gothic cathedrals is that the wall behind the altar of the new structure is of solid stone, as a background for the great tapestry that will eventually also rise from floor to roof, instead of the usual stone or wood reredos. The walls are sturdy enough to support the roof by themselves, but in the nave they are aided by a series of thin columns of concrete, which taper downward, to emphasize the height of the building, and which, by their very delicacy, refrain from competition with the stained-glass windows.

Even in its unfinished state, the interior was esthetically rich and resonant, for there is a play of textures and colors in the varied materials—the stone walls, the smooth concrete columns, the floor of highly polished black marble, the handsome wooden vaulting (in a diamond pattern) of the ceiling. Through the great rear window of the new cathedral one beholds the broken remnants of the Gothic tracery of the destroyed one, for by placing the building at right angles to its predecessor the architect has incorporated that potent symbol into his own work.

That stroke of imagination is the key to the whole design. Instead of wiping out the old monument in favor of an entirely new building, Spence strengthened his own composition by emphasizing the very event that had necessitated the new structure. On the main altar of the gaping Gothic shell are two crosses, one made from charred timbers, the other from nails from the destroyed roof. Behind the altar are the words "Father Forgive." The symbolism becomes all the more apt because, beyond the ruined walls, one beholds the figure of St. Michael, the patron saint of Coventry, on a tower.

But the architect has done more than preserve historical continuity. He has achieved what many modern critics have sadly admitted is all but impossible: he has given the painter and the sculptor an equal place in the design of his masterwork, and the success of the cathedral as a work of art to a large extent depends upon how they have measured up to this challenge. Spence chose probably three of the best artists in England among the older generation, and supplemented them with two very promising younger men. To Sir Jacob Epstein he gave the monumental sculpture of St. Michael conquering the Devil, which is on the wall to the right of the main entrance, pinned against the side of the cathedral. This is a three-dimensional work of no little power, completed just before Epstein's death, and it is weakened only by the somewhat too massive machine-finished lance of the victorious saint; in a curious way this ponderous weapon casts a devitalizing shadow over the rest of the composition. The interior, on the other hand, benefits by the esthetic vitality of the windows, which represent a progression, achieved mainly through color, from dawn to night, from birth to death—from the great aureole of light, a blaze of golds and reds, in John Piper's great window that rises above the baptismal font, to the dark blues and purples of Geoffrey Clarke's windows, colors that symbolize the rest of the Christian theme: resignation, sacrifice, pain, sin, death. (Studying the windows in the opposite direction, one becomes aware of another Christian symbolism, beginning with death and ending with the Resurrection and Transfiguration.) Piper's window is an unqualified triumph—wholly abstract in treatment, but in its context meaningful; even on a dark day it glows, and its colors, like those of the other windows, are reflected in muted but still opulent tones in the dark, shining floor.

Graham Sutherland did the cartoon for the tapestry. There was only one loom in the world—in France, of course—big enough to execute it. In trusting this work to a modern artist, Spence made a great wager with fate, for on the quality of this tapestry much of the esthetic splendor of the interior will depend. Both the daring and the humility of the choice —the humility of presenting to another artist the opportunity that most architects would covet for their own handiwork—are a demonstration of the spirit that gives the building its special quality. Here the purpose and meaning of the structure itself dominate its constructive expression and transcend the personalities of the architect and his collaborators. In this sense, and only in this sense, it is a thoroughly medieval building.

The new cathedral is itself essentially a magnificent box (say, rather, a jewelled casket), but there are two architectural features besides the ruin that give it distinction—the round chapels on each side of the building. On the entrance side of the nave stands the Chapel of Industry, which does homage to the spirit of Coventry's ancient guilds, for the Coventry mystery plays were famous in the Middle Ages. The somewhat Byzantine sculptural decoration of its interior has unhappily no freshness. But its stoic counterpart on the other side of the building, the Chapel of Unity, expresses a happy idea. While the cathedral is part of the Established Church of England, the Bishop of Coventry, perhaps touched by the plight of humanity in his bombed city, conceived of having one part of the cathedral open to all faiths—a part attached to the mother church but accessible from without by a separate entrance. The architect has designed this chap-

el as a high, almost tentlike structure, bare of all decoration
or symbolism, since no traditional fixtures of a church or temple could be added without violating the doctrines or the
prejudices of one sect or another. Here a Mohammedan or a
Communist could meet a Quaker or a Seventh-Day Adventist
without being aware of anything except their common humanity, under a nameless and imageless God.

In both conception and execution the new cathedral has
effected a union between feeling and form, between the traditional and the rational, between pious memories and modern prospects. Its originality consists in its indifference to
originality, and in its respect not for the letter of modernism
but for the spirit that giveth life. If thousands of people go
every year to the French town of Ronchamp to see Le Corbusier's little church, tens of thousands will have equally
good reason to go to Coventry—possibly with much greater
satisfaction, if only because the long nave of the church will
easily accommodate endless numbers of them. The fusion
of continuity and creativity that Sir Basil Spence has accomplished here strikes a note that vibrates longer and with
deeper resonance than many other works of modern architecture. In the structure itself, in its siting, in its chaste omissions and in its generous permissions, it has a completeness
and an organic richness that are more vital than formal perfection. Yet even in a city now as well ordered as Coventry
there is (alas!) a raucous note in the nearby townscape, for
within plain view of the cathedral a modern technical college has erected a slab sheathed in a hideous blue-green glass
that would mar even a good factory elevation—an aggres-
sive nonentity, misconceived, miscolored, and misplaced.
The most banal Victorian brick structure would have formed
a better background for the cathedral.

To pass from the cathedral to the nearby shopping precinct,
in the center of Coventry, may seem an anti-climax, but it is
not, for they both were made possible by the merciless
Blitz, and the main lines of this center are so well conceived that they make up for the mediocrity of some of
the buildings, which often—like the Hotel Leofric's second-
story dining room—do not take full advantage of the vistas
the planners have opened up. The first scheme for it was
started before the war, when the main shopping in Coventry
was still done on narrow, traffic-laden Smithford Street.

The young men who came up with a scheme for turning this quarter into a great pedestrian mall had the audacity to conceive a new kind of commercial district that would combine the pedestrian's leisurely freedom of the spacious, old-fashioned market place with the convenience and accessibility of the famous narrow shopping thoroughfares like London's Bond Street. The basic idea—a new kind of plan, then untried in any country—was to group buildings devoted to shopping, entertainment, and civic and cultural affairs into separate but related quarters in the heart of old Coventry, taking the spire of the cathedral as the esthetic and historic center. This plan kept close to the old pattern of the city but introduced order and open patches of green into the existing clutter. The merchants of Coventry, like their counterparts in Rotterdam when the postwar scheme for rebuilding that bombed-out city was broached, rejected the plan as a wasteful assault on sound—that is, stale—business practices, and they were totally unprepared for the proposed rebuilding of Coventry after the war. They fought the notion of a pedestrian shopping mall because they wished the traffic streets, which interfered with rather than served the shopper, to be fully restored. Even after the new plan had been approved they insisted that the shopping center be cut in two by a cross street, which has proved so needless that it has now finally been closed off, though it remains as a gratuitous scar.

I first saw this new center in 1946, when only a row of temporary huts had been built, and I was in on the debate between the planners and the businessmen of Coventry, when the latter held out for the old pattern of a shopping area, with a vast amount of traffic creeping through it, polluting the air and hindering the dismounted shopper. The town architect of Coventry at that time, Sir Donald Gibson, was outvoted for the moment, but today there is no question, even among businessmen, that he was right. The planning team under Mr. Gibson, led by Percy Johnson-Marshall, that conceived this quarter had been influenced by Le Corbusier. But they did not turn their backs completely on the past, nor did they shrink from laying out the mall on a firm axis just because axial plans and bilateral symmetry had become unfashionable. The axis, which is flanked by a double-decked sort of shopping promenade with a pedestrian bridge and breezeway halfway along it, terminates in one of Coventry's three historic church spires, and from the beginning of it one's eye takes in still another spire.

As in the cathedral, the old and the new are fused. The double-decking adds to both the liveliness and the convenience of the scheme, since the upper deck serves as a covered way above the ground-floor shops that protects the shopper from rain. This treatment goes back to the ancient medieval rows in Chester, a Roman town not very far away from the town-planning school in Liverpool, where some of the younger planners of Coventry were trained, and this double-deck form is still visible in Trajan's market in Rome.

The great advantage of this shopping center as compared with Rotterdam's Lijnbaan, a similar postwar reconstruction, is that it accommodates both small shops and great department stores, as well as professional offices of various kinds. And compared with American shopping centers, it has the special attraction of being in the heart of the city, reached easily by buses, which eliminates the difficulty of finding a parking place and of having to walk through a couple of acres of parking lot. One can wander through this protected pedestrian mall without being impeded or endangered or poisoned by motor traffic—a special boon for parents who have children with them, as well as for old people, who like to saunter along its broad flagstone walk and sit under the trees, surrounded by little islands of brilliant flowers, just to enjoy the stir of life there. Old people occupied not a few of the benches even at the noon hour when I visited the center.

Since most of the structures rise three or four stories above the walk, this precinct is more compact than our own sprawling conglomerations of one-story buildings, which tend to compress all open space except the parking lots. Thus Coventry has brought back both social activity and esthetically rewarding open areas to its once cluttered and sordid commercial center, and in doing so has intensified civic pride, to say nothing of an interest in even more ambitious plans. When, a while ago, traffic engineers proposed the slaughter of a fine row of trees for a road-widening project, forty-seven thousand citizens of Coventry signed a petition to prevent it. Here, at least, the papal infallibility of the traffic expert and the implacable omnipotence of the highway engineer were successfully challenged. (Home-town American papers please copy!)

This shopping center was conceived when the motorcar caused only a trickle of traffic in the average British industrial city, and the admirable further scheme for the heart of Coventry, which includes a ring road to circumnavigate it by following the line of the ancient town wall, must also include the furtherance of public transport and restrictions upon parking if the physical advantages of the shopping precinct are to be maintained. At one side of the mall stands a spacious circular food market, whose roof, reached by a ramp, holds two hundred cars, and other parking facilities are available nearby. But soon Coventry will have to choose between preserving and enhancing its historic core, now so brilliantly rejuvenated, and allowing the unregulated private car to destroy the city and the institutions that have made it so lively and attractive.

As in America, the municipal officials and highway engineers in England, whose affluence depends upon magnifying the mistakes in town planning every community has already made, are still under the illusion that the motorcar's demands for urban space can be met by many-laned roads and multi-story downtown garages, though all the money that goes into these expensive quack remedies serves only to spread the wasting disease of traffic over further areas of the social organism. These once-innocent remedies, now twenty years old, have been obsolete almost from the moment they were tried. They can end only in producing a vast wasteland of becalmed motorcars, so that the whole city becomes a parking lot. (In Los Angeles, the very engineers who have helped to devastate the city with their expressways and labyrinthine interchanges now tearfully admit that at the present rate of progression traffic will come to a standstill by 1980.)

The new cathedral and shopping precinct are critical points in the revival of Coventry, but they are merely a part of a larger complex that includes the late Victorian Gothic town hall (which survived the Blitz), a new set of municipal offices (where the planners themselves are installed), a new art museum, and a new theatre with a teen-agers' club. This close interweaving of urban functions in a central urban core contrasts favorably with the chronic American habit, now often imitated in England, of scattering civic buildings over the landscape, in the interest of cheaper land and more open space, instead of making effective use of the land near the center of town. But such a vitalizing concentration of municipal activities, while favoring the pedestrian use of the center, naturally piles up wheeled traffic unless there are restrictions. This means encouraging a major portion of the inhabitants to use public buses, and keeping private vehicles from permanently usurping the urban stage by inducing them to stay in the wings. Though current plans will enlarge the inner pedestrian area, which will remain free from traffic, they will also provide parking space for seventy-five hundred cars within a radius of half a mile of the center. This seemingly modest provision for a daytime population of some thirty thousand people may unfortunately— if it reduces the use of public transport—wreck the social concentration of the inner city and turn it into a hollow shell.

Coventry is in an exceptionally good position to control congestion, for the municipality owns some forty per cent of the land area of the city, and it is thus not, like most other cities, at the mercy of the mercenary landowner and the speculative builder. In putting up its new housing estates, the Coventry town-planning office, under Mr. Arthur Ling, has adopted the happy features of the American Radburn plan, which keeps motor traffic on the outskirts of a residential block or neighborhood and so creates an inner green for safe and pleasant pedestrian movement. A town like Coventry can, if it will, handle the problem of traffic in all its dimensions, including the distribution of industry, the provision of public transportation, the placement of schools, the density of population per acre.

With the rehabilitation they have already accomplished, the planners and administrators of Coventry have demonstrated the value of the city as a container and transformer of the varied life of a community—provided that all the forces and institutions needed for urban life are marshalled together for the benefit of the city as a whole. Now let them put the private motorcar in its place before all the civic improvements are riddled by this termite. As the home of an excellent electrically driven fork-lift truck, Coventry should shame the motor industry by offering a prize for an electric private car—more compact and maneuverable than any present "compact," as well as noiseless and entirely free from lethal exhaust—for town use. Instead of adapting the city to the space-eating automobile, only to find they have no city left, the planners should adapt the motorcar to the city, and treat our present glossily obsolete smog-making vehicles as we do animals that are not house-trained.

With half the scientific ingenuity that is expended on space rockets, engineers might long ago have produced a battery-propelled or thermo-electric motor with the range and power of a gas engine. Even in the petroleum-dominated United States, two new electric cars are already in production. But until the electric power system for cars is radically improved, the best solution for providing what private wheeled traffic is indispensable is two kinds of automobile— electric for urban areas to keep the air untainted and quiet, gasoline for long distances outside the city. With this division little would be lost in speed, much would be gained in convenience, health, and safety.

*1962*

# PART 2

# United States

## TWELVE

## What Wright Hath Wrought

There are many ways of approaching the new Solomon R. Guggenheim Museum, and perhaps the best is the round-about route that has been opened up by the timely appearance of Frank Lloyd Wright's *Drawings for a Living Architecture* in a monumental volume published for the Bear Run Foundation and the Edgar J. Kaufmann Charitable Foundation by Horizon Press. With its generous format and with reproductions of exquisite faithfulness, this is not merely a grand cross-section of Wright's work but the most intimate means of coming in contact with his mind and genius. It is not unusual for an architect to be a man of talent in the kindred arts of painting and sculpture; that, indeed, was almost the classic preparation for an architect in the early Renaissance, and architects like Le Corbusier have probably spent as much of their time at the easel as at the drawing board. What is unusual about Wright is that the sketches and the finished presentation drawings of his buildings are works of art in their own right, carrying his unmistakable signature. Both his crayon sketches and his plans express in the most sensitive way the exhilarating and positively liberating effect of his genius. The drawings show—sometimes more clearly even than the actual buildings—the combination of

formal discipline and effulgent feeling, the union of the audacious engineer, enthralled by the possibilities of technology,
and the highly individualized artist, that were the man himself. The color reproductions are particularly good. Wright
used one of the most difficult of media, the colored crayon, as
well as water color, in renderings whose handling of landscape and foliage sometimes reminds one of Dürer's sketches,
yet the drawings have a kind of architectural firmness because of the use of fine straight lines, seemingly ruled, to
convey an underlying sense of geometric structure, in sky or
background as well as in building. But the color, even when
used to embellish the plans, remains delicately lyrical, with
an early-morning freshness.

Here, before his plans and elevations were transformed
into buildings, are examples of Wright's creative intentions
at their purest. If not a single one of these projects had been
carried out, one would still know him for the original artist
that he was, the inexhaustible creator, whose formal structures
and images, far from shrinking into a convention, were un-
folding until the very moment of his death and were far
more rich and free in the last third of his life than in his
early years. Who but Wright could have conceived the
fabulous setting of his proposed Baghdad Opera House,
placed in a large, circular garden, which in turn was to be
walled in by a low, circular "ziggurat" with parking space for
over fourteen hundred cars?

There are many vital aspects of Wright's architecture—
above all, those produced by movement through space—that
cannot be translated into perspective drawings, so one must
not think of such renderings, however evocative, as an equivalent for the experience of the buildings themselves. But
these imagined forms are unique for their immediate revela-
tion of Wright's personality, with his fingertip sensitiveness,
his expansive response to nature, his delight in the intricate
play of natural and fabricated forms, his immense, unflagging
vitality—the vitality that enabled him, like his Imperial
Hotel in Tokyo, to sustain earthquake blows that would have
shattered another personality.

Wright's architectural work was just such a defiant break
with the past, just such an attempt to establish a firm American core as Whitman had conceived half a century earlier:
his whole accomplishment could be described, from first
to last, as a "Song of Myself." In these plans and renderings,

one has Wright the poet without any disturbing afterthoughts
about the relation of his architectural fantasies to the needs
and functions they served, or the conditions of climate and
weather they had to meet, or their responsibility to the neighborhood or the community, or the precedent that they helped
establish—or failed to establish—for other buildings. Here, in
fact, in terms of an old definition of architecture, is pure
"Delight," dwarfing all considerations of "Commodity" and
"Firmness." Wright's drawings live in their own world, self-
begotten, self-enclosed, often breathtaking in their originality
and endearing in their loveliness. When his designs fail esthetically—as I feel that his design for the Rogers Lacy
Hotel in Dallas, the garish Golden Beacon skyscraper in
Chicago, and the Marin Country public buildings all deplor-
ably fail—it is usually because the artist was led astray by
his sheer technical exuberance, which tempted him to ignore
his own sense of fitness and to flout other human responses.

Just because of its direct, unembarrassed presentation of
Wright's personality with a minimum of textual explication,
his *Drawings* is, I think, the most satisfactory monograph that
has been published on his architecture, though I would not
belittle the pioneer studies published by Wasmuth and
Wijdeveld. Any building of Wright's must be viewed within
the frame of his life's work that this book provides, and any
lapse must be placed within the perspective of his long series of triumphs in a career pursued without regard for historical conventions or chic contemporary stereotypes. By the
same token, when Wright failed, he failed with originality and
decision—the inverted triumph of a great acrobat who so
despises the safety nets that he would rather break his neck
than rely on them.

Wright dared greatly in all that he undertook, and
above all he dared to be himself. Loving Emerson, he must
have recognized a special personal blessing in Emerson's
statement that "whoso would be a man must be a non-
conformist." Wright lived to see the confident, self-reliant
America of Emerson and Whitman, even the mugwump
America of Howells, turn into that meek, tame, glossily corrupt totalitarian "democracy" which now lives—or half lives
—in the shadow world of the television screen. To one who
had the audacity to sin against the conventions of this society
in almost every way except its love for exhibitionism and
publicity, much may be forgiven.

Frank Lloyd Wright was a chip off the old American block. In the sense in which the term still applied before the Civil War, he might be called one of the last Americans —a distinction he shared with such a profoundly different personality as Robert Frost. In his unique development, both the good and the bad qualities one associates with that role were exaggerated: on one hand his isolationism, his anti-Europeanism, his belligerence, his lightly triggered arrogance, his colossal self-admiration, but over against this his originality, his freshness, his gay generosity, his boundless affirmation of life, his belief that the world need not remain decayed and corrupt but might be made over anew in the morning.

These thoughts on his life and character temper all that I am bound, out of my respect for Wright's greatness as an artist, to say about the Guggenheim Museum, the only example of his architecture in New York. If I have occasion to speak severely, remember that I am talking about a true artist, one of the most richly endowed geniuses this country has produced—an artist who has no need for the apologetic leniency one might accord to a lesser talent. For the most serious flaws in Wright's work, it may be that our country fully shares reproof with the artist. Had we had the proud understanding, when he was in mid-career, to encourage him with great commissions, we would have earned the right to challenge his narcissism and his complacent egocentricity and to require a more sober perfection than he, in the sheer willfulness of his genius, was prepared to achieve. Wright was at his best with appreciative but self-reliant clients, and in an equally appreciative America he might have risen to our more searching demands and thrown away the shallow showmanship that on too many occasions marred his architecture no less than his public relations.

The Guggenheim Museum is a formidable, ponderous, closed-in concrete structure of almost indescribable individuality; the main element, the art gallery, might be called an inverted ziggurat that tapers toward the bottom—not the Mesopotamian kind, which stood on a square base, but Bruegel's round version in his "Tower of Babel." Functionally, this museum, which occupies a whole block front on Fifth Avenue, from Eighty-eighth to Eighty-ninth Street, divides into two parts—at the south end a low, telescoped tower (the ziggurat) crowned by a wired-glass dome visible solely from the air, and at the north end an attached administration building only half its height, a combination of rectangular and circular forms, with portholes for windows, opening on viewless balconies with solid parapets. The ground floor of the tower is recessed under the overhanging second floor to create a deep shadow, so that the tower appears to be set on a strong horizontal base formed by the continuous concrete band of the second-floor wall, which seems, because of the shadow, to float in space.

In many of Wright's later designs, such as the unexecuted group of funeral chapels in San Francisco, such a broad horizontal base serves both to bring together separate elements and to set the building apart from the immediate landscape, as was done in such Renaissance designs as the villas in Frascati. In the Museum, the base seems wholly detached and esthetic—not functional, as in the case of Wright's early prairie houses, which rested, without the usual cellar and foundations, on a low pedestal. The main mass, the tower, is set back from the building lines at the southwest corner, where the second-story wall bulges out into a bay that emphasizes, in profile, the wider curve and sloping sides of the ziggurat.

Despite its dull color, a sort of evaporated-milk ochre, this great monolith stands out boldly from the flat, anonymous apartment houses in the neighborhood, the positiveness of the form offsetting the all too congenial mediocrity of tone. The building is so definitely a thing apart, so different from every other one on Fifth Avenue, that the sprawling, pale green letters (along the lower edge of the second-story wall) that identify it may almost be forgiven for their feebleness because they are actually not needed at all. As an external symbol of contemporary abstract art, this building has genuine fitness in its severe rationality of form. But Wright had, out of respect for the materials and constructive elements he chose, denied himself the more enlivening resources of which he was master. This building is non-traditional, non-representational, non-historical abstract art in its own right; indeed, it not merely coincides with the contents, it supersedes them. You may go to this building to see Kandinsky or Jackson Pollock; you remain to see Frank Lloyd Wright.

From the moment I examined the preliminary drawings I was disturbed and puzzled by its design, and I am still disturbed, though further reflection and observation have revealed a little of Wright's intentions and decisions. At that, almost every part of this design leads to a critical question mark. Let us first consider the exterior, and, to begin with, the choice of monolithic concrete. Whether it is in the raw state imprinted by the mold, or whether it is smoothed and painted, concrete remains a sullen material. If left in the rough, as in Le Corbusier's Maison de l'Unité d'Habitation, in Marseille, or in Louis Kahn's Yale Art Gallery, it is tolerable only at a distance; if it is smooth, unless it is mixed and poured with extreme care, cracks and splotches are bound to show from the beginning, and if the smoothness is covered with a cement paint, as in this case, it lacks texture and character. Worst of all, the flawed surface denies the solidity of the material, as if it were hastily done in plaster over canvas.

Wright was a master of texture, in brickwork no less than in stone. Yet in this building, by its nature a showpiece, he was content to emphasize the sheer elephantine solidity of the heavy concrete walls. Is it possible that this structure, seemingly designed from the foundations up as if it were a fortification, was meant to be precisely that—as indestructible as he could make it? There would be at least a strong subjective justification behind this folly. Two of Wright's early buildings, among the best of his first twenty-five years as an architect, were prematurely demolished—the Midway Gardens in Chicago and the Larkin office building in Buffalo—and now the Imperial Hotel seems doomed. Did he design the Guggenheim Museum as a super-pillbox that would resist vandalism or demolition as effectively as those surviving concrete bunkers Hitler's minions built along the Channel coast? Wright is reported to have said that if a nuclear bomb destroyed New York, his building, on its cushioned foundation, would merely bounce with the shock and survive. Thus Wright would be left, in effect, surveying the ruins, ironically triumphing over the city that had waited till the end of his life to give him this one opportunity. He may have been consoled by the thought, but, apparently to insure that triumph, he sacrificed the purposes of the Museum and created an empty monument as the sole prospective occupant of an untenanted world. In his plan for the Baghdad Opera House garage, Wright turned an embarrassment—the eventual need for motorcar parking—into a magnificent opportunity, but in the Guggenheim Museum he turned an opportunity into an obstacle. Even as a fortress, even as a bomb shelter, it falls short of perfection.

His seeming decision to leave behind an indestructible monument should perhaps enlist our sympathy, but the result does not merit our approval. From this error all the worst features of the exterior design spring. It is formidably *im*pressive, but it is not *ex*pressive of anything except the desire for monumental solidity. Montgomery Schuyler, our best nineteenth-century architectural critic, said that H. H. Richardson's overponderous buildings were defensible solely in a military sense, and the gibe applies equally to Wright's museum. Only in the intimate touches do the more lovable features of Wright's imagination emerge, such as the banks of green foliage that provide a flare of living color and texture along the Fifth Avenue approach. There is nothing else in *this* exterior to reduce the sense of grim military self-sufficiency, and the office wing is just as massive and as sparing of windows as the main structure. Except for the wealth of greenery—particularly effective in the motor court, which is framed by the entrance—there is nothing of Wright's specific imprint in the outward structure but the circular form.

In using rounded forms, Wright shares honors with Eric Mendelsohn, who first suggested the special plastic quality of concrete in the imaginative architectural sketches he published after the end of the First World War. Ever since Wright designed the Ralph Jester house, in Palos Verdes, California, back in the thirties, he was fascinated by rounded forms, curving ground plans, and circular enclosures, and he continued, with increasing felicity, to explore these architectural resources. His circular houses, such as the one he designed for his son, David, are among the best examples of his later work. But in accenting the massiveness of monolithic concrete by replacing windows with mere narrow horizontal slots between the floors of the Museum tower, Wright introduced an inflexible element into his design, for he proposed to make the amount of natural illumination, as well as the inner space, unalterable.

Again one searches for some reason besides Wright's assertion of his own ego. His circular tower creates an exhibition room whose dimensions in no way can be modified to suit the needs of a particular showing. This is an all-or-nothing building; one takes it on Wright's terms or one does not take it at all. In planning it, what Wright did was to re-design his enchanting V. C. Morris shop building, in San Francisco, which has the same system of interior circula-tion; but he hollowed out the interior and replaced the flat Morris façade with an exterior that would properly correspond with the circular interior of the Museum. Unfortunately, his interior scheme, a brilliant one for a shop, because it in-creases the temptations to buy by spreading all the merchan-dise before the eye, is a ruinous one for a museum, in which the works of art, surely, should impose their needs on the building. But Wright never had a place for the painter in any of his buildings, and it was perhaps too much to hope that there would be a place for him even in an art museum.

For all that the exterior of the Museum is contemporary abstract art, in creating it Wright hid his light, so to speak, under a concrete funnel; so that it is only in the interior that one may see it burning—in such a dazzling fashion, in fact, that it negates its function by obscuring all the other works of art that a museum supposedly exists to display. If the out-side of the building says Power—power to defy blast, to resist change, to remain as immune to time as the Pyramids —the interior says Ego, an ego far deeper than the pool in which Narcissus too long gazed. On the outside, Wright's composition puts this architecture under the wing of the New Brutalist school; on the inside, he is the old Roman-ticist, singing—as if he were alone in the wilderness—the Song of Myself, but without communicating the sense of speaking for all other men and inviting their contributions, and enhancing their personalities, too, that made Whitman's swelling ego so lovable.

Thus, though the exterior of the Museum is far from neg-ligible as "building," it is a feat for which the contractors and workers deserve heartier congratulations than the architect. More than one builder shied away from this difficult task, and the architectural pleasure evoked by the massive con-crete forms is unduly small when one considers the immense effort and expense involved. For while, as in all of Wright's buildings, the interior and exterior are conceived as organ-ically one, in this case the outer expression is mere "building" or "engineering," while Wright's special gifts—and his some-times defiant weaknesses as an architect—do not come to life until one gains the interior. In lesser degree this is true of many other domed structures, like the Pantheon, in Rome, and Santa Sophia, in Istanbul: but this distinction particularly applies to the Guggenheim Museum.

Yet once you come close to the Guggenheim Museum, Wright has you in his hold. From the time you scrape your feet on the unmistakably Wright grating in the vestibule and grasp the bronze bar that, serving as handle, stretches from top to bottom of the glass door, you are under his enchantment. Entering, you are in a monumental hall of exalted proportions. The form is circular, and the spiralling ramp that ascends it—broken by a bulging bay on each floor—creates a rotating band of light and dark, of solid and void, that terminates in the opaque, almost flat wired-glass dome. This dome, a combination of broken-spider-web space divisions and strong supporting forms, is in Wright's characteristic manner, though uncharacteristically, it closes out the sky as completely as the concrete structure closes out the landscape. As for the strong curve of the bays, it not merely enhances the dynamism of the helical ramp, which widens with each floor, but makes it psychologically overpowering—if not physiologically almost unbearable. For the abrupter fall of the ramp on this sharp curve adds to the muscular tensions created by the form of the structure and its dizzy impact on the eye. This is not a tall building—only six stories—but it gives the effect of great height. Without ornament, without texture, without positive color, in a design as smoothly cylindrical as a figure by Fernand Léger—this is how Wright shows himself here a master of the abstract resources of modern form. Here is the freedom that Mendelsohn dreamed of and first brought into existence in the Einstein Tower, in Potsdam, but here, too, is the disciplined movement that the baroque architects sometimes weakened in the exuberance of their ornament. In the very restraint of this composition, Wright, like a good disciple of Lao-tse, dramatizes its essential element—the central void, filled with light. It takes an effort to turn away from this striking composition, modelled with such boldness yet with such discipline and with such a vivid interplay of form between the curving ramp and the circular "utility stacks," which house the closets and small lavatories on each level, rising against the wall on either side of the elevator to visually tie all the floors together.

As an object by itself, the Guggenheim Museum interior

is, like the exterior, a remarkable example of abstract sculpture; indeed, it is a new kind of mobile sculpture, whose dynamic flow is accentuated by the silhouettes of the spectators, who form a moving frieze against the intermittent spots of painting on the walls. Thus Wright permitted the requirements of his composition to dominate both the works of art and the freedom of the viewer. They are needed to complete it, but apart from this they do not signify. Those who respond to the interior do proper homage to Wright's genius. If the purpose of the Museum is solely to exhibit Wright, the interior has magnificent justification for its existence. And if the spectator forgets the other works of art it contains, the building is—for him if not for the neglected artists—a compensation and a unique reward. What other monumental interior in America produces such an overwhelming effect?

But architecture is not simply sculpture, and this building was meant also to serve as a museum. In that context, it is an audacious failure. Wright has allotted the paintings and sculptures on view only as much space as would not infringe upon his abstract composition. It is an open secret that he paid no attention to the program set before him and overrode every attempt to make this great shell workable as a museum. The dominating conception would have needed complete revision if the building were to be anything but a display of Wright's virtuosity. With all the willfulness of genius, he created the minimum amount of gallery space at the maximum cost and the all but complete sacrifice of the Museum's essential requirements. This architect who stood for organic forms, who continually preached the lessons of life and growth and change, created a shell whose form had no relation to its function and offered no possibility of any future departure from his rigid preconceptions. Except for a single high-ceilinged, triangular side room opposite the main entrance, on the first floor, the sole exhibition space is that great circular wall within the tower. The continuous ribbon of promenade that winds along this wall has, for a museum, a low ceiling—nine feet eight inches—so only a picture well within the vertical boundaries thus created can be shown. The wall provided by Wright slanted outward, following the outward slant of the exterior wall, and paintings were not supposed to be hung vertically or shown in their true plane but were to be tilted back against it. The interior, under Wright's direction, was painted the same dull cream as the rest of the Museum. To make matters worse, he interposed a sloping shelf between the wall and the spectator, so that anyone interested in a closer view—whether because of myopia or a curiosity about brush stroke and treatment—could not get near a canvas. Nor could he escape the light shining in his eyes from the narrow slots in the wall. Only on the first two floors, where there are no light slots, did he forgo this embarrassing embankment.

Short of insisting that no pictures at all be shown, Wright could not have gone much further to create a structure sublime in its own right but ridiculous as a museum of art. The most pretentious Renaissance palace could hardly have served a modern artist worse. There is not a mistake in rigidity of plan, in scale, or in setting made by the pompous academic temple museums of the past that Wright did not reproduce or actually cap. Even the sculpture on view has difficulty in surviving Wright's treatment; it is in hopeless competition with the overwhelming sculptural force of the building itself. It is as if Wright had only one condition to impose on all rival artists—unconditional surrender.

With infinite labor, the Museum has since sought to neutralize Wright's blunders and to salvage the concept of the Museum as a public place for viewing works of art. But there are errors that no ingenuity can overcome, and one of them is the ramp. With it, the whole building is in motion, and the spectator must be in motion, too—part of a moving procession of people, with no place to sit down except a side bench at each floor, no place to retreat to, no possibility of changing his relation to the object viewed, except by viewing it at a distance, from the opposite side of the hall. The worst feature of the old-fashioned museum was the continuous corridor, and it is not improved here by being made a spiral. It remains only for some pious machine-minded disciple of Wright's to go one step farther and place the pictures on a moving belt, so that the spectator may remain seated. The sloping ramp and ceiling, and the slanting vertical members that divide the wall into segments, magnify the problem—the annoying distortion of view—by destroying parallels and right angles for anyone who has come to look at pictures. Who has not felt an excruciating necessity to readjust a picture when it is hung even slightly out of kilter?

In short, in the state Wright left the Museum, it was magnificent but unusable, and the very worst service James Johnson Sweeney, its director, could have done Wright's reputation would have been to open the Museum without making any changes. That might have been a justifiable revenge in return for Wright's dismissal of all suggestions that lessened his sense of omnicompetence and omnipotence, but I am glad that the Museum did not avail itself of it. Failing to enlist Wright's understanding collaboration, the Museum authorities made a gallant effort to treat his formidable shell the way an engineer might treat a mountain he cannot remove but can circumvent by a tunnel. They called in Alfred Binder, a lighting engineer, and in association with Mr. Sweeney he evolved a system of back illumination that diffuses the natural light from Wright's narrow slots in the wall and supplements it with artificial light—front lighting that focuses directly on the pictures instead of on the spectator. The cream of the interior was changed to white, and the pictures, instead of being propped against the wall, jut forth from it, supported by adjustable steel rods, as much as four feet. This device spares the visitor, as far as possible, the distortion of view caused by Wright's interior plan and presents the pictures under an intense illumination, full of radiance but not without glare. Thus the lighted wall becomes the real frame of the pictures.

My first impressions of this ingenious rectification were highly favorable, apart from my residual doubts about the value of constant artificial illumination of such intensity. But further visits have disclosed that when the sun pours through the dome the brilliance of the lighting is unkind to paintings of any subtlety, and that the glass-covered channels of the back lighting above the pictures are so near the paintings as to be distracting. Only when one sees the paintings across the wide void of the gallery, from the other side of the ramp, with the wall lighting troughs cut out by the impending ramp, does one view them in a satisfactory light. Though the present arrangement is doubtless better than Wright's cavalier treatment, it needs to be modified and perfected. Even in the high triangular exhibition room, the lights that face the spectator are irritatingly obtrusive.

Wright might have felt that these innovations ruined the architectural effect of his great spiral, but their sole effect, as far as I can see, is to alter the relation of light and dark, and sharpen the dramatic effect of the winding ribbons of space and wall. The method of displaying the pictures at a distance from the wall was employed, I understand, at the big Picasso exhibition in Rome, and it makes use of technical resources and concepts that belong as properly to our particular age as the lushly carved gilt picture frames did to the palatial mansions and pompous ceremonies they were part of. Very likely this "framing in light" will be copied by museums that do not have to meet the difficulties that Wright gratuitously imposed. On a plot as generous as this one, with Central Park to provide both a contrasting outer view and the maximum of natural light, he had a rare chance to evolve a solution that would do full justice to the art, to the museum visitor, and not least to his own imagination and invention. But by committing himself to the continuous ramp and the closed shell of the building he turned his back on that open landscape and the varied natural light that were his for the asking. As if to emphasize this perversity, he wasted half the imposing frontage on the administration offices and enclosed them in a wall as nearly windowless as the gallery. The fact that Wright threw away such advantages—which lent themselves to many alternative solutions in forms just as bold as the present one—is the bitterest pill this box holds for at least one of his admirers. Even in creating a place in which to exhibit himself as supreme master of abstract art, he hardly did justice to himself, for the self he put on display was his worse self, the exhibitionist and the autocrat, not the poetic creator of form who could evolve a hundred fresh architectural images while his rivals were painfully trying to evolve a single one.

In every aspect of architecture, except as an abstract composition in interior space, one's final judgment of Wright's Guggenheim Museum must, then, be a sadly unfavorable one, such a judgment as only an old friend may in fear and trembling impart to the living and only a life-long admirer feel free to deliver over the work of the dead. In coming to this verdict, I pass over the minor flaws—the absence of sufficient storeroom space, so that one whole floor of the spiral must be devoted to storage, and the lecture hall, too wide for its purpose, too lacking in facilities to serve as a little theatre, since it has none of the flexibility of function and seating that such a room might easily have had—for in some degree these shortcomings are all counterbalanced by many ingratiating touches. So, too, I ignore the administration building, with faults even more flagrant than those in the Museum itself, and I blame the city's building code, rather than Wright, for the lowness of the balustrade that lines the outer edge of the ramp—a lowness that seems scarcely adequate to its protective function.

There are two dominant types of architecture today, both anti-functional, both meretricious—that of the package and that of the Procrustean bed. This museum is a Procrustean structure; the art in it must be stretched out or chopped off to fit the bed Wright prepared for it. The building magnifies Wright's greatest weakness as an architect: the fact that once he fastened on a particular structural form (a triangle, a hexagon, a circle), he imposed it upon every aspect of his design, with no regard for the human purposes it presumably served. He thus sometimes turned a too strict logic into a hollow rhetoric. Despite all the sculptural strength the interior of the Guggenheim Museum boasts, the building as a whole fails as a work of architecture. And it is ironic to find that this failure is of exactly the same order—and because of the same kind of arrogance and willfulness—as that of Le Corbusier's equally ambivalent Maison de l'Unité d'Habitation. In both cases the plan is arbitrary, the interior space is tortured, and the essential functions are frustrated in order to comply with the architect's purely formal esthetic choices. This is not architectural originality but academicism.

The architects who pursue their formal aims so intently without consideration of all the public functions they serve are really claiming the privileges of the painter and the sculptor without fully accepting the responsibilities of their own profession. And they do this to their own disadvantage, for they forget that even minor irritations arising from functional deficiencies may seriously lower the esthetic vitality of their form. In the case of the Guggenheim Museum, the lapses are not minor, and Wright's hollow triumph is all the worse because he was lending the weight of his genius to the fashionable aberration of the moment—the curious belief that the functional aspects of architecture are unimportant. Instead of showing, as he well might have, how a great modern architect does justice to every aspect of a building, and not least the esthetic—without making timid compromises or irrational sacrifices or frivolous omissions—Wright turned his back on that challenge. He thus defeated his own purpose by producing a building that in order to function at all could not remain what he had planned it to be long enough to be formally opened. The old should not set such a bad example to the young, and the greatest of our architectural masters should not, while still hale and of sound mind, have added such a codicil to his last will and testament.

I can think of only one way of fully redeeming Wright's monumental and ultimately mischievous failure—that of turning the building into a museum of architecture. This would be in keeping with the form of the building and would cover up most of its mistakes. Could it be that it was this, and not abstract painting, that Wright had in mind, at least unconsciously, all the time? If so, the joke is on us, for this is the great master's monument to both his art and to himself. Its absurdities as a museum thus become its ultimate glory as a work of art: a work designed to outlast the transitory modes of contemporary art and even the city in which it is set.

*1959*

# POSTSCRIPT:

## *In Memoriam: 1869-1959*

One of our giant redwoods has fallen, and left a space we cannot fill by any quick plantation of lesser trees. For years men will build new buildings from the mere loppings of the giant's branches, without even approaching the main trunk, which remains inviolable. Like our other venerable sequoias, this tree has a name, Frank Lloyd Wright. By general agreement today, he counts as one of the greatest creative artists the nineteenth century brought forth in any field; while as architect, through the scope of his fantasy and the range of his formal experiments, he towers above his contemporaries, young and old. It took three centuries to grow this man, and it may take an even longer time to plumb the depths of his genius and to follow through to their ultimate destination all the trails he opened up.

In none of the arts has our country produced a figure of more indisputable originality than Frank Lloyd Wright, or one more deeply colored by his native soil, and by the folkways of the genial, cornfed, sky-open Middle West, the land that nourished his literary contemporaries, Carl Sandburg, Sherwood Anderson, Edgar Lee Masters, and one greater than they, Abraham Lincoln, before him. In Wright's work the old agrarian democracy finally took form in buildings so deeply indigenous that they mark a final break with our colonialism. Yet because of Wright's confident commitment to all that science and technics could offer, his creations point to a future in which mechanization and standardization and mass production would themselves come under the formative influence of art. Thus Wright embraced both sides of the New World personality: the pioneer and the inventor, the romantic and the utilitarian, the defiant rebel and the genial extravert asking nothing for himself he did not demand, as of right, for his fellow citizens.

Even in his lesser moments, this proud upstanding man was deep in the American grain. Consider well one of the last of his designs, that for a Mile-High Skyscraper—what was this but a Tall Story in every sense of the word, in the pioneer tradition of Paul Bunyan: a building whose foundations might well have been laid in "A Diamond as Big as the Ritz." Even Wright's breezy arrogance, which he preferred, he said often, to a hypocritical and dishonest humility, had the innocent if seemingly outrageous swagger of the frontiersman, ready to match his strength against all challengers. That aplomb and that daring were in the spirit of Jefferson, when, writing to one of his daughters, he observed that "it is in the nature of the American character to regard nothing as impossible." Wright indeed carried into a later age the sense of inexhaustible human possibility that quickens the pages of Emerson, Whitman, Thoreau, and even Melville.

Loving Emerson from his youth, Wright must have taken as a sort of personal blessing Emerson's dictum: "Whoso would be a man must be a non-conformist." His gifts of originality were so high, and his contempt for the derivative and the imitative so deep, that he usually disdained to pay the homage of imitation even to his own earlier work, and treated every fresh design as if it stood alone. So he kept alive, even in his old age, the creative powers, the sheer fecundity and exuberance, of his youth. Wright dared greatly in all that he undertook, and above all he dared to be himself. Even in his lifetime Wright's personality had a kind of mythic potency, magnified and marvellous; for he actually said and did and wrote and built what other men hardly dare to project in their most private dreams.

But let us now begin at the beginning. Frank Lloyd Wright was born close to the heart of mid-America itself, in Richland Center, Wisconsin, on June 8, 1869, and before he reached the end of his three-generation career, on April 9, 1959, he had planted his buildings in almost every region in America. From his father, who was a preacher and an organist, Wright inherited both his love for the music of Bach and Beethoven and perhaps the didactic tendencies of his later years; but this was mixed with traits he derived from the Welsh Joneses, his mother's family; and it was his Welsh inheritance that lay closest always to Wright's heart and prompted him to bestow on his own home the name of the fabulous Welsh bard, Taliesin.

Even before his birth Wright's mother, Anna, consecrated him to the profession of architecture, and hung pictures of great cathedrals around her young baby's crib; while the very educational toys she found for him at the Centennial Exhibition in 1876, blocks and colored paper in geometric shapes with bright primary colors, deeply influenced his ornament, on his own confession, throughout his life. From his mother, too, came his taste for the simple and the natural: food that kept its natural flavors, wood that showed its natural grain and color, structures that respected the nature of the materials. All this was deepened by his apprenticeship as a farmboy to the soil itself; for that part of his boyhood spent on his Uncle James's Wisconsin farm toughened his body and fortified his spirit, making him able to withstand adversity and invite success through his high physical vitality.

For an architect of his period, Wright had the unusual good fortune to get a grounding as an engineer in the School of Engineering at the University of Wisconsin. This supplied the needful tools for his intuitive engineer's imagination, while it made him more ready than most of his contemporaries to espouse the new processes and methods that the machine offered to an architect ready to work with them. And in addition Wright had the good fortune to complete his early architectural education by serving as chief draftsman in the office of Dankmar Adler and Louis Sullivan, two masters of the Chicago School. Once Wright set up in practice for himself, he was chiefly occupied with the transformation of the American dwelling house, carrying out more consciously and more thoroughly the work originally begun by H. H. Richardson in the eighteen-eighties. That whole story is by now too well known to be repeated here; but its outcome was to establish a new idiom in American architecture, an idiom which, like our regional landscapes and climates, was responsive to many different moods, from the Robie House to the Coonley House, from his own succession of Taliesins to the Millard House or the Kaufmann House, "Falling Water."

So rich was Frank Lloyd Wright in invention, so fertile and abundant in bringing forth fresh forms and images, that one cannot attempt even a brief summary of his achievements. The great buildings that were built, like the Larkin Building in Buffalo, and the great buildings that remain unbuilt, like the Baghdad Opera House, testify equally to his genius. Even if only his drawings remained, he would still be identifiable as a consummate artist and an original architect. What one should stress, perhaps, in conclusion is the relation of Wright innovations in architecture to those that were made in American literature during the first half of the nineteenth century. For Wright's architecture was just such a defiant break with the past, such an attempt to establish a firm American core, as Whitman had carried out in *Leaves of Grass*.

In every sense, then, Frank Lloyd Wright was a chip off the old American block. If this accounts for his isolationism, his anti-Europeanism, his rejection of the historic, the classic, the traditional, it also lay beneath his originality, his gay generosity, his imaginative audacity, his boundless affirmation of life, his sense that the world need not remain decayed and corrupt, but might be made over anew in the morning. This affiliation with an older America, while drawing freely on all the energies of our present age, accounts for many of Wright's most characteristic contributions: not least the fact that he was more at home with the architecture of the Maya, the Japanese, the ancient Mesopotamians, than he was with the Romans and the Greeks. Yet the fact that Wright's work was warmly received, from the beginning, in Europe, as well as in America, shows that in the very act of liberating architecture from the dead forms of the past, he had produced buildings that, for all their idiomatic richness, were universal in their appeal.

The movement of ideas that had begun in the works of Emerson and his contemporaries, plumbing to its depths the experience of New World man, and attempting to give organic structure to the life that was here being created, was brought to completion in the architecture of Frank Lloyd Wright. With Wright's death, a great age passes away; and in the act of his closing with beautiful finality one part of the American past, this bold spirit summons us forth on a wider quest.

*1960*

## THIRTEEN

# The Pennsylvania Station Nightmare

For perhaps two years, I have watched, with silent misgiving, the reorganization of the interior of Pennsylvania Station. As the extent of the demolition grew, my bewilderment grew with it. I could hardly believe that any rational purpose could justify the devastation that was being worked, and as the bottoms of the row of great stone columns that run from north to south across the station were chipped away and covered with a light-hued plastic, my bewilderment became incredulity. So I waited, hoping that some brilliant stroke of planning, beyond any notions I could form from the unfinished work, would turn the phantasmagoria my eyes beheld into a benign dream. But now that the scheme has taken shape, it is plain that I waited in vain. As things are going, I fully expect that Jules Guerin's begrimed mural maps, which adorn the walls above the concourse and which were once, not unjustly, described as one of the few examples of successful mural art in the country, will give way to colossal color transparencies or winking whiskey ads. The only consolation is that nothing more that can be done to the station will do any further harm to it. As in nuclear war, after complete destruction has been achieved, one cannot increase the damage by doubling the destructive forces.

The Pennsylvania Station, now half a century old, was the collaborative product of Alexander Johnston Cassatt, the Pennsylvania Railroad's president, and Charles Follen McKim, of McKim, Mead & White, who got the commission in 1902 and finished the job in 1910, after four years of building. The purpose Mr. Cassatt had in mind was to provide a magnificent, monumental structure that would serve the railroad well and embellish the city. "Certain preliminary matters had to be settled with President Cassatt before McKim could begin to think of the design," Charles Moore, McKim's biographer, notes. "The company had a notion of utilizing the very valuable air space above the station by building a hotel. Mr. McKim argued that the great Pennsylvania Railroad owed the metropolis a thoroughly and distinctly monumental gateway." And professional and civic pride won out over cupidity. But, unfortunately, the spirit of adventure had gone out of American architecture. Except for Louis Sullivan, Frank Lloyd Wright, and a handful of their followers, no one any longer had the courage or the imagination to create new forms native to our own culture and the century. So the station was cast in the classic form of the Roman baths of Caracalla; indeed, McKim had intuitively prepared himself for this commission, in 1901, by assembling a gang of workmen in those very baths, so that he could study the esthetic effect of the huge scale of the structure on the crowds passing under its arches. The punctuating beat of the rows of vast classic columns, without and within, of Pennsylvania Station turned out to be the dying note of the classic revival that had begun in 1893 with the Chicago World's Fair. But though the classic forms were symbolically dead and functionally meretricious, McKim's handling of the main elements of the design for the station was superb. The basic practical problem, created by the fact that the railway tracks, in order to pass under the East and Hudson Rivers on their way out of town, were far below ground, has, it is true, never been properly solved. Above the track level is a second level, along which one makes one's way from the trains to the subway lines on Seventh and Eighth Avenues; above this is a third level, containing the concourse and the ticket offices, and flanked by the taxicab ramps. Even this level is well below ground, and it is reached from east, west, north, and south by broad stairways from the streets surrounding the station. The ambiguity of the many exits from the trains, some leading to the second level and some to the third, is baffling to anyone attempting to meet a person arriving on a train, and creates a certain degree of confusion for the traveller seeking a taxi or a subway. Even worse, the inadequacy of the escalator system handicaps the passenger with heavy baggage much more today than it did in those fabled days when porters were numerous and did not become invisible when a train arrived. In these respects, the Thirtieth Street Station in Philadelphia and the Union Station in Washington, even with their two levels of railway tracks, are more satisfactory, despite the fact that the system of widely spaced double exits in the Philadelphia station makes meeting an incoming passenger difficult without prearrangement.

But, apart from these vexatious lapses, the general plan of Pennsylvania Station had a noble simplicity that helped it to work well. A broad, unobstructed corridor, running from east to west, was the visible expression of the station's axis, from Seventh Avenue clear through to Eighth Avenue. McKim made good use of his eight-acre site, which covered two entire blocks, by providing a sunken entrance, at the concourse level, for vehicles on both the north and the south sides of the station—far more adequate than the accommodations at Grand Central. If one approached the station by car, one had to walk but a short distance to the ticket windows and the trains. The ticket offices, the big waiting rooms, and the ample concourse, capable of embracing the largest holiday crowds, were at right angles to the axis and flanked the broad corridor. McKim, wishing to keep the axis and corridor clear, even placed the information booth in a northern corner, in a niche formed by the men's waiting room and some of the ticket booths, but wiser heads soon moved this important facility to the center of the ticket hall, so that passengers could approach it from the four points of the compass.

McKim's plan had a crystal clarity that gave the circulation the effortless inevitability of a gravity-flow system, with pools of open space to slow down or rest in when one left the main currents. Movement is the essence of transportation, and movement is what McKim's plan magnificently provided for. Amplifying this spaciousness were the great columns and the high ceilings of both the main entrance corridor (leading west from Seventh Avenue and lined with shops and restaurants) and the ticket hall, waiting rooms, and concourse—

the scale gigantic, the effect not only imposing but soothing and reassuring, as if a load were taken off one's chest. In this terminal, meant to encompass crowds, there was no sense of crowding; the ticket hall was as long as the nave of St. Peter's. The shopworn tags of McKim's classic decoration receded from consciousness, and what remained was a beautiful ordering of space, whose proportions veiled the inappropriate decorative pomp and nullified the occasional irritations of the ascent from or descent to the trains. Even the fifty-year accumulation of grime on the travertine walls of the interior has not robbed this building of its essential grandeur, which now suggests the musty subterranean passages in the contemporary remains of a Roman bath. There is never too much of that grand Roman quality in a modern city. It comes from a princely sense of magnificence, a willingness to spend munificently on a purely esthetic pleasure, instead of squeezing out the last penny of dividends. American railroad stations as late as twenty-five years ago compared favorably with those of England and the Continent, because of their interior serenity and dignity as well as the fact that they were then altogether free of advertisements—a point the European traveller often remarked on with surprise, as a pleasing contradiction in the land of the almighty dollar.

No one now entering Pennsylvania Station for the first time could, without clairvoyance, imagine how good it used to be, in comparison to the almost indescribable botch that has been made of it. To take the most favorable view of the new era, let us enter the main approach, from Seventh Avenue— the only element left that faintly resembles the original design. But the spaciousness of the corridor, with its long view, has been diminished by a series of centrally placed advertisements—a large aluminum-framed glass box for posters; then that standard fixture of today's railroad station, a rubber-tired confection from Detroit suggesting to the guileless traveller the superior claims of private motor transportation; then another poster box, holding an illuminated color photograph of a steak dinner. These nagging intrusions are only a modest beginning; in time, the top of this great, barrel-vaulted corridor will probably, like the concourse, be punctuated with transparencies and flying signs.

Happily, these obstacles serve an esthetic function; they soften the shock that one encounters at the head of the stairs to the main floor. There one discovers that almost the whole interior arrangement has been swept away. The broad east-west corridor has vanished, and in its place a huge plastic crescent canopy, brittle, fragile, and luminous, opens out, fanlike, across one's view—a canopy slanting upward at an awkward angle and suspended in midair by wires from the sturdy-looking stone columns of the original design: in all, a masterpiece of architectural and visual incongruity. This vast arched canopy drenches the space below it with diffused fluorescent light, illuminating a semicircle of ticket counters and, behind them, clerks at ranks of desks. The semicircle completely blocks the main channel of circulation to the concourse; moreover, it conceals the bottom half of the great window that once marked the western end of the station's axis. The counters of the ticket office are laid out in sawtooth indentations—open and without grillwork, like the ones in the newer banks—and a closed-circuit television set beside each counter presents the intending traveller with a visual summary of the accommodations available for the next week or so on whatever train he has in mind. This saw-toothed arrangement and the abandonment of the framed booth are the only elements in the design for which the most charitable observer can say a good word: let the reader linger over this moment of praise. The rest of this new office is a symposium of errors. To provide enough space in the rear for the booking clerks, once housed in the innards of the station, the designer wiped out both waiting rooms, for which a wholly inadequate substitute has been provided by a few benches on the concourse. To reach these, and the trains, one must walk all the way around the ticket counters. And the large central information booth has disappeared, to be replaced by a tiny counter tucked away north of the stairs from the Seventh Avenue entrance in such a fashion that people making inquiry at it obstruct one exit to the subways. "Meet me at the information booth" is now, at any busy hour, a useless suggestion. "Meet me at Travelers' Aid" would be more to the point. To conceal the information booth so neatly and to block so effectively an exit is a feat that only emphasizes the quality of this renovation—its exquisite precision in matching bad esthetics to a bad plan.

And there are other places in Pennsylvania Station where this carefree treatment has been equally successful. There are separate counters for buyers of coach, parlor-car, and sleeping-car tickets, but since the counters are identified only by numbered orange, green, blue, or red signboards, one must consult an index board beforehand. The use of colors is an excellent means of identification for all but the color-blind. Unfortunately, though, the numerals, which are white, do not show up clearly against the light green, and they virtually dissolve into the dull orange; only the red and blue backgrounds have a decent visibility. (Bold numerals, like the ones used in the central Rome railroad station, would remove the need for color identification.) No one can claim that this feeble, reticent color scheme represents an unwillingness to introduce a strong discordant note, for of such notes there is a jarring plenitude—the greenery-yallery walls next to the train hall, the stark white and black of the telephone booths, the effulgent stainless steel of the new shops and booths that have been erected on the main floor; in short, a West Forty-second Street garishness and tawdriness characterize the whole reconstruction. With this over-all design to establish the level of taste, the fevered illuminations of the soft-drink machines are fitting embellishments of the general chaos.

But these are minor matters; the great treason to McKim's original design, and the overpowering blunder, is the conception of these misplaced ticket counters, with their background of ticket clerks busily acting their parts under television's myriad eyes. If treated rationally and straightforwardly, the change-over to open counters with television equipment and doubled space for ticket selling could have been accomplished without destroying a single important feature of the whole station. But rational considerations of fitness, function, and form, with a view to the ultimate human decencies, seem as unimportant in the reconstruction of Pennsylvania Station as they do to some of our designers of motorcars. One suspects that the subversion of McKim's masterly plan was due simply to the desire to make the whole design an immense advertising display, and, in fact, this design now centers on the suspended canopy, which not merely provides a ceiling of light for the office space below but juts out many feet beyond the counters, as if it had the function it might serve in the open air—of offering shelter against rain. The purpose of such a design, psychologically speaking, is possibly to convince the railroad user either that the Pennsylvania Railroad has gone

modern and that the old station can be as pinched for space,
as generally commonplace, as a bus terminal, or else that it
can be as aerodynamic in form as an airport terminal. The
effort to shorten the time needed to make reservations is a
laudable one, though it may be doubted whether electronic
feathers will do much to improve a system whose worst bottle-
neck is not communications but wholesale advance bookings
by business corporations (often far in excess of their needs),
which create the difficulty of allotting too few spaces to too
many. But let us nevertheless assume that the new installation provides handsome gains in efficiency. These gains must
be weighed against serious losses of efficiency at other points.
There is no reason, for instance, that the booking clerks should
occupy the space once given over to waiting rooms. As a result of this pointless dramatization of the process of ticket
selling, the waiting passengers are now squeezed onto a few
benches, many of them a constant obstacle to passenger circulation.

What on earth were the railroad men in charge really attempting to achieve? And why is the result such a disaster?
Did the people who once announced that they were planning to convert the station property into a great skyscraper
market and Fun Fair decide, finding themselves temporarily
thwarted in that scheme, to turn their energies to destroying
the station from the inside, in order to provide a better
justification for their plans? Or did the management see pictures of the new Rome station and decide that it would be
nice to have a station equally up-to-date, and even more flash-
ily so? But they forgot that though the Rome booking hall is in
effect a canopy, it is a free-standing structure poised dynam-
ically on its own base, serving not as a piece of phony stage
decoration but as a shelter for its activities. To transport the
idea of a canopy into Pennsylvania Station, whose overwhelming quality, esthetically, depends upon its free command of
space, was to nullify not merely its rational plan but its
height, its dignity, and its tranquil beauty. If the planners had
cut the height of the main level in two by inserting another
floor above it, they could not have debased the original design more effectively than they have by introducing that
mask of light, suspended by wires. This glaring device was
not necessitated by the television system of communication.
The special merit of such a system is that the headquarters

of the operation can be miles away from the place where the information registers. To disrupt the whole flow of traffic through the station so as to put the system on display is a miscarriage of the display motive.

Behind this design, one must assume, was the notion that has made automobile manufacturers add airplane fins to their earth-bound products. This shows a loss of faith in their trade, on the part of railroad men, that may hasten the demise of the railways. If they had sufficient pride in their own method of transportation, they would emphasize the things that make it different from air or motor transportation—its freedom from tension and danger, the fact that planes stack up interminably over airports in poor weather, the fact that a motor expressway, according to surveys, can handle only four thousand people an hour, while a railroad line can handle forty thousand people an hour. This capacity for coping quickly with crowds that would clog the best highway facilities for hours is the special achievement of the railroad. What the railroad does superbly the motor expressway does badly, and planes, even though they travel at supersonic speed, cannot do at all. This was boldly dramatized by McKim in the great vomitoria he designed to handle the crowds in Pennsylvania Station. Everything that clutters up a railroad terminal either physically or visually must accordingly be rated as bad design, and, ultimately, because of its retarding effect on convenience and comfort, as bad publicity, too.

Some of the engineering ingenuity that was spent in devising the vast electronic jukebox of Pennsylvania Station might well have gone into repairing the crucial error in McKim's design—the failure to carry the system of circulation into its final stage; that is, an adequate method of passing immediately to and from the trains. As it is, a beautiful trip out of town can be soured in a few minutes by the poverty of mechanical means for changing levels and for transporting hand baggage. Moving platforms, escalators, light-weight two-wheeled luggage trucks, like the carts at a supermarket; identification signs for baggage lockers, so that one might recognize at a distance where one left one's bags, just by looking at the color of one's key; a well-identified enclosure for meeting—such highly desirable improvements as these are untouched by the present innovations.

The lack of improvements in these essential matters is a symptom of the bureaucratic fossilization in railroading, and that backwardness cannot be overcome by jazzing up the ticket service. If the Pennsylvania Railroad had given thought to these inefficiencies and discomforts and inconveniences, it would have treated the improvement of the ticket services with the same sharp eye on the business of railroading, and with the same readiness to keep the original design quietly up-to-date, without sacrificing the qualities in it that are time-less. Such a thorough renovation might be even more ex-pensive than the present disarrangement, but it would pay off by improving every aspect of the service, instead of simply faking a loudly "modern" setting in the hope that the passenger will forget the many ancient coaches and Pullman cars, with their shabby upholstery, that are still in service.

But no sort of renovation of Pennsylvania Station makes sense until the railroad is ready to commission the one operation that would really cause it to look fresh and bright without benefit of fluorescent lighting—a complete cleansing of its soiled interior. The plaster has begun to crack and peel in the Seventh Avenue corridor; the mural maps are al-most invisible; and, as if to accentuate the dirt, the thrifty management has merely scoured the columns and walls to a height of ten feet, making the worst of a bad job. As for the vast blaze of light from the low ceiling in the renovated portions, its chief effect at night is to make the train hall look as though it were under an air-raid blackout. If it was sad that Alexander Cassatt should have died in 1906, without seeing his great station erected, it was a mercy that he did not live until 1958, to witness its bungling destruction. It would take even mightier powers than these old railroad ti-tans wielded to undo this damage.

*1958*

# FOURTEEN

# Frozen-Faced Embassy

These last few years, the United States government has been erecting new embassy buildings all over the world, on a scale that rivals the number of Air Force bases we constructed a little earlier. In some of these embassies the spirit of the air bases seems to have affected the program of our less warlike missions, and in the design of one of the most important of these structures we have gratuitously awakened no little local resentment. This embassy is in London, the last place one would think a misinterpretation of our purposes—indeed, a literal misconstruction—could have taken place. In some cities the new embassies have added to the prestige of American architecture, for, by a happy reversal of the usual official procedures, the panel of architects who competed for the job included many of the best of our older exponents of modern architecture. There were no inhibiting provisions that these buildings should be Georgian, Early Republican, or plaster-cast Classic in outward form, so they stand on their own as exemplars of the contemporary American mode, touched with what our architects have recently learned from other lands.

In Edward Stone's adaptation of the Indian screen wall for our embassy in New Delhi, he made a graceful bow to regional tradition. Its practical outcome, by all reports, has not, though, been on the level of its esthetic success, for he unhappily forgot how difficult it is to translate ancient forms into modern materials. For Stone overlooked the fact, as did Le Corbusier and his associates at about the same time in designing the new Indian city of Chandigarh, that a concrete or stone grille, unlike its wooden counterpart, absorbs enough heat during the day to counteract even the cooling night air. Architects in America who have been copying Stone's innovation even in places where our summers are almost as torrid as India's may eventually regret their eagerness to take over this seemingly foolproof device for masking the familiar dullness of repetitive windows while avoiding the imbecility of compensating for acres of exposed glass by using tightly drawn Venetian blinds. Employed judiciously, for a rational purpose, on a single wall, the grille may be a blessing, but applied wholesale, it is both esthetically depressing and functionally absurd.

The architect of the London embassy, the late Eero Saarinen, counts, like his father before him, as one of the most distinguished exponents of current American architecture. He was the one-man equivalent of the gigantic architectural corporation known as Skidmore, Owings & Merrill, and his buildings can be found on almost every great campus in the country—recreation halls, dormitories, auditoriums, hockey rinks—to say nothing of such a structure as the General Motors Research Laboratories near Detroit, which forms almost a super-campus of its own. Unlike the S. O. & M. brand, Mr. Saarinen's trademark was a disinclination to repeat himself, yet it happens that in planning the London embassy for once he borrowed a façade he had already created for the American embassy in Oslo.

If this design were a happy one, there would be nothing against such repetition, for a well-seasoned architect, dealing for the second time with a building of a particular sort, should not be afraid to refine and perfect an earlier form, as Frank Lloyd Wright, despite his boundless powers of invention, did with his basic "prairie house" to the end of his life. For in official buildings abroad expressive design is now a matter of great importance. Our embassies are no longer simply places of official residence with an attached office; they are, rather, a complex of governmental, economic, and cultural functions, with offices, an exhibition hall, a library, and an auditorium—places in which our government not merely does business with its own citizens but attempts to make a good impression upon the country in which, for all its extra-territoriality, it is domiciled. The problem in creating such a building is not unlike the problem an American lecturer faces in addressing a foreign audience: of retaining his individuality and his national idiom without making any blatant assertion of his Americanism—being, in fact, a better representative of our many-faceted national tradition by showing his ability to find common ground with his hosts. The ambassador who has not the tact to do this should be kept at home; the embassy that cannot create a likable image of our country has not fulfilled a main purpose.

The London embassy occupies the major share of one side of Grosvenor Square—a large eighteenth-century square with long evidence of American occupation, first by our earlier embassy, then by the postwar memorial to Franklin D. Roosevelt that the grateful English erected there. The plot runs along the South Audley Street side of the square, from Upper Grosvenor Street east to Upper Brook Street, providing an all too imposing frontage on the square of some three hundred and fifty feet and a depth of some two hundred feet. Unlike the more formal squares of Bloomsbury and Belgravia, Grosvenor Square offers a considerable variety of form and color in its façades, though the buildings are mainly of the traditional, limited height. By the doubtful expedient of placing one floor half a story below the street level, and the tall ground floor half a story above that level, Saarinen respected this height limitation (the embassy shows only five stories above ground), and when the trees are in leaf in the square the foliage mercifully hides the embassy's massive uniform façade from the spectator until it hits him full in the face.

In any event, the square is so large that each side is a unit by itself, with little esthetic relationship to the other sides, except at the corner meetings. Yet, as several British architectural critics have pointed out, the device of setting the embassy building back from the sidewalks, to get light for the below-street floor, created openings that disrupt the unity of the square far more than an additional story above ground would. Not only that, but the building is further separated from the sidewalk by a formidable sloping stone-faced embankment, topped by a straw-colored metal fence. A retaining wall backs up the embankment, and between this wall and the building lies a deep if waterless moat—a drop capable of daunting any invader who dared to scale the outer barrier. From a military standpoint, the building is vulnerable only at the entrances, but for the purposes of friendly diplomacy this sidewalk barricade, which rises above the eye level, has the effect of a calculated insult—and has been so regarded by many not unduly sensitive Britons. Both the building and the barricade say, "Keep your distance! Do not enter!" though this is the precise opposite of our program for introducing the British to our educational and cultural achievements while performing the other necessary offices of an embassy.

To provide sufficient space for these cultural functions, the first two floors cover the entire plot, save for the setback; the four stories above form a rectangular U—with its base on Grosvenor Square—around a central light court. This main mass juts out several feet to overhang the lower floors and is supported by a series of boldly expressed beams. The offices of both stenographers and officials, all with outside windows, are ranged along the sides of the U. There are three entrances to the building—the central embassy entrance on the square with a double bank of elevators right at hand to give access to the whole building; a consular entrance on the south flank; a United States Information Service on the north flank.

On the principle that the positive virtues of a building should be presented first, let me dwell on the interior public spaces, which give the ground floor a monumental scale that properly contrasts with that of the upper office floors and so provides the façade with what formal distinction it has. The tall oblong windows on this level, which reach from floor to ceiling, have some justification for their existence, for though the exhibition hall, which is in the interior, is not served by them, they at least provide daylight for the library, which occupies one whole corner of the Information side of the building. This serene library, "all beautified with omissions," as Henry James said of The Great Good Place, is just what a library should be—the readers' tables close to the windows, and the stacks, holding some twenty-five thousand volumes of Americana, easily accessible. To give the authentic American touch, there is even an American Bible, but no King James Version! I cannot say as much in praise of the furniture. The clumsy, armless, almost immovable chairs were obviously chosen by someone with little experience in sitting or reading, much less in note-taking; they achieve a maximum of cushioned discomfort with a minimum of efficiency and, compared with the not altogether adequate but still commodious oak armchairs of the reading rooms in the New York Public Library at Forty-second Street, they are singularly inept.

There are today, incidentally, five badly designed "contemporary" chairs on the market for one that is even tolerably good, and the meekness with which the fashion-minded public accepts these inadequate pieces of furniture is second only to their eagerness to pay good money for the more infantile forms of modern painting. Here was a place for a dexterous innovation in modern library furniture, to match the high standard we have achieved in the conduct, if not always the design, of lending libraries. The room that vies in excellence with the library is the auditorium, for it is done with a quiet perfection that happily recalls Saarinen's smaller theatre in the Kresge Auditorium at M.I.T. Whether such a single-purpose room, for intermittent use, is justified in the embassy is another question; the Beveridge Room in the University of London, so arranged that it can accommodate as few as twenty people at a seminar or two or three hundred at a concert or a lecture, seems to me a far more adroit solution, because of its flexibility.

The fact that the exhibition hall serves frequently as an art gallery—like the lesser space at the Information entrance —is an excellent feature of the plan, since until recently America's contributions to painting and sculpture have been overlooked in other countries, a situation for which we have been partly to blame. Unfortunately, the gallery is little more than a corridor, and space that might have been used to provide temporary alcoves for a show of prints, perhaps, is sacrificed to a singularly irrelevant architectural device—a long, lengthwise trough of water, split by a wedge-shaped bank of stone that is punctuated by spouts, presumably to serve as a fountain. This trough cuts the gallery space in two without adding to its charm or usefulness. Possibly no one has yet backed into this watering trough, but it remains a clear and present danger, and, what is worse, it prevents one from going back and forth between pictures on opposite sides of the hall, as one often wishes to do when viewing a single artist's work.

The upper-floor corridors and offices are a smooth miracle of cold anonymity, as violently antiseptic as an operating room in a hospital, and even on the hot day in summer when I inspected them the absence of color and contrast was far from ingratiating. One of Conan Doyle's early villains tries to drive his girl victim insane by putting her in a white room with no hangings or decorations of any sort. This once seemed to me merely a quaint commentary on the Victorian conception of decoration, but after looking at the endless array of white cubicles in the inner row of offices on the first floor of the embassy, I began to wonder whether there mightn't be something in the notion, and I shuddered at the thought of coming into this building not out of the summer sun but out of the dark, dank fog of a London November or the cold rain that one may encounter at any London season. Under such conditions it would take more than central heating to make the embassy seem anything but bleak and forbidding. Only a distinguished architect could carry through his original errors with such consistency—and with so little misgiving about his basic premises.

On the exterior, Saarinen attempted a more positive note in the four upper stories—in the bold fashion of Le Corbusier when he was modelling his Unity House in Marseille—by alternating oblong windows in forward-thrusting stone frames and in narrow fluted frames that are not merely recessed into the walls but subdivided vertically by a bar. This pattern of alternation is carried through in the placing of the windows one above the other, so that a recessed window frame sits over a projecting window frame, and this scheme prevails through the entire façade. Such a strong modelling restores to us an almost forgotten part of the architectural curriculum—the traditional course on Lights and Shadows—and the contrasts hereby achieved will be strikingly accentuated, unless London's smoke nuisance abates further, when the Portland stone Saarinen wisely employed weathers, in standard London fashion, into streaks and patches of charcoal and gray, set off against gleaming white. Then the alternation of the flat stone surfaces of the broader window frames with the fluted units that border the other windows, top and bottom, may become far more effective than it is now.

All in all Saarinen used his best talents to give this façade the character of an old-fashioned masonry structure, and if one of the youngest leaders of the "Brutalist" school has complained that the embassy is too monumental, the fact is that at least its masculine strength compares most favorably with the slickly neuter glass walls that have dominated the buildings of the past decade. With the admirable structural consistency that was so marked in Frank Lloyd Wright's work, Saarinen even carried the heavy beams of the lowest projecting floor out to the exterior, not alone to support the overhanging stories but to create a bold, serrated edge that sets off the recessed windows of the setback ground floor as effectively as an old-fashioned cornice. Esthetically, this is a far sounder feature of the façade than the overeffortful window frames, but the architect, alas, softened the effect by covering his beams with straw-colored anodized aluminum sheathing. The use of this feeble color throughout the building wherever a metallic covering is needed is an unfortunate lapse; it not merely looks fatally cheap, like imitation gold, but it offers insufficient contrast with the diluted cream of the unweathered exterior stone.

What the architect sought here is obvious: he made a desperate attempt to conceal the incurable monotony of his façade by breaking away from the glib modern curtain wall, yet without going back to the simple repeating pattern of window and masonry wall that marked the buildings on the decently unobtrusive eighteenth-century London squares. In the older order of London, architects concentrated their efforts at individuality and distinction on the entrances of the houses, with their delicate fanlights and inviting classic porticoes; at most, they gave the special dignity of column and pediment to the building at the center of a row of houses, just because of its position. Saarinen sought to overcome the dull uniformity of a long, unbroken façade by making every other window stand out, but the power of his forms only increases the building's obsessive repetitive beat. In contriving this form of esthetic escape, he chose a solution that was not quite so arbitrary as that in his elevation for the new girls' dormitory at the University of Pennsylvania, in which, for no reason except superficial decoration, quite inadequate horizontal windows alternate with equally meaningless vertical ones. The truth of the matter is that if the functions within a building are themselves unduly repetitive, one cannot save the situation by over-emphasizing that embarrassment.

In point of fact, Saarinen embraced the bureaucratic functions of the embassy and their corresponding office structure too eagerly, and neglected to express the cultural functions that could have given life to this unnecessarily monotonous and sterile building. One would hardly guess from this façade that the embassy is not a mere office building. The library, the exhibition hall, the auditorium, the more public features of the building were all at the architect's call, waiting for appropriate architectural expression—indeed, demanding it—to dramatize the building's special ties to the great city and to those many Englishmen who are eager to come closer to our country's culture.

That culture in all its brief historic exuberance stands in memorable contrast to the conformities and standardizations of our more recent affluent, bellicose, and brutalized society; and this vitality and variety should not be hidden behind a uniform façade. On his own confession, Saarinen knew that the administrators of the Grosvenor estate planned to rebuild the other sides of the square to a height of nine stories; so, quite apart from the embassy's privilege of extraterritoriality, there were no spatial limits to his handling of the varied functions of the embassy. By rejecting any formal expression of the cultural functions of his building, Saarinen repeated in his own fashion the mistakes of the United Nations headquarters in both New York and Paris: he gave precedence and eminence only to the bureaucratic function, thus bowing too complaisantly to the ruling force of our age and simply overlooking, or bluntly denying, our not inconsiderable cultural advantages.

When the plans for the embassy were made public, it appeared that a dominant feature of a purely decorative order, trite but overwhelming, had indeed been provided, in the form of a seemingly huge golden eagle with outspread wings perched high above the main entrance, and a great deal of criticism was roused in London, even in usually friendly circles, over this flaunting of our national bird. But when this pale eagle finally materialized it had shrunk into tame inoffensiveness, and now blends quite innocuously into the anodized aluminum of the rest of the decoration. What still causes great resentment among many Britons—justifiably, it may as well be said—is the embankment of concrete. For this feature, I have been told, the State Department is responsible, unbelievable as that may seem. This device is a far remove from the Renaissance habit of placing a free-standing building on a plinth or base whose bold intervention between the ground and the structure not merely raised the building but set it off without violating its esthetic composure. Many far less offensive barriers were available, even under the conditions Saarinen faced. One that instantly suggests itself is the cheerful London fashion of a bastion of flower boxes, which offers at most seasons the touch of color and organic form that is now lacking at every point. Even for an embassy in Moscow, this quasi-military design would have been an unfriendly, if perhaps prudent, gesture; among our British friends and allies it is much worse. At the moment the State Department is urging people to smile in their passport photographs, our London embassy presents a cold, unsmiling face, a face unfortunately suggesting national arrogance and irresponsive power. We should amend this image even if this demands that we take a long look at ourselves, to find out why the official Face of America and the Voice of America today so often contradict our historic character and our present ideal professions.

No architect can solve that problem singlehanded.

I do not wish to leave this discussion of the work of a dead man, who cannot defend himself, without citing a quite different appraisal, from a contemporary English architect who is full of admiration for this building. Though dubious about the pallid metal trim, he praises the use of the Portland stone and the effort to achieve a strong, characterful façade. He feels that the decorative treatment of the interior is exquisitely chaste—read "hospital coldness" in my report—and he regards the detailing of the structure and the craftsmanship as setting a standard well above most contemporary work in his country. He is charitably willing to overlook the sidewalk barricade—though he winces at it—and he thinks that the building will settle down into the townscape of Grosvenor Square as a happy addition, full of character if not charm. Since he is one of the most attractively English of Englishmen, this is a most objective judgment, if not a representative one. I wish I could share his sentiments. But to me the whole style and message of the building seem as ominous as the depersonalized sort of thinking that comes out of our Air Force research centers. It has the dehumanized nonchalance of a thermonuclear Kahn. By the very perfection of its technique and the emptiness of its performance, it seems to say—as, indeed, our newer technologies often seem to say—that, quite apart from possible nuclear catastrophes, our civilization has come close to a dead end. At this juncture, we shall have to surrender what is left of our more humane values or retrace our steps to the point where we took the wrong road. One is not as yet easily persuaded that this blank, bureaucratic-military mask is the true face of America; certainly it does not represent the America we love, the America that other countries once found both enviable and lovable.

*1962*

# FIFTEEN

# The Case Against "Modern Architecture"

Three quarters of a century ago, the tides of modern architecture were rising, as the great technical resources that engineers like Telford, Paxton, and Brunel had introduced were applied, at last, to other forms of building. This was the period when Jenney, Sullivan, and their colleagues developed steel-frame construction and found a form for the skyscraper, when Eiffel produced his tower and Freyssinet his Hall of Machines, and when the new spirit that H. H. Richardson had brought to the design of traditional domestic buildings in stone and wood was spreading everywhere, from the houses of Ashbee, Voysey, and Parker in England to the far shores of California, where at the turn of the century Maybeck had begun work.

For reasons that no one has successfully uncovered, this wave spent itself during the decade before the First World War: except in the design of purely utilitarian structures, there was a return to the pseudo-historic and outwardly traditional, at least in the decorative facing of buildings: skyscrapers with Gothic pinnacles vied with those that were crowned with Greek temples of love; and the splendid train hall of the Grand Central Station, now effaced by a loud smear of advertisement, was betrayed earlier by its imitative Rennaissance façade. When modern architecture came back in the twenties, first in France with Le Corbusier and Lurçat, and in Germany with Mendelsohn and Gropius, in Holland with Dudok, Wijdeveld, and Oud, it was forced to refight the battle that had already seemed won in 1890.

Within the last thirty years, modern architecture has swept around the world. The victory of the modern movement over its traditional enemies has been so complete that special courses must now be offered, outside the usual architectural school curriculum, to provide architects with sufficient historic knowledge to maintain and restore ancient monuments preserved for their historic value. Yet many ominous signs have appeared, during the last fifteen years, that indicate that the victorious forces do not know how to make full use of the victory; that contradictions and conflicts have developed among various groups of architects sufficient already to have broken up the once united front of the C.I.A.M.; that, indeed, the differences that have come forth within the ranks of the modern architects are quite as serious as those that divided the pioneers of modern architecture from the traditionalists who sought to continue the old forms and the eclectics who sought to mask the new ones.

The order and the consensus that modern architecture seemed ready to establish in the thirties is still far to seek: indeed, some of the most brilliant exponents, like the late Eero Saarinen, boasted a theory of form that denied the need for continuity and made of each separate project an essay in abstract design, without any affiliation to the work of other architects in our period or to the architect's own designs, before or after. As in the advertising copy of our period, the successful modern architects have been saying, in effect: "And now! a new taste sensation." Or, "You, too, can be *years ahead* with the latest model."

This situation has given hope and comfort to minds that are so radically committed to past forms that they would solve the problems that modern architecture faces by merely erasing the history of the last century and going back to the classic shells of antiquity, particularly Roman antiquity. This is the last hope of Henry Reed; too empty and vulnerable to merit more than a passing smile. But though Mr. Reed's remedies are absurd, the situation in modern architecture is in fact profoundly unsatisfactory: almost as chaotic and irrational as the political situation of the modern world, in which the heads of state solemnly threaten each other to solve their problems, if the other side does not yield, by mutilating the human race and wiping out civilization.

The very fact that one can make such a comparison points to certain underlying errors about the nature of technical and social progress that crept into modern architecture almost from the moment that the conception of new forms, which reflected the needs and ideals of our period, became articulate in the writings of a few architectural critics and thinkers, like Adolf Loos and, much later, Le Corbusier. The moment has come to examine these conceptions and to reformulate the ideas and ideals that have, up to this moment, governed the development of the whole movement. We shall perhaps find, when we do so, a need for restoring some of the values that were too ruthlessly discarded in the development of modern form.

Beneath the belief in modern architecture lay certain preconceptions about the nature of modern civilization; and these preconceptions have proved so inadequate that it is time to give them a thorough overhauling.

Perhaps the most central of these beliefs was the belief in mechanical progress. Concealed within this notion was the assumption that human improvement would come about more rapidly, indeed almost automatically, through devoting all our energies to the expansion of scientific knowledge and to technological inventions; that traditional knowledge and experience, traditional forms and values, acted as a brake upon such expansion and invention, and that since the order embodied by the machine was the highest type of order, no brakes of any kind were desirable. Whereas all organic evolution is cumulative and purposeful, in that the past is still present in the future, and the future, as potentiality, is already present in the past, mechanical progress existed in a one-dimensional time, the present. Under the idea of mechanical progress only the present counted, and continual change was needed in order to prevent the present from becoming *passé*, and thus unfashionable. Progress was accordingly measured by novelty, constant change, and mechanical difference, not by continuity and human improvement.

In every department, the nineteenth century ruthlessly swept away old ideas, old traditions and institutions, and not least old buildings, confident that nothing would be lost that the machine could not replace or improve. Have we forgotten that the central shrine of our Independence and our Constitution, Independence Hall, was almost sold off to the highest bidder in the early part of that century? But this anti-traditionalism imposed a penalty upon modern architecture; and that is, it was deprived by its own assumptions of either recognizing its essential continuity with the past or of building upon its own tradition. In wiping out the past, unfortunately, the cult of the machine surreptitiously destroyed its own future—and left only an under-dimensioned present, scheduled, like any speculative building investment, for quick replacement.

Beneath this belief in mechanical progress as an end in itself was still another conviction: that one of the important functions of architecture was to express its civilization. This conviction was a sound one; and indeed, even without conviction, that condition whether openly recognized or unconsciously fulfilled is unavoidable. But those of us who insisted upon the value of this expression were perhaps unprepared for what it would reveal about "modern times." We used the word modern as a "praise-word," in Robert Frost's vocabulary; and we overlooked the possibility that modern technics, which had given us instant communication, would also provide us with instantaneous mass extermination: or the fact that while its hospitals, medical services, and sanitary precautions would reduce older forms of disease, technical progress would also pollute our food, befoul the air with smog, and produce new tensions and new diseases and new anxieties, as crippling as those that have been banished. Modern psychology has introduced man to the depths of his own nature, in all its immense variety and creative potentiality; but it has also produced the bureaucratic personality, sterilized, regimented, overcontrolled, ultimately hostile to every other form of life than its own: cut off from human resources and human roots.

Since modern architecture has begun to express modern civilization, without the hypocrisy and concealment that the eclectic architects used to practice, it is not perhaps surprising that the unpleasant features of our civilization should be as conspicuous as its finest and most admirable achievements. We have been living in a fool's paradise, so far as we took for granted that mechanical progress would solve all the problems of human existence, by introducing man into the brave new, simplified, automatic world of the machine. If we look at our buildings today, with open eyes, we shall find that even in handling the great positive forces of our time, with admirable constructive facility, the greater number of them have neglected even the scientific data they need for a good solution. There is hardly a single great innovation in building these last thirty years—total air-conditioning, all-day fluorescent lighting, the all-glass wall—that pays any respect to either the meteorological, the biological, or the psychological knowledge already available, for this knowledge calls for radical alterations in their present use. And still less do these innovations heed human activities or personal desires.

In so far as modern architecture has succeeded in expressing modern life, it has done better in calling attention to its lapses, its rigidities, its failures, than in bringing out, with the aid of the architect's creative imagination, its immense latent potentialities. The modern architect has yet to come to grips with the multi-dimensional realities of the actual world. He has made himself at home with mechanical processes, which favor rapid commercial exploitation, and with anonymous repetitive bureaucratic forms, like the high-rise apartment or office building, which lend themselves with mathematical simplicity to financial manipulation. But he has no philosophy that does justice to organic functions or human purposes, and that attempts to build a more comprehensive order in which the machine, instead of dominating our life and demanding ever heavier sacrifices in the present fashion, will become a supple instrument for humane design, to be used, modified, or on occasion rejected at will.

Despite the shallowness of the theory of mechanical progress, the first erections of modern architecture, beginning with the Crystal Palace in 1851, rested on a firm foundation: the perception that the technology of the nineteenth century had immensely enriched the vocabulary of modern form and facilitated modes of construction that could hardly have been dreamed of in more ponderous materials, while it made possible designs of a far more organic nature than the heavy shells that constituted buildings in the past.

In their pride over these new possibilities, the engineers who turned these processes over to the architect naturally over-emphasized this contribution and when Louis Sullivan proclaimed that form followed function, his successors falsely put the emphasis on mechanical form and mechanical function. Both are in fact essential to the constitution of modern architecture; but neither by itself—nor both together—is sufficient. Frank Lloyd Wright understood this from the beginning, and insisted, quite properly, that he was something more than a "functionalist," though in the last phase of his great career, as in the Johnson Laboratory and the Guggenheim Museum, he succumbed to the fascination of an elegant mechanical solution, treated as an end in itself.

In the new beginning that dates from Le Corbusier's *Vers une architecture,* the machine occupied a central place: its austerity, its economy, its geometric cleanness were proclaimed almost the sole virtues of the new architecture. Thus the kitchen became a laboratory, and the bathroom took on the qualities of a surgical operating room; while the other parts of the house, for a decade or so, achieved excellence almost to the degree that they, too, were white, cleanable, empty of human content. This was in fact a useful period of cleansing and clarification. A few critics, notably Henry-Russell Hitchcock, recognized that this was the primitive state in the evolution of an historic style; and that, at a later date, certain elements, like ornament, that had been discarded in this new effort at integrity, might return again—though in fact they had never been abandoned by Wright.

Unfortunately, this interpretation of the new mechanical possibilities was in itself dominated by a superficial esthetic, which sought to make the new buildings *look* as if they respected the machine, no matter what the materials or methods of construction; and it was this superficial esthetic, openly proclaiming its indifference to actual mechanical and biological functions or human purposes that was formally put forward, by Philip Johnson and his associate Hitchcock, as The International Style, though it was Alfred Barr who coined the dubious name. From this, only a short step took the architect, with Mies van der Rohe to guide him, from the Machine to the Package. Mies van der Rohe used the facilities offered by steel and glass to create elegant monuments of nothingness. They had the dry style of machine forms without the contents. His own chaste taste gave these hollow glass shells a crystalline purity of form: but they existed alone in the Platonic world of his imagination and had no relation to site, climate, insulation, function, or internal activity; indeed, they completely turned their backs upon these realities just as the rigidly arranged chairs of his living rooms openly disregarded the necessary intimacies and informalities of conversation. This was the apotheosis of the compulsive, bureaucratic spirit. Its emptiness and hollowness were more expressive than van der Rohe's admirers realized.

Here perhaps was the turning point in the development of modern architecture. The principle of functionalism, stated even in its crudest terms, was sound as far as it went; and if modern architecture was to develop further, that principle needed to be applied to every aspect of architecture. It was necessary to develop functional analysis to its limits, not merely embracing the physical elements of building, but the internal services; not merely the external structure, but the plan, and the relation of the building to its site; and the site itself to the rest of the urban or rural environment. And even this is only a beginning, because human purposes modify all these functional characteristics; so that the so-called open plan for the dwelling house turns out to be far from acceptable as a universal solution, once one takes account of the need for privacy, solitude, withdrawal, or of the differences between the extroverted, the introverted, and the integrated personality. As one adds biological and social functions, and personal desires and needs, to those of the purely physical requirements of structure, one must get, as a resultant design, a much more complex and subtle result, than if one centered attention upon only one set of conditions.

How far modern architecture has withdrawn from the effort to achieve such organic richness one learns from recent architectural exhibitions, which have shown modern buildings as spatialized abstractions, in utter isolation. Some of the most famous architects of our time defiantly throw away their best opportunities: thus more than one new business building has been placed in the middle of a large country estate, with all the advantages of a lovely landscape, only to turn its back completely to its surroundings, defiling the approach with an acre of parking lot, whilst the building itself, air-conditioned and curtained in Venetian blinds, mocks its open site, its possible exposure to sunlight and fresh air, by turning inward upon a closed court. The result is the characterless package, which has become the main hallmark of fashionable architecture for the last decade.

Is Le Corbusier's Unity House at Marseille an exception

to this rule? Far from it. Its powerful concrete façade, with variations produced by the ill-conceived and almost abandoned market area, esthetically distinguishes it from the less expensive and less sculptural façades of similar buildings; but for all that, it is a mere package, because the plan of the individual apartments is cramped and tortured to fit the arbitrary allotment of space, in a fashion that is as archaic as that of a New York brownstone front that has been built over the back yard and is full of narrow, dark rooms, without exposure. The genius of Le Corbusier here consisted in making a mere package look like a real building; and the feebleness of current architectural criticism is recorded in the chorus of praise that this extravagant piece of stage decoration still calls forth.

Meanwhile, the advance of technology has presented the architect with a vast array of new metallic alloys and new plastics, with new structural materials like prestressed concrete, with now large-scale elements useful for modular designs, and with new mechanical devices that add to the total cost of the structure, as well as the upkeep. On the assumption that mechanical progress is itself more important than human purposes, the architect has felt, it would seem, almost a moral obligation to use all these materials and methods, if only to maintain his status as a creative designer. In this respect, the architect finds himself in almost the same unfortunate position as the physician, overwhelmed by the enormous number of new antibiotics and other drugs that are thrust on the market by the great pharmaceutical organizations, and often unable to follow through one remedy before a new one is thrust on him.

Who would dare to single out the most notorious examples of the salesmanship that have often led the architect to make unfortunate choices? To make a detailed examination would in fact bring one close to legal libel. But what has happened with many new materials and forms has also taken place with a respectably ancient material, glass; and this will serve to bring out the underlying irrationality of much superficially modern design.

Glass is plainly an indispensable part of the architect's equipment; but it has two great drawbacks. One is that it seriously lessens the ultra-violet rays, which kill bacteria and in contact with the skin supply Vitamin D to the body:

hence a solid wall of glass is less desirable than openable windows that admit direct sunlight. The other weakness of glass, when used as a wall, is the excessive admission of radiant heat in the warmer seasons and the excessive seepage of indoor heat in colder weather. In attempting to make glass do duty as both wall and window the modern architect had succeded in fulfilling neither function satisfactorily. Instead, he has produced the most flagrantly uneconomic and uncomfortable buildings of modern times, which can be inhabited only with the aid of the most expensive devices of heating and refrigeration: esthetically dull, technically absurd.

The irrationality of this whole system of construction is visible today in every city from New York to San Francisco: glass-sheathed buildings without any contact with fresh air, sunlight, or view, since at most times of the day glass sheathing is made endurable only through the use of Venetian blinds or their vertical modern equivalents over the whole façade. To make this form even more ridiculous, the window is often carried down to the floor: a device that on the lower stories not merely reveals the natural litter and trash on the floor itself but, in providing light that has no visual value below desk level, it also deprives the office of needed wall space that windows set above the level of a four-drawer filing case would permit. Frank Lloyd Wright, in his Larkin Building in Buffalo, long ago demonstrated the desirable relation of high window to usable outside wall in an office building.

I am aware that the reaction against the all-glass façade has already begun, as in the design of the new John Hancock Life Insurance Building in San Francisco. But so far this reaction is a superficial one, since it merely returns to the traditional alternation of window and wall; and it has not yet gone on to explore a possibility that modern construction methods present: not merely the restoration of the openable window, but likewise the provision of an entirely new feature, a movable insulating wall-panel inside, which will slide open and shut to the full width of the window, in a fashion that will make unnecessary the once-daring, but now sadly obsolete, Venetian blinds. So much for the misuse of an older technical achievment.

But the advances of technology, which have opened those breathtaking possibilities for new forms that Eric Mendelsohn so brilliantly anticipated in his imaginative sketches back in the twenties, have also revealed the possibility of two new architectural perversions. One of them is the utilization of sensational methods of construction merely to produce equally sensational forms, which have no purpose other than that of demonstrating the esthetic audacity of the designer. The external shell of the new opera house at Sydney reveals this order of design; so, for that matter, does the too-often-quoted Guggenheim Museum in New York, and even more Wright's new municipal building in Marin County; and all over the country today, one finds new churches whose very form of construction reveals nothing except a desire to compete on equal esthetic terms with the supermarket and the hot-dog emporium. This is not functional and purposeful creativity: it is the creativity of the kaleidoscope, so far the most successful of all inventions for imitating creativity by juggling mechanical forms.

When a child is bored or an adult is ill, the esthetics of the kaleidoscope is enchanting; and I do not underestimate its fascination. Nor would I deny that, related to our emergent needs, many new forms must and will appear in modern architecture, which will reveal meanings and values, intuitions about the nature of the cosmos or the condition of man, they are not present in any earlier architectural system. But creativity, in order to be assimilated, requires an underlying basis of order; and what is more, the most original form needs to be repeated, with modifications, if its full value is to be absorbed by the user and the spectator.

The desire for architectural originality through a succession of kaleidoscopic changes, made possible by modern technological agents, when the inner purpose and contents are ruled out of the equation, inevitably degrades the creative process. Such technical facility, such esthetic audacity, poured forth on a great scale, promises only to enlarge the domain of chaos. Already the architectural magazines show projects, and even buildings, that look as if they were ingeniously cut out of paper and twisted together, shapes full of fantasy and capable of giving childish pleasure—provided they are not carried out in more solid constructions.

One may explain this excessive virtuosity, with which modern architecture is now threatened, by two conditions. This is plainly, on one hand, a revolt against the excessive regimentation that has gone on in every part of our lives:

that regimentation whose symbol is the vast repetitive inanity of the high-rise slab. And on the other hand, it is due to the fact that genuine creativity, which takes into account all the possibilities of structure, the nature of an institution's function and purposes, the values that the client draws from the community and in turn must give back to the community, is a slow process. Because such knowledge and such facility cannot be improvised in a few weeks, the creative architect must build from structure to structure on his own experience, and absorb that of other architects, past and present. It is far easier to create a sensational shell, with the constructive facilities now available, than to fulfill all the functions of architecture. An engineer of genius, like Nervi, has shown the way toward more solid achievement; but even he has succeeded best when the inner content of the building was as simple as tiers of spectators watching sport, or an exhibition or market hall whose contents could be adequately enclosed by a mere shell.

But there is an alternative to kaleidoscopic creativity that would be equally disastrous to architecture and to the human spirit, though the threat comes from the opposite point of our machine economy. Instead of an endless succession of superficial new forms, dazzling Christmas packages that have no relation to contents, we are threatened by another form of technologic facility, whose present favored form is the geodesic dome. Under this potential technical triumph, buildings as such would disappear, except perhaps as improvised rooms within a mechanically controlled environment, dedicated to producing uniform temperature, lighting, and ultimately, with the aid of drugs, surgery, and genetic intervention, uniform human beings.

Whether aboveground or belowground, this development would bring to an end, in a world of colorless uniformity, the long history of man's building: he would return to the cave from which he originally emerged, none the richer or wiser for his experience. I will not examine this particular possibility in detail, except to note that many minds are now busily engaged in preparing for this grand act of suicide. So committed indeed are many architects in our day to the automatism of the machine, that they fall under a compulsion to follow the process to its limit, even though that final stage is a colorless and dehumanized existence, just one breath more alive than the world that might emerge from a nuclear catastrophe.

If modern architecture is not to continue its disintegration into a multitude of sects and mannerisms—international stylists, empiricists, brutalists, neo-romantics, and what not—it must rest on some principle of order; and that order must ally architecture to an equally coherent theory of human development. The notion of mechanical progress alone will not do, because it leaves out the one element that would give significance to this progress, man himself; or rather, because it makes the human personality a passive tool of the process that should in fact serve it.

Man himself is an organism whose existence is dependent upon his maintaining the delicate balance that exists between all the forces of nature, physical and organic, from sunlight and air and the soil, the bacteria, the molds, and growing plants right up to the complex interaction of thousands of species. Despite the great advances in technology, man controls only a small part of these processes: for neither destruction nor mechanical substitution is in fact a mode of control. From this complex biological inheritance man extracts and perfects those portions that serve his own purposes. Organic order is based on variety, complexity, and balance; and this order provides continuity through change, stability through adaptation, harmony through finding a place for conflict, chance, and limited disorder, in ever more complex transformations. This organic interdependence was recognized and expressed in every historic culture, particularly in its cosmic and religious conceptions, with their genuinely sacred buildings, and though these buildings have outlived their technologies they still speak to the human soul.

Greenough's original analysis of form, on a basis of the biological and physiological nature of organisms, did justice to both process and function, but overlooked their transformation through a still higher and more complex category, that of human purpose. Man is not just an actor and a fabricator: he is an interpreter and a transformer. On the higher levels of existence, form determines function, no less than function form. At this point the continued development of the whole man takes precedence over the continued development of his instruments and his machines; and the only kind of order that can ensure this is one that provides a many-sided environment capable of sustaining the greatest variety of human interests and human purposes. An environment or a structure that has been reduced to the level of the machine, correct, undeviating, repetitious, monotonous, is hostile to organic reality and to human purpose: even when it performs, with a certain efficiency, a positive function, such as providing shelter, it remains a negative symbol, or at best a neutral one.

There are three sources for this larger order: nature is one, the cumulative processes of history and historic culture are another, and the human psyche is the third. To turn one's back upon these sources, in the name of mechanical progress, for the sake of purely quantitative production, mechanical efficiency, bureaucratic order, is to sterilize both architecture and the life that it should sustain and elevate. An age that worships the machine and seeks only those goods that the machine provides, in ever larger amounts, at ever rising profits, actually has lost contact with reality; and in the next moment or the next generation may translate its general denial of life into one last savage gesture of nuclear extermination. Within the context of organic order and human purpose, our whole technology has still potentially a large part to play; but much of the riches of modern technics will remain unusable until organic functions and human purposes, rather than mechanical processes, dominate.

An organic approach will handle, with equal dexterity, but with greater freedom of choice, every kind of function: it will not automatically reject daylight in favor of a facile mechanical substitute, or fresh air, renovated by vegetation, for a purely mechanical system of modifying the air. But neither will it turn banks into frivolous glass-enclosed pleasure palaces, office-building entrances into cathedrals, or churches into airport terminals. On the contrary, purpose and function will provide an organic criterion of form at every stage of the design process; and in the end this will produce, not merely an esthetic variety and exuberance that are now almost unknown, but even mechanical economies that have been flouted by our compulsive overcommitment to the machine.

There are two movements now visible that indicate a beginning in the right direction, which will lead, not away from functionalism, but toward a multi-functional approach to every architectural problem.

One of these movements, visible in the architectural schools today, is the students' demand for architectural and town planning history. The desire behind this is not for forms to imitate, but for experience and feeling to assimilate, for spiritual nourishment beyond that which is offered by the immediate environment or a brief present moment. This is a healthy reaction against the notion that the experience of a single generation, or a single decade in a generation, is sufficient to provide the knowledge and insight man needs to create a human environment of sufficient richness and depth.

The other movement became visible last summer in the meeting of the younger architects who have broken away from the Old Masters of the C.I.A.M. In their attempt to redefine the province of architecture today they expressed many differences with the generation of Le Corbusier and Gropius, as well as personal and characterological differences within their own ranks; but at the end they were united, in a large degree, on one final conclusion: that architecture was more than the art of building: it was rather the art of transforming man's entire habitat. This concept has already struck root in California, for the school of architecture at Berkeley has been reconstituted and renamed the School of Environmental Design.

If human development does not become sterile and frustrated through an excessive effort to conquer nature without drawing upon all the resources of history and culture to rehumanize man, the architecture of the future will again become a true polytechnics, utilizing all the resources of technics, from the human hand to the latest automatic device. It will be closer in spirit and richness of form to the work of Frank Lloyd Wright and Bernard Maybeck than to the masters of the C.I.A.M.; and it will go beyond them, because it will draw upon the richer human resources now worldwide in cultural scope, which are happily available for collective as well as individual expression.

*1962*

## SIXTEEN

# Historic Philadelphia: I

The civic and architectural sprucing up of Philadelphia, for some time most conspicuous in the area around the recently demolished Broad Street Station, differs from the revivals that are likewise taking place in Pittsburgh, Chicago, St. Louis, New York, and Boston. For this revival is not merely concerned with making the new quarters of the city more habitable; it is also devoted to rescuing its historic monuments from a century and a half of unseemly neglect. Now, however, the focus of this activity in Philadelphia is Independence Hall, and the issues raised by the planning and restoration that have gone on in the area around it bring up many important questions about the dynamics of city development —including how historic a historic city can afford to be. This is a matter that also vexes the municipal authorities of Amsterdam, Venice, and the old City of London, and if anybody thinks there is only one answer to this question, he hasn't ever walked around it and viewed its many sides.

The move to reclaim the Independence Hall district was launched in 1942, and it has been gathering vigor ever since. The original proposal was to give Independence Hall and the buildings adjoining it a setting worthy of such a historic monument. With the aid of an eloquent plea by Carl Van Doren, appropriately the author of an excellent biography of Benja-

min Franklin, this plan elicited not merely patriotic encourage-
ment but a considerable slice of money from Congress. This
set in motion a much larger scheme—of dealing, in a sym-
pathetic way, with the horde of notable old buildings still
sprinkled through the area, some interesting for their human
association and some significant for their architectural features, such as the pattern of red-and-black bricks that
characterizes some of the most venerable dwellings. The recognition of this need was belated. Up to 1942, the prevailing attitude toward historic monuments in Philadelphia was
symbolized by the fact that the house of President Madison had become a ragpickers' headquarters. The Independence Hall area, the core of pre-Civil War Philadelphia,
contains more historic buildings than a similar acreage in any
other American city, largely because so much history was
made there between the meeting of the first Continental Congress and the removal of the capital to New York. The
problem of counteracting the ravages of time is a complicated one, and it requires more thoughtful consideration, if
not more heated debate, than anyone has yet given to it.

Since Independence Hall has at last been made a national
monument, under the protection of the National Park
Service of the Department of the Interior, the rehabilitation of the area around it in some degree concerns all of us,
not merely the citizens of Philadelphia. The amount of land
to be dealt with runs into acres; the buildings whose fate
must be decided run into scores; the cost of acquisition, to
say nothing of refurbishing the buildings, will run into many
millions; and the decisions made will form a precedent for
other cities. In England and France there is now something like a national policy on historic monuments—though
established only after much wanton damage had been done
—but our own purposes are still unclear, partly because
there is a considerable body of citizens who hold the quaint
view that American history stopped short in the eighteenth
century. And even our concern for the eighteenth century is
a late autumnal flower.

Perhaps the best way to understand the whole problem of
reconstruction would be to take a quick look at the Independence Hall area and its scattered treasures in the earlier
stages of their development. When William Penn took over
the colonization of Pennsylvania on a grant from Charles II,

he proposed to build a model city that would remain a "green countrie towne," with gardens, orchards, or fields surrounding each residence. Behind this generous purpose was, no doubt, Penn's memory of the plague that swept through the crowded and overbuilt center of London from 1664 to 1666, and the terrible disinfectant of the Great Fire of the latter year. His plan, so precise that it might have been plotted on coordinate paper supplied by Penn's mathematical near-contemporary Descartes, bears a close resemblance to one of the numerous plans for the reconstruction of London after the fire. That plan was devised by one Richard Newcourt, who was sensible enough to divide his blocks, somewhat larger than the Philadelphia ones, by laying them out around a central core (it is not certain whether this was to be an open square or occupied by a building of some sort), from which four narrow streets ran, at right angles, to the perimeter.

Penn's good intentions about air and open space and a rural setting were only partly fulfilled, largely because he overlooked the economic realities of urban growth. In addition, he did not reckon with the prejudices of the Contributorship, the fire-insurance monopoly established in Philadelphia in 1752. At the moment the founding fathers, in 1774, were beginning their move to oust the British, the insurance brokers, not to be outdone, undertook to get rid of trees, and refused to insure a house that was near any. (This had its parallel in New York City, where, a century later, a vigorous and successful effort was made to rid Broadway of its trees, under the guise of "improving" the city.) Indeed, they went so far, in 1782, as to secure the passage of an ordinance ordering all trees in streets, lanes, and alleys of the city to be removed as a nuisance and a fire hazard. In the end, civil amenity won out, for in 1784 the tree lovers, who had succeeded in getting the ordinance repealed, formed a rival insurance company, the Green Tree, whose cast-iron emblem of a tree is still visible on the façades of many old Philadelphia buildings.

Like Newcourt's plan, that of Penn's planning commissioners called for four open squares, symmetrically disposed to form the corners of a rectangle in the broad strip of land between the Delaware River, on the east, and the Schuylkill River, on the west. All these squares, incidentally, exist today, although Logan Square, at the northwest corner of the rectangle, has been absorbed into Logan Circle and the Benjamin Franklin Parkway, which runs northwest from City Hall. City Hall, by the way, occupies the fifth square of Penn's scheme, placed at the center of his rectangle. At the southwest corner is Rittenhouse Square. The other squares—Franklin, at the northeast corner, and Washington, at the southeast corner—are really formal urban parks. Independence Hall, set in a smaller green park of its own, is just diagonally across the street, to the northeast, from Washington Square.

It was only in the past dozen years, as I have said, that an articulate and active group of Philadelphians, alarmed by the steady decay of the district around Independence Hall, was able to persuade the Commonwealth of Pennsylvania and the United States Congress to take an interest in reclaiming the area. Urged on by the group, the Commonwealth has undertaken to acquire a strip of land, one block wide, running north from Independence Square to Franklin Square, along the eastern perimeter of Penn's rectangle, and the federal government has undertaken to acquire three blocks of land running east from Independence Square as far as Second Street. The new approaches to this square thus form a vast L. The three blocks to the east of the square are, by the way, especially rich in venerable buildings and historical interest. The downstroke of this L, the land acquired by the Commonwealth, has been converted into a green mall; what is to be done with the area acquired by the federal government is slowly being determined, though the main outlines are by now fairly well set.

The National Park Service has jurisdiction over this historic core. But, in addition, the Park Service has possession of, or authority over, a wide scattering of other buildings with varied historic claims, most of them worthy of respectful preservation in some form but difficult to include in any unified plan until the entire district can be treated as a whole, with federal financial aid. Should this area be reclaimed as a residential district, there are rows of admirable early-nineteenth-century houses, in various stages of destitution and prostitution, that might be turned into charming apartment houses. This would do far more to preserve at least a faint aura of the past than any amount of pseudo-Colonial face lifting.

The city began to rise along the river front and port of entry on the Delaware, moving mainly from north to south along the river, which was not in accord with Penn's plan, but also pushing westward. Penn wanted Philadelphia to run east and west, and he made Market Street, the central east-west thoroughfare, a hundred and ten feet wide, a great breadth in the seventeenth century; this was enough to permit a series of market stalls and a market hall in the middle of it, at the Delaware end, extending for three whole blocks. Around the beginning of this century, the citizens of Philadelphia began to move farther north, south, and west, particularly west, and much of the original area of settlement became a grubby backwater. Even such a venerable body as the American Philosophical Society, Franklin's true and legitimate child, was on the point, in 1911, of abandoning its snug and modest Independence Square quarters, reeking with history, for the baroque emptiness of Logan Circle. How happy its members can now be that they resisted this temptation!

The first attempt to provide a proper setting for Independence Hall followed shortly on the building of the Hall itself, with the laying out of Independence Square. The lots that composed this square were originally held by a group of Welsh settlers in Radnor, for Penn assigned a certain number of building lots within the city as a bonus for those who took up land for agriculture in the countryside. But because all this space was available, one is tempted to ask why the designers of the State House—as Philadelphians continued to call Independence Hall till the end of the nineteenth century—placed it so close to Chestnut Street, instead of setting it back sufficiently to provide in front of it a plaza for public ceremonies, as well as visual insulation from nearby buildings. Slowness in acquiring the land was very likely responsible, for though the land for the building was acquired in 1730, it took years to assemble the rest of the square and remove the existing structures.

A truly faithful restoration of State House Yard as of 1776 would disclose a flat, unplanted waste surrounded with a high brick wall. The first landscaping of Independence Square did not, in fact, take place till 1784, when its central walk, leading to a monumental gateway on Walnut Street, became a fashionable promenade. The original architectural drawings for the State House date back to 1732—a sketch and a plan that seem as naïve in outline as a schoolboy's project, which testifies to the abilities of the carpenters and masons, who had no need for specific directions once the general form was given. These drawings show a main building joined by loggias without arches to two flanking buildings, the latter with gabled roofs instead of the hipped ones that were finally used. At first, the State House had not a tower but a turret, a miniature of Wren's Tom Tower, at Oxford. The building was probably the handiwork of a master carpenter, Edmund Woolley, one of that Worshipful Company of Carpenters who had carried to this country the practices of the medieval guilds.

The buildings in the Independence Hall group were not all built at one time, but they were all built in the same general manner, and red brick and wood trim were the principal materials. A sketch in a *Gentleman's Magazine* of 1752 shows the main building, with arched arcades on either side, leading to the two small wings, pretty much as one sees them today. The turret had, by 1752, become a tower, but it must have been shabbily constructed and cared for, or made of unseasoned wood, for it had to be removed as early as 1781. What one sees today in its place is the steeple William Strickland designed in 1828, during one of the first of many restorations. It is fortunate that, despite these changes, so much of the original design remains, at least on the exterior.

Most people may imagine, if they have not looked into the history of these structures, that at least since the signing of the Declaration of Independence the building where the founding fathers met must have been treated with fond, not to say worshipful, respect. But to fancy this is to forget that the progressive minds of the eighteenth century, and even more those of the nineteenth century, were in revolt against the past, including their own past. They were on the side of innovation rather than tradition; they were more interested in making history than in preserving it. Without any pious inhibitions, our ancestors demolished one Philadelphia historic monument after another, from Franklin's house (destroyed in 1812) to Washington's Presidential mansion (destroyed in 1832). In fact, the first generations to inherit these monuments practiced vandalism on a large scale, as blithely oblivious of their offenses as so many juvenile delinquents.

After the legislature of Pennsylvania had moved to Lancaster and the federal government had finally settled in Washington, the State House was spiritually as well as physically deserted. In 1802, it was granted rent free to Charles Willson Peale, to serve as a portrait gallery and a cabinet of natural curiosities, possibly the first museum of art and natural history in the country. A plan dated as late as 1824 shows on the second floor of the State House a Mammoth Room and a Quadruped Room—not, one presumes, an oblique reference to the legislators. The progressive Peale, in 1816, installed a gasworks in the tower, perhaps the first in America, to light his museum, and it is only by a miracle that in its three years of operation this plant did not take fire and ruin the building.

But that was not the only threat to this historic shrine. In 1816, the legislature of Pennsylvania, wanting money for a new capital in Harrisburg, decided to sell Independence Square and its buildings, hoping to realize a hundred and fifty thousand dollars on the deal. Happily, the city of Philadelphia was allowed to acquire the whole estate for a mere seventy thousand dollars. Had it not been for that, it is doubtful if Independence Hall would have escaped the wrecking crew. As it was, part of its panelling was gutted by an astute contractor, who made a job for himself by replacing it with a bang-up "modern" interior in plaster and paint. (The panelling was later replaced intact.) This does not end the long list of indignities this national monument has suffered. In the eighteen-fifties, no one seems to have felt that it was disrespectful to put a municipal dog pound in the cellar, though there were, I am pleased to record, protests against putting a refreshment stand in the main hall.

This cavalier treatment of Independence Hall in the nineteenth century provides a disgraceful contrast to the fidelity with which the original plans were carried out in the eighteenth century. Congress Hall, just west of Independence Hall, was erected in 1789, followed, on the east flank, by a City Hall, built in 1791. For a moment, the whole site was regarded as a major civic center; the American Philosophical Society was given a plot just south of the City Hall, and in 1787 its headquarters added its modest architectural weight to the scene. Except for New Haven, with its churches on the green, I can think of no other American city before the nineteenth century whose group of public buildings rivalled this one. Unfortunately, the magnates who presided over the growth of commercial Philadelphia during that century not only lacked historic piety; they had no use for the classic virtues of unity, emphasis, and coherence. For the sake of economy, the city fathers engaged Robert Mills, later the designer of the Washington Monument, to eliminate the arcades—locally they were always to be called piazzas—on either side of the State House, and to replace them with buildings that afforded space for juries, the county commissioners, and similar functionaries. It was not till 1896 that, at the instigation of the Daughters of the American Revolution, these office buildings were replaced by the present arcades, much on the original pattern, though without the outside stairs that led to the second stories of the wings. This was a happy restoration, not just because it was a return to the structures visible in 1776 but because these loggias afford glimpses, through the archways, of the parklike Square beyond; they thus increase the apparent size of Independence Hall and give the whole design a special distinction. But if the faithful reproduction of antiquity is to be the sole guide to restoration, the Sons of the American Revolution will have to re-erect a brick necessary—as a public lavatory was called in the eighteenth century—in the yard.

By something more, perhaps, than mere coincidence, the major architectural changes in Independence Square are connected with crises or memorable moments in our country's history. Thus Congress Hall was begun when the Constitutional Convention was sitting in the State House; the rescue of the State House dates from 1816, directly after the end of the War of 1812; and the first gesture of historic respect came in 1824, with the welcoming of General Lafayette under a special arch built by Strickland in front of the shrine of independence itself. So, again, the recognition of these buildings as a national rallying point probably dates from President-elect Lincoln's raising the national flag over the Hall on Washington's Birthday in 1861; the first large restoration of the whole group, bringing the buildings closer to their eighteenth-century form, was completed in 1898, the year of the Spanish-American War; and, finally, the present immense effort at reconstruction and visual replenishment began with the institution of the Independence Hall Association in 1942, a few months after Pearl Harbor. But it was not until 1943 that Independence Square was officially recognized, by a compact between the City of Philadelphia and the Department of the Interior, as a "national shrine." Even the revival of interest in Independence Hall during the Centennial Exhibition of 1876, the anniversary of the Declaration of Independence, did not effect this change, though it did result in a belated and somewhat frustrating attempt to restore the interior furniture to a rough approximation of what it was like when the founding fathers met there. Readers of Henry James's short story "The Birthplace" will recognize some of the moral dilemmas, as well as the antiquarian difficulties, still presented to an honest guide by successive restorations of these buildings.

Even if the problems of rehabilitating this area were confined to Independence Hall and its adjacent buildings, their solution would still involve delicate and debatable decisions. Should the architects merely attempt the preservation of the existing structures, so that every addition and replacement is honestly visible, standing out in contrast to the original? Or should they essay a "complete restoration," the kind that seeks to make the restored building just as fresh as the original, or a little more so, as if these monuments had been mummified and time had actually stood still? On such matters, I, for one, would follow the great example of William Morris—who revered genuine historic monuments, even if battered, and who loathed counterfeits all the more because of their waxen perfection—and stand firmly with the first school.

In either event, the general purpose should be plain: to preserve these buildings from further decay, and to stimulate the imagination of those who visit them to consider the great events that they still point to and in a way symbolize. And in either case there is no question of improvement. Doubtless someone could design a more graceful steeple than the one that Strickland inexplicably placed on the Hall; the tower of Dartmouth's Baker Library, a plainly imitative building, could be counted as such an improvement. If one may judge from earlier prints, the first steeple did not have such a poorly proportioned and divided base, or else the delineator corrected this in his drawing. There are Colonial buildings, like the State House in Boston, that have greater felicities of detail. But even to mention such purely esthetic considerations, to say nothing of proposing an improvement, would be as unseemly as correcting a Stuart portrait of Washington to lessen the severe expression caused by his clumsy false teeth. We love such historic buildings for what they are, as we accept the homeliness of Lincoln, wart and all; and love would not have them different.

Independence Hall and its adjacent structures are examples of Georgian decency and quiet dignity, without a touch of the grandiose. The scale of the chief structure, two stories high, is as domestic as that of Mount Vernon, and far more so than some of Jefferson's later classic mansions; it was this homely, non-classic, almost anti-classic quality in Georgian work that Jefferson despised. His State Capitol at Richmond exemplifies what he regarded as proper civic dignity. Unfortunately, not everyone today understands these simple Georgian virtues. Even those who plainly love and honor these buildings have, in their conception of an appropriate setting, done violence to the architectural genius of these buildings; they have, in fact, in an excess of zeal, nearly killed their shrine with kindness, or at least with the sort of princely generosity of space that baroque architects quite naturally accorded to a king's palace. This is such a typical temptation, such a natural miscarriage of love, that it will be worth going into at some length; for the misuse of openness is almost as serious an error as its denial, though somewhat easier to correct. And this brings us to the first great problem of this restoration: what constitutes an "adequate setting"?

*1956*

# SEVENTEEN

# Historic Philadelphia: II

The present project of rehabilitating the area around Independence Square in Philadelphia began with an effort to provide a suitable approach from the north to the Square and the string of historic buildings that adjoins it to the east. The plan to reconstruct the district was set in motion a dozen years ago by a group of Philadelphia citizens headed by Judge Edwin O. Lewis. Ever since the Civil War, the changes that had been effected thereabouts had been mainly for the convenience of business, with no thought of providing a fine setting for the most venerable of all our national monuments. From the red-brick-and-brown-sandstone Bourse, on Fifth Street north of Chestnut, to the twenty-story granite Penn Mutual Building, bulking over the south end of Independence Square, the needs of business, and business only, governed the development of the district. This commercial exploitation was too erratic to give any unity to the neighborhood, for alongside the big insurance offices many historic dwellings remain, sinking stage by stage from indigence to squalor, from squalor to grimy destitution, like old pensioners, too decrepit to perform any offices but the most menial ones, not even lucky enough to succumb to the commercial fever and be put out of their misery. The nearest anyone came to considering Independence Hall was when the twelve-story

Curtis Publishing Company Building and the Public Ledger Building, both at the west side of the Square, were deferentially given façades of red brick with white marble columns, under the delusion that this—plus a few suitable moldings and cornices and facings—made them appropriately "Colonial." All that can be said about the mishmash of business buildings that invaded the quarter is that when the visitor at last reached Independence Square, the contrast between eighteenth-century courtesy and nineteenth-century competition was a violent one. This ugly setting, though not designed to bring out the virtues of the jewel, at least gave it the benefit of that contrast.

Since Judge Lewis's committee got under way, the whole situation has changed. The Commonwealth of Pennsylvania, the same but different Commonwealth that back in 1816 considered selling off Independence Square and all its buildings, including Independence Hall, to the highest bidder, has taken on the responsibility of clearing a swath of land three blocks long north of the Square in order to form the approach I have spoken of—a formal park now called Independence Mall. Following this, the national government (in the guise of the National Park Service) has taken possession of a swath of land running east from Independence Square, to be made over into what it has designated as Independence National Historical Park. The refurbishing of this area brings up many fundamental problems in city design, such as what activities and what manner of architecture are appropriate in such a historic neighborhood. Those concerned with this matter divide into several groups. There are the people who are interested in creating a handsome frame for the old picture, and the people who would like to create a greatly enlarged picture, filled with pseudo-Colonial reproductions that would "blend" with the originals. There are also those whose bump of historic respect disappears between 1800 and 1840, and those who believe that characteristic mementos of each generation should be cherished until they become a positive nuisance or, though perhaps intact, an obstacle to a fresher act of creation. Then there are the "total preservationists," who would permanently maintain these significant examples even if they impede a sound new development. Each of these groups favors a different answer to the problem. Cutting across these divisions is a natural conflict of interests between the state authorities, who got there fustest, and the federal officials, who have the mostest men—and, incidentally, most of the historic buildings. As a result, not only has the project grown since 1942 but its plans and purposes have shifted, and are still shifting, as one pressure or another prevails.

Originally, the only visual approach to Independence Hall was a long, diagonal walk that still leads across Washington Square (which is southwest of Independence Square and just across the street from it) and through the informally planted interior of Independence Square itself, a park that looks much the way New York's Washington Square once did. When the trees are in leaf in this park, one sees only parts of the Independence Hall group of buildings—a patch of brick wall or a bit of white spire—until one is close enough to take in the main structure as a whole. Independence Square has gone through almost as many alterations as these buildings, but when it was planned, landscape architecture, while flourishing in England, had no practitioners in America, and the artlessness of its present design, though different from the original planting, is in keeping with the air of domesticity that is a part of Georgian architecture.

There is nothing magnificent in this approach; its charm is its unpretentiousness, just as Georgian buildings please by their modest details—a porch, a fanlight, a Palladian window —rather than by any larger structural assertions. By the time Independence Hall is in view, it almost seems bigger than it is, and that, too, is quite fitting. However inadequate the planting in the park as it is today, its general design seems to me more fitting than the exact historic resurrection of the 1784 plan that the National Park architects are now considering. That restoration, which calls for a central alley and wavy side paths, ignores the diagonal approach from Washington Square, and it fails to provide open space in front of the Independence Hall tower for outdoor public ceremonies—a provision all the more necessary because the happy suggestion, made as early as 1915, of a permanent reviewing stand in a plaza in front of the Hall was not taken seriously by the designers of Independence Mall.

The unassuming and intimate air of Independence Hall is precisely what the Mall cannot claim. Naturally, one has no quarrel with the generous public spirit that is responsible for this lordly gift of land. Whether visitors in cars approach downtown Philadelphia from the west, via the Schuylkill Ex-

pressway and Pennsylvania Avenue, or from the east, over
the Benjamin Franklin Bridge, it is in the area of the Mall
that they would logically park their cars before going on, by
foot, to see Independence Square. Along the route of this
pilgrimage, every device of architecture and landscape gardening should be utilized to make the walk a rewarding
one.

But the value of space is not dependent solely upon the
quantity available. Too much space has a peculiar effect
upon a reasonably well-educated architect; it induces swollen
sensations of grandeur, and it reminds him, automatically, of
the long, axial approaches, like those at Versailles and Karls-
ruhe, that were used with such formal distinction by the
great baroque architects. The first study for the Mall, made
by the Philadelphia architectural firm of Harbeson, Hough,
Livingston & Larson, in 1944, called for an approach of this
nature, and its general conception is being carried out—
with sundry modifications, not all of them improvements—by
Mr. Larson. The result, even before the work is complete, is
striking; such vigorous order, such freedom from the haphaz-
ard and the formless, falls gratefully on eyes constantly as-
sailed in Philadelphia by incongruous clutter. But is this
long formal park the right approach to the modest Georgian
buildings of Independence Square?

It is a little unjust to deal with an only partly completed
design, but it is possible to estimate the total effect, on the
basis of what has been completed and the unpublished plans
for the rest. The Mall, as I have said, will occupy three city
blocks. The block just north of Independence Square
has already been cleared and planted; its design will be repeated in almost every detail in the northernmost block, on
which no work has yet been done, for its welter of dilapi-
dated buildings is still standing. This is also true of most of
the center block, the proposed site of an underground parking
garage, an idea that has now apparently been abandoned by
the state authorities.

If one could grant the validity of the dominating concept
of design, one might easily accept the way it has been carried out. There are a few minor annoyances, like the little
service buildings, which have been treated to suggest guard-
houses, but there are also certain admirable features. A ribbon of greensward, ninety feet wide, runs down the middle of

the portion already planted to within a hundred feet of Chestnut Street, on which Independence Hall faces. This green carpet is flanked on each side by a broad flagstone alley, for pedestrians, which is lined with a double row of trees, and the alleys in turn are flanked by slightly raised esplanades, planted with magnolias, fruit trees, and ornamental dwarf trees, pleasantly grouped in a fashion that invites the pedestrian to rest. In twenty years, when the trees that form the arcade have grown bigger, they will close off the scraggly rooftops on either side of the Mall until the pilgrim comes within a long stone's throw of his objective. This uniform pattern is all that is left of the original concept, so elegant on paper, which treated the whole Mall as a unified area, with a grand circle at the northern end and a grander semicircle at the southern end. But though they tried to cling to this concept, the architects had to come to terms with the facts that denied it. For these three separate blocks are neither functionally nor visually one; not even from the spire of Independence Hall could they be seen as they appear on the architectural rendering of the project, with the traffic arteries that cut across the vista artfully presented without any hint of traffic. What this grand opening up of space will reveal, when it is completed, is the ragged sky line of industrial Philadelphia.

Functionally, there was much to be said for all the proposed utilities. The parking garage, an information center, and a restaurant, which were to have occupied the middle block of the Mall, would at least be in the right place for the convenience of the visitor. What needed revision was not these utilitarian features but the conception of the grand axial approach. All that is now left of this bad compromise between "form" and "function" is a square pool with thirteen jets of water gaily spouting in it. The National Park Service wants its information center not here, along the logical approach to Independence Hall, but much farther to the east, near the waterfront, so that the guided tourist will reach the national shrine more circuitously, through the oldest and most historic part of the city. To prompt the tourist to acquiesce in this arrangement, the National Park people will offer him parking space next to the new Custom House, near the historic Philadelphia Exchange, which will become the information center, and to "feed" the tourist they will "reconstruct" the ancient City Tavern (1773), at Second

Street and Moravian, without, however, offering the visitor any actual food. Whether all this is a sound conception, even for the guided tourist, is dubious. But I trust this federal scheme will not keep the Commonwealth of Pennsylvania from reviving its plan for its own garage, to take care of those reckless vagrants who want to commune with their ancient heritage in their own wayward fashion. The money required for this project will not be wasted; as the pilgrimages to this spot become more popular, two parking facilities will be barely sufficient on a busy day. Some million and a quarter visitors already flock to this shrine every year.

Eliminating the information building and restaurant from the scheme for the Mall will, by the way, only emphasize a basic fault. Their disappearance will remove the major interruption in the architects' contemplated long vista, but it will make all the more apparent the fact that the movement of pedestrians *across* the Mall will be impeded except where the streets intersect it. Redesigning the Mall to permit crosswalking by people who do not intend to go to Independence Hall would increase the utility of these three blocks of park as recreation space. This is something that might well be emphasized in the rehabilitation of the district. And the happy decision to retain the Free Quaker Meeting House—once scheduled for removal—at the northeast corner of the middle block of the Mall surely accentuates the need for another mode of park design here.

The situation faced by the designers of the Mall may be profitably compared with that faced by Sir William Holford in his recent design for the precinct around St. Paul's, in London. Like Independence Hall, St. Paul's is a hallowed monument, and it is set in a district even more dedicated to commercial activities. But unlike our first Capitol, the cathedral is a large and imposing structure that, until the University of London's Bloomsbury skyscraper was built, in the nineteen-thirties, had no rival on the London sky line. For more than two hundred years, people dreamed of lifting St. Paul's out of the clutter of buildings that hemmed it in, and Wren's plans for rebuilding the City of London sought to open up the site with two converging avenues. In 1940, the Blitz succeeded in doing what no planner had ever persuaded the city to do—it razed almost all the buildings in the area around the cathedral. In his early plans for this area,

Holford sought to take advantage of this openness, and he was even tempted, by the very style of St. Paul's, to outformalize Wren by providing a semicircular colonnade to define strongly the open space in front of the building. But he could not down his misgivings about this treatment, and in a revised plan he was driven to minimize, rather than maximize, the direct exposure of the cathedral, planning the approach to it through a series of lanes and openings between buildings of different heights, the whole completely dissimilar in esthetic effect from the spacious symmetrical and standardized arrangements dear to baroque architects.

Quite another treatment is called for in Philadelphia, precisely because the individuality of the city must be taken into account. But a planner who had equally freed himself from baroque political and spatial perspectives would, I believe, turn up with an entirely different solution, and a much more fitting one. He should respect tradition in the design of the Mall, but the tradition that should be understood and carried further is that of Philadelphia itself, with its ample squares, its uniform roof lines, and its intimate gardens, not that imposed by the servants of an absolute monarchy seeking to translate into space the mystique of absolute power and centralized political control. Was it not in revolt against that absolutist tradition in politics that Independence Hall itself acquired its special meaning for Americans?

Just because it would be lost, on account of its diminutive size, if it were as closely surrounded by business buildings as St. Paul's, Independence Hall needs a setting of green to insulate it from the contemporary city. But this setting must take account of the east-west traffic lanes which are probably too important to be broken by converting the Mall from three separate square blocks into a single oblong superblock. The answer, then, is to accept the blocks as the units of design, and to organize and furnish them in such a fashion as to give each its individual content instead of trying to relate them visually to the historic buildings they lead to. Then Independence Hall would come, as it still does when one approaches it through its own square, as a happy surprise, in a friendly and intimate setting of its own, without pretensions to an architectural magnitude it does not possess. Even if the cross-traffic did not ruin the long, spectacular approach through the Mall, the very length of that approach will impose upon this unassuming Georgian building an esthetic burden that only a vast palace or temple of far greater architectural merit could hope to carry off. One will be looking at the Hall through the wrong end of the telescope.

The problem of designing a pleasant and fitting approach to a building whose architectural boasts are much more modest than its historical claims is so new that one should not be cast down because this first exploration was tempted down a visual alley that turned out to be a blind one. But the results show how dangerous it is to adopt a purely formal scheme, based on a historically remote tradition, as a safe way for avoiding often unpleasant modern clichés. The proper key for such a design is not wholly a visual one. The designers would have come out better if they had thought not of a modernized baroque scheme but of the little shrine itself, what it means, and in what mood and for what purpose the visitor approaches it. Surely the purpose is not just to reach Independence Hall; one could do that quicker on a moving platform. Nor is the purpose just to stretch one's legs after being cooped up in a car. Here, rather, is an opportunity gently to remind the passerby, at every turn, of the relevant facts of American history and to prepare his mind for more immediate confrontation with the past in the old buildings themselves—Philosophical Hall, Carpenters' Hall, and, finally, Independence Hall. Instead of concentrating on an axial approach, the architects might have created, quite in the spirit of Philadelphia, a series of connected enclosed areas, strung along a series of short, continually shifting axes, each forming a sort of outdoor room, with the shrubbery and the trees providing a screen against the surrounding areas of the city. Symbolically, each of the enclosures might have been dedicated to one of the thirteen founding states, and a series of fountains, by a play of water, if not by the rhythm of sculpture, might have given the whole design an animation and a vitality it now lacks.

In short, it seems to me that a good design for this Mall would not merely emphasize the separateness of the squares but would invite the visitor to dawdle and reflect, going and coming; to awaken his own historic associations, his state and regional pride, his ancestral pieties. Such an approach might irritate the tourist who speeds from one historic spot to another, and stops just long enough to buy a batch of picture postcards or snap another spool of film. But that kind of tourist could be painlessly taken care of in an air-conditioned chamber in that underground garage, where he could enjoy a rapid guided tour of Independence Hall on a television screen before rushing off to the next spot. Fortunately, there are plenty of people who, with a little inducement, might linger even longer than they now do.

Perhaps it is too late to canvass fresh suggestions for the part of the Mall that is already complete. But is it really too late to think twice about the rest of it—or, for that matter, about other parts of the project?

*1957*

# EIGHTEEN

# Historic Philadelphia: III

The most striking improvement that has been brought about in the effort to rehabilitate the district surrounding Independence Square, in Philadelphia, is Independence Mall, the long and dignified northern approach to the historic buildings that are spread across the north side of that square. The Mall, now under construction, is the Commonwealth of Pennsylvania's contribution to the belated reorganization of this area. But another project is under way, and still others should be planned if the original purpose of this rehabilitation —to give some of the most important of our national historic buildings a fine setting—is to be achieved. The more difficult half of this reconstruction, in the area to the east of Independence Square, has not yet been begun by the National Park Service, which has been assigned this task by the federal government. Except for the matter of preserving one historic building on the site of the Mall, the Free Quaker Meeting House, at the corner of Fifth Street and Arch, the problem of handling the area the Mall is to occupy was, architecturally, a simple one. As soon as the other structures that still stand there have been cleared away, there will be nothing to curb the designer except the three thoroughfares —Chestnut, Market, and Arch Streets—that cross this plot of land.

The area under federal control, on the other hand, offers many thorny problems, for a unifying landscape plan must be created to provide a setting for three famous buildings—what is usually called the Old Custom House, designed by William Strickland and erected in 1819-24, as the Second Bank of the United States, at a cost of nearly half a million dollars, a munificent sum in those days; Carpenters' Hall, just to the east of it; and, architecturally the most interesting of the lot, Strickland's Philadelphia Exchange, still farther to the east. This federal project, officially designated Independence National Historical Park, covers the three big blocks or "squares" as they used to be called in Philadelphia, to the east of Independence Square, as well as the Square itself.

In addition to a handful of historic structures, the farthermost block also boasts a much later pink elephant, the new Custom House, a towering hulk, sound in plan but banal in decoration, that is almost as much an esthetic liability to this particular sky line as the John Hancock Mutual Life Insurance Building is to Boston's. Deciding whether everything *in situ* but these three famous buildings should be summarily demolished was not easy, for other interesting structures had to be considered, among them a characteristic bank by Frank Furness, in the manner of his Pennsylvania Academy, as well as an early cast-iron building (1850), at Third and Dock Street, and the Jayne Building, at 242 Chestnut Street, an almost archetypal American skyscraper, eight stories high, built in 1849—all of them with claims to historical respect, though not because of associations with the American Revolution or subsequent political events. Furness' bank and the cast-iron building, as it happens, have already been demolished, and the future of the Jayne Building is in doubt.

The most important building in this area, because of its nearness to Independence Square and its unique historical associations, is Carpenters' Hall, at the foot of a narrow blind alley that runs south from Chestnut Street. This was the seat of one of the last guilds that functioned in this country, the Carpenters' Company, set up in 1724, an organization that still has a local aura—influence would possibly be too strong a word—comparable to that of the great Livery Companies in the City of London. (No one, I have been told, is likely to get far in the building trades in Philadelphia without becoming a member of this company.) Carpenters' Hall is the building in which the more subversive fathers of our country met in secret session, in 1774. They were egged on by one of the Carpenters' Company leaders, who represented the "mechanics' interest" in the Revolution, as Sam Adams in Boston represented the merchants' interest. The Hall is memorable but not monumental. Judged by a cold eye, it is a somewhat gawky building, handsomer within than without, that would be helped rather than handicapped if some of its neighbors had been allowed to survive this reconstruction. Furness' bank, the Guarantee Safe Deposit & Trust, which formed the eastern side of the alley on which it is situated, shielded the Hall from any too distant and comprehensive effort to take it in. New Hall, a sort of annex to Carpenter's Hall, formed the western side of the alley and served as a lesser shield. But New Hall was demolished many years ago, and now the bank, too, has disappeared. In Colonial days, it was the retired position of Carpenters' Hall—what Henry James called its "beautiful posteriority"—that made it just the place to hold clandestine meetings. The National Park Service architects seem under a certain pressure, possibly only subjective, to expose this worthy monument as if it were a prime esthetic object. The exposure would not only be cruel; it would obliterate the great historical point about its position. And it would be even worse if—like modest Independence Hall, which is to be dwarfed by the grandiose approach of the Mall—this little building were to be diminished by being placed at the end of a long, wide axis running east from Independence Hall, and further diminished by a vista that revealed the classic Doric amplitude of the Old Custom House, which lies between it and Independence Square.

The answer, it seems to me, is to cut completely loose from the enthralling spatial stereotypes of the baroque tradition, which postulates the sort of approach typified by Independence Mall. The approach from the west to Carpenters' Hall should be an intimate one, perhaps through a cordon of trees and a series of small, partly walled gardens that would delight the eye with their richness of color and intricacy of foliage, all of which would provide a pleasing contrast to the more formal clumps or colonnades of trees that should set off the fine austerity of the Old Custom House. As for the approach from the north, I look with a dubious eye upon the Park Service's plans to construct a replica of the original New Hall, even though this reproduction is to serve as a museum for the Marine Corps. Such faking seems to me inexcusable, no matter how abundant the historical data or how careful the "reconstruction." Since so much that is historically genuine remains, why should anyone debase its value by minting and scattering about false coin that the innocent will take as real money?

Instead, there should be a modern version of the alley on which Carpenters' Hall sat—perhaps a covered arcade, just two parallel stone walls, which might be helpfully inscribed with a brief account of the historic events that took place there. What I am pleading for is the suppleness of design that Olmsted and Vaux used so well, within their Victorian limitations, in their plan for New York's Central Park, in which they passed easily from the romantic informality of tree-bordered meadows of the strict spatial order of the Mall. No uniform approach can do justice to the historic variety that the architect must deal with in the necessarily spotty rebuilding of ancient Philadelphia; rather, the designer must be able to combine jigging folk melodies with austere formal hymns in a single composition. And he should remember the characteristic intimacy of the small Philadelphia gardens that are still visible along the many downtown alleys and streets, and seek to turn what has so often been a mean constriction of space into a positive advantage.

The Old Custom House, set above Chestnut Street on a pedestal of steps, is one of the best examples of Greek Revival architecture in this country. It is a Doric temple—a Parthenon, in fact, though without the sculpture or the golden goddess—beautifully proportioned, its form altered only by the introduction of windows on each side, to serve its original banking functions. This building presents no problem at all, not even the problem of preservation, except perhaps for the heavy weathering of the fluted shafts. The Schuylkill marble used on its face has a warmth often lacking in limestone, and the building is still as useful as it is spacious; for that matter, it is now headquarters for some of the Park Service staff. It needs only an adequate setting of trees to temper its bleak side walls; an early print shows that trees once actually did perform this function.

The recent demolition of the ten-story Drexel Building, which bulked between the Custom House and Independence

Square, does, however, pose a question of some importance—
the relation of this classic structure to its far less monumental
political neighbors to the west. The plan devised by Mr.
Grant Simon, the architect who drew up the first scheme for
the reconstruction of the Independence Park area, made out
of the open space created by this demolition a hollow oblong,
bordered by a triple row of trees, and this seems better than
the present plan, by another hand, which would leave open
the wide, uninteresting west face of the Old Custom House, a
façade that was never meant to be so exposed.

East of Carpenters' Hall, on Third Street, stands the First
Bank of the United States, usually called the Girard Bank,
a classic building (1795) more than a generation earlier
than Strickland's Old Custom House and not so handsome
or quite so well preserved, albeit worth preserving, even
though its leafy Corinthian capitals are an invitation to the
untidy domesticity of pigeons. The Simon plan, which gave
each of these buildings an independent setting, is closer to
the right solution than the current one, which attempts to
unite them in a fashion that flouts both their original character and their form, and does not conceal the quite mediocre
side faces of the First Bank.

In the block east of the First Bank, between Third and
Second Streets, the problem changes. More than a quarter
of this block is occupied by the new Custom House, which
will not be removed for many years. At the southwest corner
of the block is another Strickland masterpiece—the Philadelphia Exchange. This building stands by itself on a triangular
island, which came into existence when Dock Street, whose
course follows the bed of an old creek, sliced diagonally
through the block and severed this island from it. Dock
Street was the first departure from rectangularity in the original plan for Philadelphia, and it remained the only one until Benjamin Franklin Parkway was laid out, in the grand
manner, a hundred and twenty-five years later. The Exchange,
an oblong building three stories high, is well proportioned
and gracious in line. The front façade bows out into a sort of
semicircular apse, two stories high and punctuated by columns. The columns stand on a platform, also semicircular,
formed by the ground floor, and support a sloping roof
whose juncture with the main roof is capped by a little
tower, a free adaptation of the famous monument of Lysicrates
in Athens. In its quiet ornamental detail and the fine propor-

tions of the side windows, arranged in triplets, this building is an outstanding representative of the Greek Revival period in architecture. It can quite literally stand alone without embellishments of any kind; the trees that used to line its south flank were for once superfluous. Unfortunately, this handsome structure has been treated over the years with almost as much disrespect as Independence Hall. Half a century ago, its classic interior was gutted; worse, a cordon of ramshackle market stalls was thrown around the circular façade, to accommodate the provision merchants who then used it. Here restitution, not minute restoration, is called for. But even after this is achieved, for what purpose should such a building be used?

The Park Service plans to make the Exchange an information center—a prospect that fills me with more than a vague dread. Just as people who invest in power mowers promptly extend the green of their lawn in order to justify their investment, the Park Service, once entrenched in the guided-tour business, may be tempted to add other counterfeit shrines to its project for the nearby City Tavern, which it plans to reconstruct as a picturesque but empty relic—not even as the useful restaurant for tourists and local businessmen one might well welcome here, in competition with the famous fish restaurant that survives in the neighborhood. The Exchange may, in addition, house a library, a museum, an auditorium for motion pictures, and the historic Peale Collection. Thus the whole center of gravity may be shifted away from Independence Hall to the subordinate buildings, and the dutiful sightseer may finally reach that original symbol of our freedom only after he has lost the last vestiges of his own, which he will have exchanged for a headache and tired feet.

There is certainly a place for a modest information center, but the site originally proposed for it, on the Mall, was a far better choice. Certainly, too, it is better to have some activity in the once so active Exchange than to turn it into another ghostly architectural corpse, for the way to keep most old buildings, if they are not in fact holy icons, fragrant with the past, is to keep them alive. But in this instance we may, in rectifying the callous nihilism and neglect of the nineteenth century, end up with an odd collection of museums, busy with educational activities, cleaned and scoured and "restored," but without a trace of their original historic characters. One would, I submit, do more honor to Strickland's design by restoring the Exchange to working order for appropriate business enterprise, since there is no dearth of historical reminders in the area about it. Electric lighting, steam heating, modern lavatories, and partitions will not take anything essential away from the exterior esthetic value of this building, whereas an exact period restoration of the interior will be simply a pious fake, and a bore to all but a few confirmed antiquarians glorying not so much in the past as in an exhibition of their knowledge of the past.

The bold act of creating open space on two sides of Independence Square does more than merely settle (or partly settle) the problem of approach; it also provides a firebreak around the highly flammable historic buildings it contains—a precaution whose necessity was demonstrated a while back when embers from a blaze across the street set fire to the roof of Congress Hall, which adjoins Independence Hall on the west. Such an opening has already been carved around Christ Church (1727), on the site of the first (1695) Anglican church in Philadelphia. But what shall be done to enhance the beauty of the other venerable buildings that have been preserved, such as the Old Swedes' Church (designated as a National Historic Site in 1942), the diminutive Dilworth-Todd-Moylan house, the home of Dolly Madison (now cowering behind a big luncheonette sign), and the fifteen old houses (now under the jurisdiction of the Park Service) along Walnut and Locust Streets, as well as along Manning Street, or Marshall's Court, as it has recently been rechristened? The question is not whether these buildings are to be preserved but how they can best be preserved—and appreciated.

Unluckily, the historical piety that spurred this wholesale reconstruction and renewal may become an obstacle to finding a sensible solution. Betteredge, the old butler in Wilkie Collins' *The Moonstone*, had sardonic comments to make upon "decoration fever," but what would he have said of "restoration fever," which can be even more upsetting? There is an immense difference between preservation, which may prolong the life of a treasured building, and restoration, which is an attempt to give a corpse an imitation bloom of life or to impose a counterfeit antiquity on something painfully put together with the aid of modern scholarship and modern tools. Much can be said for judicious—I stress "judicious"—

preservation. It would have been possible, as late as the eighties, to preserve a whole group of congenial buildings (now vanished) to the east of Independence Hall, including Dr. William Thornton's fine Library Hall. Independence Hall could not have had better neighbors, esthetic or historic. But it is usually best to let bygones be bygones. Not the least disastrous effect of restoration fever is that restorationists become anti-historic, in that they want to halt the flow of history at the particular moment they value.

In the case of the one ancient institution—apart from the old insurance companies—that has remained alive through the years of decay in this area, the American Philosophical Society, whose Philosophical Hall flanks Independence Hall to the east, there was good reason to permit the addition, on the opposite side of the street, of a badly needed building to house its famous collection of books and manuscripts. But it was a meretricious proposal to house that collection in the reproduction of the original Library Hall that is now being built, for that original design poorly fits a modern library's purposes. There is no more reason a new library across the way from the Philosophical Society should look like that old building than there would have been to make the Old Custom House look not like a Greek temple (the "modern" of the eighteen-twenties) but like the red brick Old City Hall. In the interests of history, living history, the new library should have been a good example of today's architecture, a witness to the skill and taste of our time, as Carpenters' Hall and the Old Custom House are to the skill and taste of their own periods. In his sketches in 1950 for the Museum for the State of North Carolina, in Raleigh, the late Matthew Nowicki showed how an entirely modern building could be made to harmonize with an old classic building without imitating a single detail.

People who do not respect their own age accept too easily counterfeits of the past, not realizing that the "little difference" they see between a well-preserved original and a modern copy is all the difference in the world. Thus the Park Service's present plan to build a replica of the original tavern erected on Second Street in 1773 is a libel on history, whereas a thoroughly modern library building that was part of the continuing life of Independence Square would do honor to the historic spirit. Only those who fully understand this distinction should be entrusted with the care of our national historic monuments.

Quite early in the day, Mr. Charles E. Peterson, originally in charge of the federal portion of the Philadelphia project —he left that post to become supervising architect of all the National Historic Sites projects—disposed of the effort to turn it into another Williamsburg by pointing out that there is no uniform style for treating almost two centuries of architecture, which have produced a marked succession of styles. This was the proper answer to those who, in their concentration on 1776 and all that, looked with disdain on such a Victorian masterpiece as Notman's Athenæum Library, on Philadelphia's Washington Square, though this structure has the noble proportions of Barry's Reform Club in Pall Mall. If Mr. Peterson's wise lead is followed, the general rehabilitation of this area will not bring about a reign of compulsive Colonialism. There will be, rather, a wider variety of buildings, carried over from the past or newly built, each representing a significant moment in our national development. Only after 1840 did a truly indigenous architecture spring up in America, and one of the merits of Mr. Peterson's approach is that it would ensure the preservation of at least one of Frank Furness' characteristic works in this area.

Even before Chicago, Philadelphia was one of the germinal points in modern architecture, mainly because of the self-confidence and vigor of Frank Furness. An English critic recently dubbed a contemporary Philadelphia architect the leader of the Brutalist school, and "brutalism" is exactly the word for describing the Furness influence. In buildings like the Provident Trust Company, on Chestnut Street between Fourth and Fifth, he pushed ugliness to the point where it almost turned into beauty, or at least a brutal creativity. If this bank were in the National Park area, I would strongly favor its preservation, and there is much to be said for acquiring a national option on it at this early date. It is nothing less than a second Declaration of Independence, and it admirably demonstrates some of the consequences, both good and bad, of the first.

The preservation itch, if not the restoration fever, has, alas, even attacked the admirers of the post-Colonial and post-Federal progenitors of modern architecture. Last fall, a number of these people banded together, through the Philadelphia chapter of the American Institute of Architects, to plead (in vain, it turned out) for the preservation of the Jayne Building, the cast-iron building I have already mentioned, and the Furness' bank. Though I share their respect for these indigenous products, I shrink from this kind of idolatry. I would apply to the urban scene William Morris' words about interior decoration: "Have nothing in your home you do not believe to be beautiful or know to be useful." These buildings could not claim preservation on either count. The Jayne Building has interest only as a façade, the cast-iron building was interesting as an early technical curiosity, the bank was interesting as one of a group of similar buildings by the same hand. Much as I cherish the Jayne Building in memory, because of its possible effect on Louis Sullivan, when he worked in Furness' office across the street, I believe that its destruction would be a relatively small price to pay for turning its deep site into a handsome garden. On this matter I stand firmly with the present administrators of the Park Service and against the "total preservationists." Again I would like to quote, this time from *The Culture of Cities*: "If the city is to escape being a confused rubbish heap, the function of preservation and storage must be taken over by the museum. . . . By confining the function of preservation to the museum, we thus release space in the rest of the city for the fresh uses of the living." Those of us who have long labored to rescue the industrial and commercial buildings erected between 1850 and 1890 from undeserved neglect have a special duty to avoid misplaced piety and esthetically callous antiquarianism. Our job is to work for a more positive and healthy attitude toward the whole problem of urban renewal in this area.

But the greater danger comes from the Colonial restorationists, who do not realize that one Williamsburg is enough for even a big country. If they were content with such genuine improvements as the recent removal of the grotesque third story that was added to Philosophical Hall in the nineties, one would go along with them, even on such an expensive enterprise. But they also wish to turn new buildings into imitations of the old. The respectable firm of architects that restored Philosophical Hall designed the bank recently erected catercorner from Congress Hall, at Sixth and Chestnut Streets, and gave it an elegant Georgian mask. Commendably, the bank is built to the scale of the Independence Square buildings. But by the very effort to identify itself with the old structures, the new building takes away their historic distinction—the fact that they *belong* to the eighteenth century, and that their classic ornament is native to a generation that quoted Latin authors, imitated the heroes of Plutarch, and carefully conned, in the Federalist Papers, the political lessons of Greece and Rome.

Nothing could do more to make our national shrine seem commonplace and undistinguished than to surround it, as it is now partly surrounded, with dubious approximations of Georgian architecture, coarsened in every feature, internally adapted to the age of fluorescent lighting and air-conditioning. Even where this is done to the hilt, as in Williamsburg—to the point of dressing the custodians up in Colonial costume—the facts of contemporary life keep breaking through to spoil the harmony, for the designers cannot reproduce the eighteenth-century face or the eighteenth-century voice, and so at some point the illusion of historical intimacy must ironically collapse. What our historic buildings need, if they are to stand out in all their brave uniqueness, is just the opposite of this: the benefit of the contrast provided by a modern urban setting, whose fresh comeliness and order do justice to what Colonial and Federal Philadelphia bequeathed to us. The lovers of the old demand too little by asking only for red brick and classic moldings, white trim and graceful urns when a new building goes up in this area. Apart from the falsification and affectation, this would still leave far too many nests of squalor and disorder. What has been done so far in creating a coherent setting is only a small part of what, with imagination and spirit, we could and should still do in a series of generous urban renewal projects.

*1957*

# NINETEEN

# Historic Philadelphia: IV

Many interests must be reconciled in the effort to provide a worthy setting for the group of historic monuments that form the core of Independence National Historical Park, the federal government's project to rehabilitate the area immediately to the east of Philadelphia's (not to say the nation's) Independence Square. The antiquarian and the go-getter, the patriot and the profiteer, as well as the present miscellaneous occupants of the district—from the humble owners of dusty machine shops to the proud purveyors of life and fire insurance—all have a stake in this. The open expression of their differences, the consciousness that they exist and must be respected, are part of the workings of a democracy, and though all this may slow up decisions, it ensures a certain solidarity of assent when final action is taken. Since the plans for the rehabilitation were not begun until 1942, some of the differences of opinion have yet to be smoothed out: one can still feel tensions, ideological if not personal, between various groups, some content to dote on past glories, others eager for future achievements. Fortunately, many of the larger decisions are still open to discussion, and some already made should be reconsidered and drastically revised during the coming generation.

Those who, down through the years, concerned themselves

with preserving and conserving the historic architectural treasures of this neighborhood had, until 1948, fought a delaying action, but a losing one, for one historic building after another near Independence Hall was torn down or gutted to make room for some vagrant industry that needed cheap, if restricted, quarters. Suddenly, by one of those quick reversals of sentiment foreign observers are tempted to label American, the gallant defenders of our national shrine found themselves —by virtue of a sumptuous appropriation by Congress—with more land and more buildings than they were prepared in their minds to make use of. Because of the public interest their efforts have generated, they can obviously now go much further than their original demand—which was merely for an "adequate approach" to Independence Hall itself.

What should be demanded now is not a limited formal approach but a more comprehensive setting for the entire urban complex, historic and modern, that makes this a unique quarter. Attaining this involves not just the pious preservation of the old but vigorous acts of creation that will bring fresh urban color and beauty into the entire neighborhood. It calls for a program to take over and replan, as a whole, not merely the acreage the federal and state governments have already acquired in their efforts at rehabilitation but a far larger part of old Philadelphia. This area, half a mile wide, east to west, from Second to Eighth Street, and amost a mile long, south to north, from Lombard to Race Street, would have the Independence Square project as its center, and it would embrace just about all of the city's ancient monuments, public and private, that deserve a better fate.

So far, the reconstruction of the district has been treated principally as a problem of insulation—an effort to keep the twentieth century from intruding on the eighteenth, or at least persuading it to put on a hired fancy-dress costume, dated eighteenth century but fabricated of nylon and held together with zippers, whenever it comes near the older quarters. More realistically, an effort has also been made to control the height of buildings in this area, and thus prevent the erection of any more structures that would dwarf the old monuments, which is what a group of nearby office buildings already does.

For the attempt to make any new buildings in this area conform to a purely arbitrary (indeed, mythical) Colonial style, there is nothing good to be said, as the existing office

buildings that have been designed in this fashion prove.
Those that have recently been put up in the vicinity of
the venerable Philadelphia Exchange, for example, do no
honor to its austere post-Georgian design. Yet there are still
many people who believe that this fraudulent masking of
history should characterize the whole neighborhood, and if I
read the evidence correctly, there are officials in the National Park Service, which is in charge of the Independence
National Historical Park project, who share this unfortunate
belief. For them, the whole problem of an approach can be
solved by setting aside a few gardened open spaces and
reaching an agreement that any new buildings shall be done
in red brick, with white trim, small-paned windows, and classic pediments, cornices, and columns, behind which the usual
panoply of modern mechanical conveniences can brazenly
flourish. While one need not question the pious intentions of
these Colonial conformists, one is impelled to suggest that
something better than this superficial scene-painting is called
for if the new buildings are to be worthy of the old.

On this matter, the executors of the project received excellent counsel from a committee of the American Institute
of Architects: G. Holmes Perkins, Dean of the School of Fine
Arts at the University of Pennsylvania, and two other men,
both now dead—Fiske Kimball, a conservative and a great
authority on Colonial and Federal architecture, who loved
McKim, Mead & White as well as Cézanne, and George
Howe, who began as a traditionalist and blossomed, in middle life, into a leader of the moderns. Perkins, on the other
hand, is young enough to have been born into the modern
movement, during the great travail in the architectural schools
in the thirties. In a statement of principles to govern the
whole area, these three men set down the following guide-
lines: First, there should be no effort to make new buildings
"Colonial," if only because, in scale and plan and construction and purpose, there is no relationship whatever between
modern business structures and their predecessors. Second, old buildings later than the eighteenth century should, if
physically and economically sound, be saved. "To wander
about among structures of successive styles and periods," they
observed, "is to feel the exhilaration of moving in architectural history. The nineteenth-century buildings were designed
by some of the most dedicated and original architects our
country ever produced. They are the very symbol of the

continuity of our hard-won independence." On that basis, the committee came out for straightforward contemporary design of any new buildings, with limitations on bulk and with deeper setbacks than are called for by city ordinance, to preserve the scale of the bordering streets. The committee also urged the planting of trees. If this last bit of advice had been available when the Curtis and Public Ledger buildings were built, on the west side of Independence Square, the historic buildings that they dwarf would today enjoy the amount of visual elbow room they need and the ratty sky line around them would be mercifully less apparent.

But the stylistic problems of new construction cannot be separated from the whole business of urban redevelopment, the orderly rearrangement of an entire neighborhood. Congressional acceptance of the concept of urban redevelopment as a national responsibility—as well as a municipal necessity, if blight and bankruptcy are not to destroy our urban centers—is favorable to the idea of large-scale planning. The Independence Hall area needs something more than negative protection and piecemeal rebuilding; the private enterpriser who plans to build here cannot afford to think in terms of public benefits unless his rivals are bound, by law, to think in the same terms. If the original aim of the lovers of Independence Hall is to be adequately fulfilled, the L-shaped core of green that—by virtue of the federal and state rehabilitation projects—is to flank this national shrine must be esthetically supported by a series of other schemes, designed to make this part of the city so attractive both for living in and for doing business in that there will be a steady building up of population, to take advantage of the unique facilities that this area already offers. In other words, to preserve the best of the past—and the past at its best—one must do justice in no grudging way to the needs of the future.

But let us consider the suggestion that a larger area be included in the rehabilitation scheme. (Perhaps one should consider this with a historical map at one's elbow; Mr. Grant Miles Simon, a Fellow of the American Institute of Architects, compiled an exhaustive one for the American Philosophical Society's 1952 book, *Historic Philadelphia from the Founding Until the Early Nineteenth Century*.) I have set the eastern boundary of this larger area at Second Street, because between it and Water Street, an eighth of a mile farther east, lies the old port district, a miscellany of markets, storehouses, and related petty industries that belong to such a locality. Except for a few scattered buildings, and a group of mean little dwelling houses done in the eighteenth century, called Elfreth's Alley, about which Philadelphians seem inordinately proud, there is almost nothing in this section that calls for preservation in the face of more imperative commercial use. The only exception is the little Market Hall (or Head House, as it is usually called nowadays), which stands in the middle of Second Street where Pine Street intersects it, at the southeast corner of the area under consideration —a building that should be treated tenderly and remain undisturbed even if, to facilitate the flow of traffic, this means widening the street it now inconveniently divides.

Immediately to the south of Independence National Historical Park, down as far as Lombard Street, a distance of perhaps half a mile, is a district that should not be left to time, chance, and the conflicting aims of real-estate operators. This district has become nondescript—a mixture of seedy residences, lunchrooms, factories, lofts, tombstonemakers' sheds, old burial grounds, and historic churches, among them St. Paul's Protestant Episcopal Church (1761) and the Spruce Street First Baptist Church (1830), now a Rumanian synagogue. This part of Philadelphia is still known as Society Hill, and it still contains many houses that justify the name —from the famous Shippen-Wistar house, now occupied by an insurance company, to rows of elegant dwellings of impeccable craftsmanship, which need only a little loving care to be nursed back to life. This area, thanks to numerous graveyards as well as the National Park, already possesses more viewable, if not otherwise usable, open space than any other part of the city except the borders of Fairmount Park. That is a huge asset for future residential development.

The outer fringes of Society Hill, the transitional zone that borders the business district, are natural sites for residential buildings, and nothing would provide a better setting for Independence Hall than rehabilitating the area south of the Square with hotels, apartment houses, and residences. This reconstruction should be not an imitation of the eighteenth century but an effort to give what is left of the early Philadelphia a setting that would in twentieth-century fashion fulfill William Penn's conception of his city as a "greene countrie towne." Generally, the first step in establishing a mod-

ern residential neighborhood is to eliminate half the streets
and create a system of superblocks, turning the space so
saved into gardens, green promenades, and playgrounds.

Luckily, some of the blocks in this area are larger than
the usual Philadelphia block, and these could be treated as
if they were superblocks, linking together existing gardens
with greensward, turning grimy alleys into grasslined pedestrian malls, extending the open spaces provided by old burial
grounds with tree-lined walks, planning houses and apartment
buildings in an open pattern instead of lining them up along
the old street fronts, though retaining the established building lines where certain ancient houses are to be preserved.
Continuity of open spaces is perhaps even more important
for urban beauty than mere quantity. Thus, without breaking
up the present street pattern, a new kind of park would be
possible—an idea the National Park Service apparently already has in mind for at least one of these blocks. I am glad
to report that, thanks to the far-sighted City Planning Commission, buoyed up by the success of Penn Center (the hotel, office-building, and bus-terminal scheme that has lately
risen on the site of the Pennsylvania Railroad's old Broad
Street Station), a somewhat similar treatment of the area
south of Independence Square is now being considered.

The municipality, happily, has the power to provide guiding lines for the treatment of both open spaces and buildings
by real-estate operators and builders, who will thus be able to
do a better job, since desirable minimum standards of performance will be required of everyone. Both hotels and apartments are, by the way, sorely needed in Philadelphia, where
a sudden clotting of conventions leaves the city without a vacant room for the casual visitor. Introducing an urban renewal
project in this area for such a purpose would prevent unsuit-
able industrial and commercial development from coming too
close to the historic monuments, and it would also encourage
an influx of restaurants, amusements, and shopping facilities
for the visitor to historic Philadelphia who might want to
linger a little. Nothing tempts such dawdling, as the ancient
cities of Europe well know, so much as a mixture of history
and beauty. Philadelphia, which boasts history galore, has
only to add the missing element—beauty—to become a center for tourists that will rival New York, Boston, Washington,
and San Francisco.

But the beauty must not be that of Williamsburg, a dead

beauty preserved in embalming fluid. It must be a living beauty that strengthens its links with the past through successive acts of creation and that respects the needs and purposes of our own day without attempting to deform them in the mold of an earlier period. The differences between historic Philadelphia and contemporary Philadelphia should be respected and even emphasized, not suppressed. To invoke the admirable example of Venice: the vitality of the Piazza San Marco as a pictorial composition derives from the historic and esthetic differences between the Byzantine cathedral, the Gothic Doges' Palace, and the Renaissance library across the way from it, to say nothing of the great skyscraper of a campanile that towers above them. Each of these structures represents a different period and a different phase of culture: the total result required almost a thousand years. So in Philadelphia. Even an occasional high building on the edge of the historic area will do less esthetic damage—provided clamorous sky signs are forbidden—than hedging it with rows of spurious Georgian business buildings.

The hardest problem in the rehabilitation of historic Philadelphia is the treatment of what is now, unfortunately, a commercial and industrial area on both sides of Independence Mall, which runs north from Independence Hall toward Franklin Square. The removal of the clutter of similar buildings that remain on the site of the Mall will only expose an unkempt sky line, dominated, to the east, by the Philadelphia Bourse and an equally high building, as well as, behind them, by a brand-new office building, in green and lavender-gray glass, which has arisen apparently in an effort to take swift advantage of the civic improvements that are afoot. There are plenty of historic buildings in this area: a ghost building, Franklin's house, demolished in 1812, may be restored, if the plans can be discovered—not to mention little museums, like the Betsy Ross House, and institutions, like the famous Christ Church and the Friends' Meetinghouse, on Arch Street. There is no single solution for this vast area to the east; the best that one can hope for is the gradual removal in planned stages of the machine shops and miscellaneous industrial buildings.

But the blocks that line Independence Mall, on the other hand, call for bold planning and constructive action. The open space created by the Mall will offer only a modicum of its potential delight as long as the sordid buildings that now range alongside it remain. This, it seems to me, is the perfect site for a new kind of urban unit, whose needs should long ago have been considered in modern city design; namely, a "federal city." If you look under the heading "United States" in any big city telephone book, you will find a multitude of federal agencies scattered over the city. In Philadelphia, some of them occupy whole office buildings; others have taken over apartment houses badly needed by the civilian population, which is what the Navy did in elegant Rittenhouse Square. The grouping of a large number of these agencies in buildings designed for them is long overdue, and what better place could be found for concentrating the complex governmental functions of the modern state than the flanks of Independence Mall? Buildings ten or twelve stories high—neutral in color and window treatment, like those now rising in Penn Center, but, one hopes, measurably superior in design—would screen the Mall and Independence Square from the architectural disorder of the rest of the city, and at this height they would be in scale with the Mall, as neither higher nor lower structures would be. The city, or the Commonwealth of Pennsylvania, or both, might join in this project, and the building up of this governmental enclave or *"cité"* could be done in stages.

To round the historic project out, the part farthest from Independence Hall might be fittingly dedicated to new municipal or state structures. Such planning is neither purely functional nor purely formal; rather, it recognizes in the complicated functions of modern business and administration a special incentive to create a new sort of formal order, as appropriate to the requirements of our own day as the Independence Hall group was to those of the eighteenth century. It would be an extravagant muffing of opportunities to introduce into this part of the city all the new open space created by the Mall without following through by laying down a plan for a new form of modern city. This is a large order. But nothing less than that—a whole series of renovated urban neighborhoods, not a superficial, spotty linear approach—can preserve Philadelphia's historic heritage.

Federal legislation now helps a municipality gather together and replan large parcels of land in blighted areas, and thus our cities have an instrument to effect unified reconstruction. The one thing that is lacking is sufficient imagination to use this opportunity; so far, imagination has confined itself to suburbia: its grandiose highway systems and its vast shopping centers. Historic Philadelphia now has the unique privilege of being able to do justice to its venerable past and to open up a new future in the very heart of its ancient settlement. Open minds, ready to face the future as boldly as William Penn did when he planned his city, are the main requisite. In the lively, confident atmosphere of present-day Philadelphia, such minds are not lacking, even in the business community, so perhaps history will yet be made there as well as remembered.

*1957*

# TWENTY

# The Skyway's the Limit

The destruction of New York, which I have reported upon at intervals, has recently been arrested in one tiny spot and speeded up on a large scale in another. If the intelligence that operated to bring about the small victory of preventing the complete annihilation of Washington Square had been brought into play against the scheme for the Narrows Bridge, from Brooklyn to Staten Island, that plan might have sunk into the Bay itself, and the Bridge with it. The best contributions to metropolitan architecture today have the exquisite appropriateness of a fine meal bestowed upon a prisoner who is to be executed next morning. As with so many other irrational phenomena of our day, like the building of bigger and better nuclear bombs or of wilder and more whimsical counterfeits of motorcars, people have come to regard the pathological as normal, and the more senseless a proposal is in terms of vital human needs, the more likely they are to give hundreds of millions of dollars for its execution.

The battle of Washington Square has for the moment passed into history, though I fear that it will have to be fought over again more than once, even after Mr. Robert Moses disappears from the scene. At that, this battle was a belated one, for it was back in the eighties, when the east and west sides of the Square were being wrecked to make way for bulky apartment houses and for the tall office buildings that have since become Washington Square College of New York University, that the engagement should have been fought. For a long time, Washington Square has not been entirely of one period or mode; the early buildings of the University represented the fashionable Gothic of the fifties, which was quite at variance with the Colonial air of the old brick dwellings on the Square. These new buildings, nevertheless, at least respected the human scale.

Even as late as the eighties, the taste for the architecture of the young Republic was not highly developed, and the esthetic value of open squares had not yet been accented by the rise of population densities in middle-class urban quarters. I have not looked into contemporary accounts to see whether there was any opposition to the new buildings, but I suspect that fewer people were sad over the demise of the modest original ones, erected on the Square in the forties, than were happy over their successors—fine apartment houses with elevators, in the best Parisian mode. For back in the eighties, indeed, up to half a century ago, whole thoroughfares like King Street, in the old Ninth Ward, were lined with houses even handsomer than those on Washington Square. Yet many of those Ninth Ward houses were destroyed by the cutting through of the Seventh Avenue extension, which—like so many similar cuttings and widenings—left ugly strips of unhealed scar tissue on either side.

As late as 1920, when people had begun to appreciate the surviving architectural and civic qualities of Washington Square, there was still a chance of preserving the north side of it intact by zoning it for single residences or by declaring it a public monument. Instead, the buildings on the west side of this entrance to Fifth Avenue were converted, with due legal permission, into an apartment house, and that paved the way for the even bigger buildings that have replaced *it* and that have destroyed the north side of the Square as a framed entrance to Fifth Avenue. As a historic monument, Washington Square has gone the way of Rittenhouse Square, in Philadelphia, and the pious effort of New York University to restore the historic flavor by masking its Law School under a Georgian skin is not merely futile but distracting; the best that one can hope for the Square's architectural framework now is the addition of good modern buildings, since its historic scale and grace have been destroyed.

But the case for Washington Square as a public open space and as both a campus for Washington Square College and a neighborhood recreation area is quite another matter. In these respects, too, the defacement and degradation of the Square have gone on for a long time. It was, it is true, a convenient terminus for the Fifth Avenue bus line, but Cooper Square offered an equally serviceable turnaround, and at the time the franchise was given to the bus company, adequate facilities could have been provided there, to prevent any encroaching on Washington Square. Recently, the total ruin of the Square was threatened by an ingenious proposal of Mr. Moses to push a four-lane highway through it in order to open up a clear passage to the lower part of the city and, not too incidentally, to give the people living in the group of tall, expensive apartments just south of the Square—the group called Washington Square Village—a Fifth Avenue address, which Mr. Moses, in one of his Pooh-Bah roles, had promised the owners. This proposal not only threatened Fifth Avenue, clogged by its already congealing traffic, with an additional load coming up from Canal Street, but cut the Square into two unrelated halves, which endangered pedestrians and children and reduced, by many hundred square feet, an inadequate—and therefore doubly precious—recreation space. This proposal to add more asphalt and wheeled traffic to what remained of the Square was nothing less than civic vandalism.

At first, no one but the immediate residents of Greenwich Village seemed against this proposal, for in our age nearly everybody believes in serving automobile traffic and almost nobody has an interest in serving any other urban need. Our cities are being replanned for passing cars, not for permanent residents, and the more cars that can be induced to clutter the arteries of a city and make residence less desirable, the more "progressive" the planning is deemed. The opposition to Mr. Moses' plan by local groups began timidly; in the initial flurry of resistance they were ready to settle for a narrower roadway through the Square, such as the one proposed by the Borough President.

Fortunately, the very stubbornness of Mr. Moses and his inaccessibility to even small modifications gave time to reinforce the opposition with a sounder scheme. Backed by the doughty neighborhood newspapers, one of the groups suggested that all traffic be barred from the Square. Instead of settling for a minimum further damage to the Square, the whole neighborhood rallied around this much bolder program, and what seemed at first like a losing fight became a substantial victory: the Square has now been closed to traffic. This should lead to the complete rehabilitation of its interior, which desperately needs the services of an imaginative landscape architect to create a series of tree-shaded outdoor "rooms" for students, nursemaids, chess players, and neighboring families, who do so much to give the Square its life and color.

All this is a heartening sign of the way in which a stir of intelligence and feeling not only can rally far more support than one would expect (the Fifth Avenue Hotel even gave the insurgent group a room to meet in) but can bring to a halt the seemingly irresistible force of a group of experts and "authorities."

But this setback to ill-conceived planning does not mean that more menacing errors will not be made elsewhere. In fact, a far more extensive and destructive proposal has just been voted into existence—the three-hundred-and-twenty-million-dollar bridge across the Narrows.

The basic principle of this bridge derives not from the city planners but from highway engineers, though, to their shame, many city planners have accepted it as if it were unchallengeable. In the utopia that highway engineers have been busily bulldozing into existence, no precinct of the city and no part of the surrounding countryside are to remain inaccessible to automobile traffic on a large scale. This means that people who live in cities are not to be permitted the refreshing contrast of escaping to an island, to a mountaintop, or even to a swath of open country whose isolation from urban traffic makes it possible to still engage in farming or fruit raising. By means of many-laned highways, every acre everywhere is to be made accessible for the real-estate speculator and the subdivider, and in another generation a drab, standardized, low-grade settlement, lacking both the advantages of the country and those of the city, will stretch along the Eastern seaboard from Maine to Florida.

Because this principle has been treated as sacred, our growing cities have already lost most of the recreational advantages that the surrounding countryside once afforded them, and one suburb after another has filled in the natural greenbelt that—when the railroad stations were a few miles apart and commuters lived within walking distance of them— gave it a pleasantly rural flavor. This has happened all over the country. Some of the most beautiful and thriving regions known to man—the San Bernardino Valley, the Santa Clara Valley, and Marin County, in California—have gone the same way as the nearer reaches of Long Island. Now, with the Narrows Bridge and the belt highways that will serve it, those parts of Long Island that are still rural are to be opened up to a vast volume of through traffic seeking to by-pass New York on the way to and from New England, and the irresponsible operations of the building speculators will absorb land that should, for the benefit of the citizens of New York, be kept intact permanently as a farming and rural recreation area. Since the preservation of the rural matrix requires special legislation, the securing of that legislation is the indispensable preliminary to any kind of large-scale planning or highway building.

Unfortunately, there is a huge vested interest in raising hell with nature, and there is very little money—in fact none at all —in letting well enough alone. So it is easy to see which side loses out in a country dominated by the meretricious conception of an ever-expanding economy. Environmental massacre and mal-construction can be organized for profit. And while engineering genius has pretty well taken care of the problem of moving traffic quickly between cities, scarcely any intelligence at all has been applied to the planning of cities and their environment so that this traffic, where it enters the cities, will not make them unattractive for permanent residence. Planners who believe that they are being most daring and progressive have done little better than to stereotype the designs that Le Corbusier made almost forty years ago, designs that have been copied frequently enough to make anyone who has examined the results think twice before repeating them. One look at the cluster of skyscraper offices that now rise in the "rehabilitated" area of Pittsburgh known as The Point should convince them of their error; a handful of skyscrapers standing in a glittering freight yard of parked cars is a contribution to neither business nor urban beauty.

This oversolicitude for motor traffic, this sheer indifference to the comfort of urban living, shows itself all too plainly in the design for the Narrows Bridge. This must be a high-level crossing, in order to let vessels pass beneath. It is eventually to accommodate six lanes of traffic on each of two levels, so the elevated approaches to the bridge must be twelve lanes wide. To clear an area large enough to accomplish this end, nearly eight thousand people must be displaced in the Bay Ridge area of Brooklyn. This says nothing of the many other people whose lives or properties will be unfavorably affected by the elevated highway through their neighborhood. At the very moment, as I have remarked before, that we have torn down our elevated railways, because of their spoilage of urban space, our highway engineers are using vast sums of public money to restore the same nuisance in an even noisier and more insistent form. But what is Brooklyn to the highway engineer—except a place to go through quickly, at whatever necessary sacrifice of peace and amenity by its inhabitants?

This terrifying project was not voted into existence without severe opposition, properly led by the Borough President of Brooklyn. Three things probably accomplished its success. For one thing, it is part of a larger and even more disastrous program for expanding our federal highways, a project that is working similar havoc in every part of the country—slashing through old neighborhoods, stealing land from public parks, dumping traffic in urban centers that are already overcrowded. As part of the federal program, the approaches to the Narrows Bridge will be the recipient of state and national funds, which will defray no small part of the project's excessive cost—incidentally, roughly equal to the cost of digging the Panama Canal. That bait is a difficult one for the hungry local sharks and minnows to resist. Moreover, the Port Authority, the City of New York, and the State Highway Commission have already linked together a series of parkways and throughways that enable a motorist to go from Coney Island to Buffalo without encountering a traffic light. Once a system like that takes shape, it has an abstract, hypnotic fascination, which leads to the next step of complementing it by a system that will lead the motorist from Washington to Maine with the same smooth facility. That it is not worth while to scramble the living quarters of tens of thousands of people to achieve such a goal does not occur to the real beneficiaries of the system, to whom it means jobs and prestige, contracts and profits. Thus, at a time when our cities can be made livable again only by isolating their residential neighborhoods from through traffic and rebuilding our decaying systems of mass transportation, our public authorities are busily breaking down the structure of neighborhoods and parks and devoting public funds to private transportation and private speculative building at random. As a formula for defacing the natural landscape and ruining what is left of our great cities, nothing could be more effective.

The opponents of the Narrows Bridge made a mistake that the people who saved Washington Square did not. In their fight against the Bridge, many of them urged the building of a Narrows tunnel as an alternative. But once a mass flow of vehicular traffic was established across the Narrows, by whatever means, it would have to be carried through Brooklyn on elevated highways to join the existing traffic system, and little would have been gained by this scheme. The argument against the Narrows Bridge should have been directed against any connecting link that would further clog the highways of Long Island and further increase the mass flow of traffic into two of the last great recreation reserves near New York—Staten Island and Long Island. Traffic for traffic's sake does not make sense except to highway engineers and the Port Authority.

The part that this quasi-public body has played in furthering the disintegration of New York as a going metropolis has not been sufficiently appreciated. The Port Authority was created as an adjunct to our state-bounded governmental units, to promote the welfare of our whole vast port area by treating it as a single unit. Because this activity was regarded as a public benefit, the Authority was granted public powers denied to a private corporation. Such an agency is supposed to have economic vigor and to be solvent, but this does not mean that its obligation to make a profit is superior to its public duties. In the course of time, the Port Authority has turned increasingly into a money-making enterprise, using public-planning activities of the widest order to further ends not easily identifiable with the health, welfare, or prosperity of the New York region. By now the great need of the City of New York—indeed, of the whole area—is the swift rehabilitation of its underequipped and insufficiently used system of rapid mass transportation. Instead of applying its resources to meet this pressing need, the Authority has persistently aggravated the city's difficulties. By concentrating on such profitable enterprises as toll tunnels and toll bridges, the Authority has diverted traffic from our mass-transportation facilities and grossly increased the vehicular congestion in the city. While an express highway can handle only four thousand passengers an hour in private motorcars, against forty thousand on a comparable rapid-transit system, the Authority stubbornly concentrates on inefficient time-wasting and space-eating private transportation. The reason is simple: the Authority can make no profit from public transportation, while the over-use of private facilities, though it may wreck the city, causes the Authority to flourish.

The Port Authority has gone even further, by using its profits to defray the losses on its airports—though despite their present crippled state, the railroads bring ten thousand people into New York for every thousand who enter by air. In short, this is the subsidization of chaos, and the result is already predictable—a sprawling mass of expressways, cloverleaves, bridges, viaducts, airports, garages, operating in an urban wasteland, with the municipality sinking ever deeper under the burden of taxes imposed to bring even the illusion of relief from the inevitable congestion and disorder. The ultimate form of such a topsy-turvy city is an acre of buildings surrounded by a square mile of parking lot. If public transportation ceases, pedestrian traffic will come back again, in the form of even longer walks to parked cars—about which suburbanites who invade the theatre district by automobile already know. The paradoxical result of this concentration on motorcars is a curbing of freedom of movement, a removal of alternate choices of transportation, the steady reduction of the speed of local travel, and the total defeat of the city itself as a place that offers the maximum possibilities for face-to-face meeting, social cooperation, and transactions of every kind.

Obviously the Port Authority is not the only problem child in this drama; the state and federal highway authorities have been equally successful in promoting a single type of transportation exclusively instead of helping to keep alive as many methods of moving as possible, in order to distribute the load and make the mode and the speed suit the occasion. In addition, the habit of tying the welfare of the nation to the maximum production of motorcars has helped, and the popular fascination with new technical facilities valued for their newness rather than their efficiency has robbed many people of ordinary common sense. If the process goes on, we will wake up one morning to discover that our city has become as helpless and useless as a stranded whale, unable either to swim back to the sea or crawl forward on land. That will be the end—and no jet planes or moon rockets will save us.

*1959*

# TWENTY-ONE

# Landscape and Townscape

During the last generation a change has taken place in our conception of open spaces in relation to the urban and regional environment. People in the nineteenth century were conscious, primarily, of the hygienic and sanitary function of open spaces. Even Camillo Sitte, a leader in the esthetic appreciation of cities, called the inner parks of the city "sanitary greens." In order to offset the increasing congestion and disorder of the city, great landscape parks were laid out, more or less in the fashion that the aristocracy had promoted for their private country estates. The recreational value of these landscape parks was indisputable; and in addition they served as barriers against the spread of the city as an unbroken urbanoid mass. But except for the leisured classes, these parks were used chiefly on Sundays and holidays; and no equivalent effort was made to provide more intimate open spaces in each neighborhood, where the young might dig and romp, where adults might relax, from time to time, all through the week, without making a special journey.

Given the high densities for dwellings that have prevailed in big cities, it was natural, no doubt, that there should be an emphasis on the biological necessity for open spaces: this recognized the value of sunlight, fresh air, free movement in promoting health, and the psychological need for the sight and smell of grass, bushes, flowers, trees and open sky. The park was treated, not as an integral part of the urban environment, but as a place of refuge, whose main values derived from the contrast with the noisy, crowded, dusty, urban hive. So impoverished were most cities, except where they inherited aristocratic parks, open residential squares, and playing fields from previous centuries, that open spaces came to be treated as if their value was directly proportional to their area—without too much regard for their accessibility, their frequency of use, or their effect in altering the texture of urban life. Those who felt increasingly deprived of the gardens and parks essential to urban living moved, if they had the means, to a spacious leafy suburb; and in the very act of seeking this all-too-simple solution, they permitted the city itself to become further congested and pushed the open country ever further away from its center.

Today our appreciation of the biological function of open spaces should be even deeper, now that their function in sustaining life is threatened by radioactive pollution and the air itself around every urban center is filled with scores of cancer-producing substances. But in addition, we have learned that open spaces have also a social function to perform that the mere demand for an open refuge too often overlooks.

To understand how important the social role of open spaces is, we must take into account three great changes that have taken place during the last century. First, the change in the mode of human settlement brought about by fast transportation and instantaneous means of communication. As a result, physical congestion is no longer the sole possible way of bringing a large population into intimate contact and cooperation. From this has come another change: a change, wherever sufficient land is available at reasonable prices, in the whole layout of the city: for in the suburbs that have been growing so rapidly around the great centers the buildings exist, ideally, as free-standing structures in a parklike landscape. Too often the trees and gardens vanish under further pressure of population, yet the sprawling, open, individualistic structure, almost anti-social in its dispersal and its random pattern, remains. The third great change is the general reduction of working hours, along with an increasing shift of work itself from industrial occupations to services and professional vocations. Instead of being faced with a small leisured class, we have now to provide recreational facilities for a whole leisured population. And if this emancipation from incessant toil is not to become a curse, we must create a whole series of alternatives to the sedatives and anesthetics now being offered—especially the anesthesia of locomotion at an ever higher rate of speed and an even lower return in esthetic pleasure and meaningful purpose. In meeting this challenge, we may well re-examine the experience of the historic aristocracies who, when not engaged in aimless violence and destruction, devoted so much of their energies to the audacious transformation of the whole landscape. Once we accept the challenge of creating an environment so rich in human resources that no one would willingly leave it even temporarily on an astronautic vacation, we shall alter the whole pattern of human settlement. Ebenezer Howard's dream of garden cities will widen into the prospect of a garden civilization.

Now very little of the planning that has been projected or achieved during the last generation has taken this new situation into account. Indeed, the chief work that has been done in urban extension and in highway building has been under a curious compulsion to serve the machine rather than to respond to human needs. Unless fresh ideas are introduced, the continued growth of loose suburban areas will undermine our historic cities and deface the natural landscape, creating a large mass of undifferentiated, low-grade urban tissue, which, in order to perform even the minimal functions of the city, will impose a maximum amount of private locomotion, and, incidentally, push the countryside even further away from even the suburban areas.

This kind of openness and low density is another name for social and civic disintegration, such as we find in cities like Los Angeles. Meanwhile, the great landscape parks in the heart of our old cities too often become neglected, though a long motor ride often leads to a far less attractive destination. While this is happening, the more distant recreation areas by woods, lake, or sea are left to stagger under a weekend congestion that robs that facility of its recreative value, for the motorcar brings to such distant areas the combined population, not just of a single city, but of a whole region.

As a result of these changes, in particular our overattention to movement and our underattention to settlement, the very words park and field have taken on new meanings. "Park" now usually means a desert of asphalt, designed as a temporary storage space for motorcars; while "field" means another kind of artificial desert, a barren area planted in great concrete strips, vibrating with noise, dedicated to the arrival and departure of planes. From park and field unroll wide ribbons of concrete that seek to increase the speed of travel between distant points at whatever sacrifice of esthetic pleasures or social opportunities. And if our present system of development goes on, without a profound change in our present planning concepts and values, the final result will be a universal wasteland, unfit for human habitation, no better than the surface of the moon. No wonder people play with projects for exploring outer space: we have been turning the landscape around our great cities into mere launching platforms, and our long daily journeys in the cramped interiors of motorcars are preparatory trips for the even more cramped and comatose journeys by rocket.

Perhaps the first step toward regaining possession of our souls will be to repossess and replan the whole landscape. To turn away from the processes of life, growth, reproduction, to prefer the disintegrated, the accidental, the random to organic form and order is to commit collective suicide; and by the same token, to create a counter-movement to the irrationalities and threatened exterminations of our day, we must draw close once more to the healing order of nature, modified by human design.

The time has come then to conceive alternatives for the classic and romantic clichés of the past, and for the even more sterile clichés of the mechanical "space-eaters," who would destroy all the esthetic resources of the landscape in their effort to enable tens of thousands of people to concentrate at a distant point at the same time; and who, when their weekend tourists finally reach such a point, can only reproduce the congested facilities and the banal amusements of the community they have made such a desperate effort to escape. It is not by a mere quantitative increase in the present park facilities, but by a comprehensive change in the whole pattern of life that we shall realize to the full the social function of open spaces.

And first, one must think of open recreation spaces, outside the existing urban areas, as no longer adequately represented by a few landscape parks or wild reservations however large: nothing less than a whole region, the larger part of which is in a state of natural growth and useful cultivation, will suffice to meet the needs of our new-style recreation, open to the larger part of the population. The most important public task, around every growing urban center, and far beyond, is to reserve permanent open areas, capable of being maintained for agriculture, horticulture, and related rural industries. These areas must be established in such a fashion as to prevent the coalescence of one urban unit with another. Within its metropolitan area, this has been the notable accomplishment of Stockholm, and in no small degree of the Netherlands as regional entity. Witness the call of the bulb fields at flowering time in spring.

Though the provision of urban greenbelts in part meets our new requirements, we must now think not of greenbelts alone but of a permanent green matrix, dedicated to rural uses whether it comes under public control or remains in private hands. For weekend recreation, the whole regional landscape has become, in fact, the landscape park. That area is far too large to be acquired for park purposes alone; for its upkeep, if solely under state or municipal control, would overburden the largest budget. But by firm legal regulation, the land may be zoned permanently for rural uses in a fashion that will maintain its recreational value, provided both highway system and recreational facilities are planned so as to disperse the transient population of visitors.

The new task for the landscape architect is to articulate the whole landscape so that every part of it may serve for recreation. Besides persuading public authorities to stabilize agricultural land uses by zoning and urban tax abatement so that it will not, without public authorization, be used for residential or industrial building, the task of the landscape architect will be to design footpaths, picnicking grounds, pedestrian pleasances along riverfronts, beaches, and woodland groves in such a fashion as to give public access to every part of the rural scene, without undue disturbance to the daily economic round. One must think of continuous strips of public land weaving through the whole landscape and making it usually accessible to both nearby residents and to holiday visitors. There is the beginning of this new process of using the whole landscape as a recreational facility in the layout of bicycle paths in the Netherlands; and there remains in certain parts of England, as a residue from an older era, a system of public footpaths over hill and dale, through field and wood, that needs only to be broadened into somewhat wider strips, no more than twenty or sometimes fifty feet, to provide amply for public needs without encroaching too heavily on agricultural uses.

The same kind of planning would even apply to the motor road, once the object was to achieve, not the maximum amount of speed, but the maximum amount of relaxation and beauty in slow drives designed to open up views, and persuade the motorist, not to seek a more distant point at high speed, but to linger where shade and rich foliage and spicy air are his without further effort. Even in the design of faster highways, those recreational values that have nothing to do with speed can be brought into play by the resourceful landscape architect. Thus the design of the Taconic Parkway in New York State, following the ridgeway in great curves, heavily planted with flowering bushes, opening wide views from time to time over the valley below, offers special rewards to the sensitive motorist.

While our facilities for mass transportation are responsible for opening up the whole region as a recreational area and public park, the landscape architect must boldly challenge the transportation authorities and highway engineers who have made a fetish of speed and who, in order to justify the extravagant costs of their enterprise, seek to attract the heaviest load of traffic. Speed is the vulgar objective of a life devoid of any more significant kind of esthetic interest. But if our rational object is to disperse traffic and avoid congestion, we must round out our highway system, not by building more speedways, but by laying out or rehabilitating minor roads designed for just the opposite purpose; namely, to tempt the motorist to slow down, to stretch his legs and relax, to spend more time in enjoying the natural beauties near at hand, and less time in trying to reach some more distant point where thousands of other motorcars will converge.

Our ability to turn the whole regional landscape into a collective park, with its recreation facilities dispersed and easy to reach, will be determined by the success of public authorities in making misused or untidy parts of the landscape more attractive, and by setting aside as public recreation grounds a sufficient number of small areas to prevent any congestion or overuse in any particular spot. The government might well offer subsidies to individual farmers and landowners for participating in larger public landscaping schemes, as well as by paying outright for widened rights of way and proiding the gates and stiles and fences needed to keep the urban visitor within bounds. Something of the same system that the Italians have worked out to police their roads, with individual stations at intervals, occupied by a permanent roadworker and his family, might well be applied to ensure the proper care of the landscape.

In this task of applying landscape design to the whole region, in order to make it available to every kind of recreation, we must find a place for both the extrovert and the introvert; for those whose enjoyments are often enhanced by a public setting and the presence of other people, and those whose deepest impulses lead to withdrawal and solitary exploration and quiet contemplation. Today, in most countries, we tend to overplay the role of mass movements and mass satisfactions and mass attendance at spectatorial sports. We forget the need to offset the pervasive compulsions of the crowd by providing plenty of space for solitary withdrawal. But man, as Emerson observed, needs both society and solitude; and no small part of the social function of open spaces is *to remain open*, not crowded with people seeking mass recreation.

Now in this regional provision for open spaces I can detect no difference whatever between the needs of the most congested metropolis and those of the country town or the open suburb. For mass transportation, by rail, by public bus, and by motorcar, has extended the field of recreation far beyond the local community and has, at least potentially, widened the area of choice. The surest mark of bad planning is that, in the very effort to meet one kind of mass demand, the planner is tempted to set up a single standard of success, that of quantitative use, and to overlook the need for variety and choice. If this goes on, our mass recreation areas will become as standardized, as monotonous, as lacking in psychological stimulus of any kind, as the urban quarters people want relief from. Good planning, on the other hand, as it widens the field of recreation, in order to meet the demands of a bigger population commanding greater leisure, must be more concerned to achieve a fuller differentiation of both human activities and landscape forms, bringing out the unique resources of each spot—here a winding river, there a striking view, or in another place, an historic village with a good inn, whose character must be preserved by swinging motor roads and carparks widely around the village, instead of letting them pile up in its center. The autumn visits to the vineyards that used to go on in the Napa Valley of California, like the visits to the blossoming apricot orchards once possible in the Santa Clara Valley, may have more recreational value than a visit to an idle landscape sacred to park custodians. In allowing such land to be swallowed up by speculative builders our "great metropolises" are depleting their most precious recreational resources.

So much for the larger conception of open spaces, as conceived on a new regional pattern, with a permanent green matrix of open areas, preserved for both local residents and visitors. If we take the necessary political measures to establish this green matrix, a large part of the pressure to escape from the congested city to a seemingly more rural suburb will be relieved, for the rural values that the suburb sought to achieve by strictly private means—and actually could achieve only for a prosperous fraction of the population— will become an integral feature of every urban community.

Two complementary movements are now necessary and possible: one is that of tightening the loose and scattered pattern of the suburb, turning it from a purely residential dormitory into a balanced community, approaching a true garden city in its variety and partial self-sufficiency, with a more varied population and with sufficient local industry and business to support it; and the other is that of loosening the congestion of the metropolis, emptying out part of its population, introducing parks, playgrounds, green promenades, private gardens, into quarters that we have permitted to become indecently congested, void of beauty, and often positively inimical to life. Here, too, we must think of a new form of the city, which will have the biological advantages of the suburb, the social advantages of the city, and new esthetic delights that will do justice to both modes.

Now the great function of the city is to give a collective form to what Martin Buber has well called the I-and-Thou relation: to permit—indeed, to encourage—the greatest possible number of meetings, encounters, challenges, between varied persons and groups, providing as it were a stage upon which the drama of social life may be enacted, with the actors taking their turn, too, as spectators. The social function of open spaces in the city is to bring people together;

and as Raymond Unwin demonstrated at Hampstead Garden Suburb—and Henry Wright and Clarence Stein even more decisively at Radburn—when both private and public spaces *are* designed together, this mingling and meeting may take place, under the pleasantest possible conditions, in the neighborhood. Unfortunately, the very congestion of the city produced a reaction on the part of sensitive people that made them overemphasize a purely quantitative ideal of open spaces; and under the influence of suburban practices, which made privacy and spatial aloofness a mark of upper-class status, many of our new communities in both America and Europe are far too loose and sprawling to serve their social purposes. Socially speaking, too much open space may prove a burden rather than a blessing. It is the quality of the open space—its charm and its accessibility—that counts for more than gross quantity.

The problem of the archetypal suburb today is to trade some of its excessive biological space (gardens) for social space (meeting places): that of the congested city is just the opposite, it must introduce into its overbuilt quarters sunlight, fresh air, private gardens, public squares, and pedestrian malls, which will both fulfill the social functions of the city and make it as favorable a place as was the older suburb for establishing a permanent home and bringing up children. The first step in making our older cities habitable is to reduce their residential densities, replacing decayed areas now occupied at a density of two hundred to five hundred persons per acre with housing that will permit parks and gardens as an integral part of the design, at densities not higher than a hundred, or at most, in quarters with a large proportion of childless people, of one hundred and twenty-five to one hundred and fifty persons per acre. Let us not be deceived by the appearance of the spatial openness that can be achieved by crowding many families into fifteen-story apartment houses. Abstract visual open space is not the equivalent of functional open space that may be used as playgrounds and private gardens. Here again a variety of uses—and therefore a variety of esthetic forms—is the mark of skillful planning and expressive design. Row after row of great slabs or towers, even though set apart far enough to avoid casting a shadow on each other, create a poor environment for any kind of recreation, for they rob the area of sunlight and destroy the intimate and familiar human scale, so vital to the young child, and so pleasant, for that matter, to the adult.

In the restoration or fresh creation of urban open spaces there is room for much fresh experiment and bold design, which will depart both from traditional models and those that have become the fashionable clichés of contemporary form. And in this field each city should suggest a different answer: what is appropriate for Amsterdam with its great water resources would not be equally possible in Madrid. We do not merely need grand plans, conceived freshly, for entirely new neighborhoods where we have cleared away acres of slum. We also need piecemeal solutions that can be applied on a small scale, seizing each small opportunity that will go toward the fulfillment over the years of a much larger design.

When I ask myself what immediate improvement would make my own city, New York, more attractive to live in again, I find two answers: rows of shade trees on every street, and a little park, even a quarter of an acre, in each block, preferably near the middle. When I think of another familiar city, Philadelphia, I would turn the back alleys into green pedestrian malls, threading through the city, now widening into pools of open space surrounded by restaurants, cafés, or shops, all insulated from motor traffic. And what applies to individual blocks applies to neighborhoods. To have any value for recreation they, too, must be insulated from the traffic avenues and motorways: the parts of the neighborhood should be joined together by green ribbons, pedestrian malls, and pleasances, such as that admirable park Olmsted designed for the Back Bay Fens of Boston, taking advantage of a little river and a swamp to create a continuous band of green, uniting more than one neighborhood.

The one great requirement for open spaces in urban centers is to insulate them from the fumes, the noise, and the distracting movement of motor traffic. The neighborhood, not the individual building block, is now the unit of urban design, and all fresh schemes for both open spaces and for traffic, to be worthy of approval, must separate the pedestrian completely from the motorcar. When this can be done from the beginning as was first decisively achieved at Radburn, New Jersey, the motor roads that give access to buildings may be reduced in area and partly eliminated; while the space that is so saved within the superblock and the neighborhood may be dedicated to a public park. When these measures are taken, a much more economic and socially valuable use of the land can be made, without the wastage in excessive roads and setbacks and verges one finds in the British New Towns—admirable though they often are in their adequate, indeed sometimes overgenerous, provision for greenbelts and private gardens.

What I have been saying about the social function of open spaces can now be briefly summed up. For weekend recreation we must treat the whole region as a potential park area and make it attractive at so many points that the hideous congestion of the slowly unwinding procession of weekend traffic will be minimized, or disappear entirely in a more lacy network of regional distribution. As for daily use, the same requirements for open space now apply to both the most congested cities and the most sprawling suburbs: for the first must be loosened up for the sake of health and pleasure, while the second must become more concentrated and many-sided, for the sake of a balanced social life. In the cities of the future, ribbons of green must run through every quarter, forming a continuous web of garden and mall, widening at the edge of the city into protective greenbelts, so that landscape and garden will become an integral part of urban no less than rural life, both for weekday and holiday uses.

*1960*

# TWENTY-TWO

# The Highway and the City

When the American people, through their Congress, voted a little while ago (1957) for a twenty-six-billion-dollar highway program, the most charitable thing to assume about this action is that they hadn't the faintest notion of what they were doing. Within the next fifteen years they will doubtless find out; but by that time it will be too late to correct all the damage to our cities and our countryside, not least to the efficient organization of industry and transportation, that this ill-conceived and preposterously unbalanced program will have wrought.

Yet if someone had foretold these consequences before this vast sum of money was pushed through Congress, under the specious, indeed flagrantly dishonest, guise of a national defense measure, it is doubtful whether our countrymen would have listened long enough to understand; or would even have been able to change their minds if they did understand. For the current American way of life is founded not just on motor transportation but on the religion of the motorcar, and the sacrifices that people are prepared to make for this religion stand outside the realm of rational criticism. Perhaps the only thing that could bring Americans to their senses would be a clear demonstration of the fact that their highway program will, eventually, wipe out the very area of freedom that the private motorcar promised to retain for them.

As long as motorcars were few in number, he who had one was a king: he could go where he pleased and halt where he pleased; and this machine itself appeared as a compensatory device for enlarging an ego which had been shrunken by our very success in mechanization. That sense of freedom and power remains a fact today only in low-density areas, in the open country; the popularity of this method of escape has ruined the promise it once held forth. In using the car to flee from the metropolis the motorist finds that he has merely transferred congestion to the highway and thereby doubled it. When he reaches his destination, in a distant suburb, he finds that the countryside he sought has disappeared: beyond him, thanks to the motorway, lies only another suburb, just as dull as his own. To have a minimum amount of communication and sociability in this spread-out life, his wife becomes a taxi-driver by daily occupation, and the sum of money it costs to keep this whole system running leaves him with shamefully overtaxed schools, inadequate police, poorly staffed hospitals, overcrowded recreation areas, ill-supported libraries.

In short, the American has sacrificed his life as a whole to the motorcar, like someone who, demented with passion, wrecks his home in order to lavish his income on a capricious mistress who promises delights he can only occasionally enjoy.

For most Americans, progress means accepting what is new because it is new, and discarding what is old because it is old. This may be good for a rapid turnover in business, but it is bad for continuity and stability in life. Progress, in an organic sense, should be cumulative, and though a certain amount of rubbish-clearing is always necessary, we lose part of the gain offered by a new invention if we automatically discard all the still valuable inventions that preceded it.

In transportation, unfortunately, the old-fashioned linear notion of progress prevails. Now that motorcars are becoming universal, many people take for granted that pedestrian movement will disappear and that the railroad system will in time be abandoned; in fact, many of the proponents of highway building talk as if that day were already here, or if not, they have every intention of making it dawn quickly. The result is that we have actually crippled the motorcar, by placing on this single means of transportation the burden for every kind of travel. Neither our cars nor our highways can take such a load. This overconcentration, moreover, is rapidly destroying our cities, without leaving anything half as good in their place.

What's transportation for? This is a question that highway engineers apparently never ask themselves: probably because they take for granted the belief that transportation exists for the purpose of providing suitable outlets for the motorcar industry. To increase the number of cars, to enable motorists to go longer distances, to more places, at higher speeds, has become an end in itself. Does this overemployment of the motorcar not consume ever larger quantities of gas, oil, concrete, rubber, and steel, and so provide the very groundwork for an expanding economy? Certainly, but none of these make up the essential purpose of transportation. The purpose of transportation is to bring people or goods to places where they are needed, and to concentrate the greatest variety of goods and people within a limited area, in order to widen the possibility of choice without making it necessary to travel. A good transportation system minimizes unnecessary transportation; and in any event, it offers a change of speed and mode to fit a diversity of human purposes.

Diffusion and concentration are the two poles of transportation: the first demands a closely articulated network of roads—ranging from a footpath to a six-lane expressway and a transcontinental railroad system. The second demands a city. Our major highway systems are conceived, in the interests of speed, as linear organizations, that is to say as arteries. That conception would be a sound one, provided the major arteries were not overdeveloped to the exclusion of all the minor elements of transportation. Highway planners have yet to realize that these arteries must not be thrust into the delicate tissue of our cities; the blood they circulate must rather enter through an elaborate network of minor blood vessels and capillaries. As early as 1929 Benton MacKaye worked out the rationale of sound highway development, in his conception of the Townless Highway; and this had as its corollary the Highwayless Town. In the quarter century since, all the elements of MacKaye's conception have been carried out, except the last—certainly not the least.

In many ways, our highways are not merely masterpieces of engineering, but consummate works of art: a few of them, like the Taconic State Parkway in New York, stand on a par with our highest creations in other fields. Not every highway, it is true, runs through country that offers such superb opportunities to an imaginative highway builder as this does; but then not every engineer rises to his opportunities as the planners of this highway did, routing the well-separated roads along the ridgeways, following the contours, and thus, by this single stratagem, both avoiding towns and villages and opening up great views across country, enhanced by a lavish planting of flowering bushes along the borders. If this standard of comeliness and beauty were kept generally in view, highway engineers would not so often lapse into the brutal assaults against the landscape and against urban order that they actually give way to when they aim solely at speed and volume of traffic, and bulldoze and blast their way across country to shorten their route by a few miles without making the total journey any less depressing.

Perhaps our age will be known to the future historian as the age of the bulldozer and the exterminator; and in many parts of the country the building of a highway has about the same result upon vegetation and human structures as the passage of a tornado or the blast of an atom bomb. Nowhere is this bulldozing habit of mind so disastrous as in the approach to the city. Since the engineer regards his own work as more important than the other human functions it serves, he does not hesitate to lay waste to woods, streams, parks, and human neighborhoods in order to carry his roads straight to their supposed destination.

The fatal mistake we have been making is to sacrifice every other form of transportation to the private motorcar—and to offer, as the only long-distance alternative, the airplane. But the fact is that each type of transportation has its special use; and a good transportation policy must seek to improve each type and make the most of it. This cannot be achieved by aiming at high speed or continuous flow alone. If you wish casual opportunities for meeting your neighbors, and for profiting by chance contacts with acquaintances and colleagues, a stroll at two miles an hour in a concentrated area, free from needless vehicles, will alone meet your need. But if you wish to rush a surgeon to a patient a thousand miles away, the fastest motorway is too slow. And again, if you wish to be sure to keep a lecture engagement in winter, railroad transportation offers surer speed and better insurance against being held up than the airplane. There is no one ideal mode or speed: human purpose should govern the choice of the means of transportation. That is why we need a better transportation *system,* not just more highways. The projectors of our national highway program plainly had little interest in transportation. In their fanatical zeal to expand our highways, the very allocation of funds indicates that they are ready to liquidate all other forms of land and water transportation. The result is a crudely over-simplified and inefficient method of mono-transportation: a regression from the complex many-sided transportation system we once boasted.

In order to overcome the fatal stagnation of traffic in and around our cities, our highway engineers have come up with a remedy that actually expands the evil it is meant to overcome. They create new expressways to serve cities that are already overcrowded within, thus tempting people who had been using public transportation to reach the urban centers to use these new private facilities. Almost before the first day's tolls on these expressways have been counted, the new roads themselves are overcrowded. So a clamor arises to create other similar arteries and to provide more parking garages in the center of our metropolises; and the generous provision of these facilities expands the cycle of congestion, without any promise of relief until that terminal point when all the business and industry that originally gave rise to the congestion move out of the city, to escape strangulation, leaving a waste of expressways and garages behind them. This is pyramid building with a vengeance: a tomb of concrete roads and ramps covering the dead corpse of a city.

But before our cities reach this terminal point, they will suffer, as they now do, from a continued erosion of their social facilities: an erosion that might have been avoided if engineers had understood MacKaye's point that a motorway, properly planned, is another form of railroad for private use. Unfortunately, highway engineers, if one is to judge by their usual performance, lack both historic insight and social memory: accordingly, they have been repeating, with the audacity of confident ignorance, all the mistakes in urban planning committed by their predecessors who designed our railroads. The wide swaths of land devoted to cloverleaves, and even more complicated multi-level interchanges, to expressways, parking lots, and parking garages, in the very heart of the city, butcher up precious urban space in exactly the same way that freight yards and marshalling yards did when the railroads dumped their passengers and freight inside the city. These new arteries choke off the natural routes of circulation and limit the use of abutting properties, while at the points where they disgorge their traffic they create inevitable clots of congestion, which effectively cancel out such speed as they achieve in approaching these bottlenecks.

Today the highway engineers have no excuse for invading the city with their regional and transcontinental trunk systems: the change from the major artery to the local artery can now be achieved without breaking the bulk of goods or replacing the vehicle: that is precisely the advantage of the motorcar. Arterial roads, ideally speaking, should engirdle the metropolitan area and define where its greenbelt begins; and since American cities are still too impoverished and too improvident to acquire greenbelts, they should be planned to go through the zone where relatively high-density building gives way to low-density building. On this perimeter, through traffic will bypass the city, while cars that are headed for the center will drop off at the point closest to their destination.

Since I don't know a city whose highways have been planned on this basis, let me give as an exact parallel the new semicircular railroad line, with its suburban stations, that bypasses Amsterdam. That is good railroad planning, and it would be good highway planning, too, as the Dutch architect H. Th. Wijdeveld long ago pointed out. It is on relatively cheap land, on the edge of the city, that we should be building parking areas and garages: with free parking privileges to tempt the commuter to leave his car and finish his daily journey on the public transportation system. The public officials who have been planning our highway system on just the opposite principle are likewise planning to make the central areas of our cities unworkable and uninhabitable. Route 128 in Boston might seem a belated effort to provide such a circular feeder highway; but actually it is a classic example of how the specialized highway engineer, with his own concerns solely in mind, can defeat sound urban design.

Now it happens that the theory of the insulated, high-speed motorway, detached from local street and road systems, immune to the clutter of roadside "developments," was first worked out, not by highway engineers, but by Benton Mac-Kaye, the regional planner who conceived the Appalachian Trail. He not merely put together its essential features, but identified its principal characteristic: the fact that to achieve speed it must bypass towns. He called it in fact the Townless Highway. (See *The New Republic,* March 30, 1930.) Long before the highway engineers came through with Route 128, MacKaye pointed out the necessity for a motor bypass around the ring of suburbs that encircle Boston, in order to make every part of the metropolitan area accessible, and yet to provide a swift bypass route for through traffic.

MacKaye, not being a one-eyed specialist, visualized this circuit in all its potential dimensions and developments: he conceived accordingly a metropolitan recreation belt with a northbound motor road forming an arc on the inner flank and a southbound road on the outer flank—the two roads separated by a wide band of usable parkland, with footpaths and bicycle paths for recreation. In reducing MacKaye's conception to Route 128, without the greenbelt and without public control of the areas adjacent to the highway, the "experts" reduced the multi-purpose Bay Circuit to the typical "successful" expressway: so successful in attracting industry and business from the center of the city that it already ceases to perform even its own limited functions of fast transportation, except during hours of the day when ordinary highways would serve almost as well. This, in contrast to MacKaye's scheme, is a classic example of how not to do it.

Just as highway engineers know too little about city planning to correct the mistakes made in introducing the early railroad systems into our cities, so, too, they have curiously forgotten our experience with the elevated railroad—and unfortunately most municipal authorities have been equally forgetful. In the middle of the nineteenth century the elevated seemed the most facile and up-to-date method of introducing a new kind of rapid transportation system into the city; and in America, New York led the way in creating four such lines on Manhattan Island alone. The noise of the trains and the overshadowing of the structure lowered the value of the abutting properties even for commercial purposes; and the supporting columns constituted a dangerous obstacle to surface transportation. So unsatisfactory was elevated transportation even in cities like Berlin, where the structures were, in contrast to New York, Philadelphia, and Chicago, rather handsome works of engineering, that by popular consent subway building replaced elevated railroad building in all big cities, even though no one could pretend that riding in a tunnel was nearly as pleasant to the rider as was travel in the open air. The destruction of the old elevated railroads in New York was, ironically, hailed as a triumph of progress precisely at the moment that a new series of elevated highways was being built, to repeat on a more colossal scale the same errors.

Like the railroad, again, the motorway has repeatedly taken possession of the most valuable recreation space the city possesses, not merely by thieving land once dedicated to park uses, but by cutting off easy access to the waterfront parks, and lowering their value for refreshment and repose by introducing the roar of traffic and the bad odor of exhausts, though both noise and carbon monoxide are inimical to health. Witness the shocking spoilage of the Charles River basin parks in Boston, the arterial blocking off of the Lake Front in Chicago (after the removal of the original usurpers, the railroads), the barbarous sacrifice of large areas of Fairmount Park in Philadelphia, the partial defacement of the San Francisco waterfront, even in Paris the ruin of the Left Bank of the Seine.

One may match all these social crimes with a hundred other examples of barefaced highway robbery in every other metropolitan area. Even when the people who submit to these annexations and spoliations are dimly aware of what they are losing, they submit without more than a murmur of protest. What they do not understand is that they are trading a permanent good for a very temporary advantage, since until we subordinate highway expansion to the more permanent requirements of regional planning, the flood of motor traffic will clog new channels. What they further fail to realize is that the vast sums of money that go into such enterprises drain necessary public monies from other functions of the city, and make it socially if not financially bankrupt.

Neither the highway engineer nor the urban planner can, beyond a certain point, plan his facilities to accommodate an expanding population. On the over-all problem of population

pressure, regional and national policies must be developed
for throwing open, within our country, new regions of
settlement, if this pressure, which appeared so suddenly, does
not in fact abate just as unexpectedly and just as suddenly.
But there can be no sound planning anywhere until we
understand the necessity for erecting norms, or ideal limits,
for density of population. Most of our congested metropolises
need a lower density of population, with more parks and
open spaces, if they are to be attractive enough physically
to retain even a portion of their population for day-and-
night living; but most of our suburban and exurban communities must replan large areas at perhaps double their present
densities in order to have the social, educational, recreational, and industrial facilities they need closer at hand. Both
suburb and metropolis need a regional form of government,
working in private organizations as well as public forms, to
reapportion their resources and facilities, so as to benefit the whole area.

To say this is to say that both metropolitan congestion and
suburban scattering are obsolete. This means that good planning must work to produce a radically new pattern for urban growth. On this matter, public policy in the United
States is both contradictory and self-defeating. Instead of lowering central area densities, most urban renewal schemes, not
least those aimed at housing the groups that must be subsidized, either maintain old levels of congestion, or create
higher levels than existed in the slums they replaced. But the
Home Loan agencies, federal and private, on the other hand,
have been subsidizing the wasteful, ill-planned, single-family
house, on cheap land, ever remoter from the center of our
cities; a policy that has done as much to promote the suburban drift as the ubiquitous motorcar.

In order to cement these errors in the most solid way possible, our highway policy maximizes congestion at the center
and expands the area of suburban dispersion—what one
might call the metropolitan "fall-out." The three public agencies concerned have no official connections with each other:
but the total result of their efforts proves, once again, that
chaos does not have to be planned.

Motorcar manufacturers look forward confidently to the
time when every family will have two, if not three, cars. I
would not deny them that hope, though I remember that it

was first voiced in 1929, just before the fatal crash of our economic system, too enamored of high profits even to save itself by temporarily lowering prices. But if they don't want the motorcar to paralyze urban life, they must abandon their fantastic commitment to the indecently tumescent organs they have been putting on the market. For long-distance travel, a roomy car, if not artfully elongated, of course has many advantages; but for town use, let us insist upon a car that fits the city's needs: it is absurd to make over the city to fit the swollen imaginations of Detroit. The Isetta and the Goggomobil have already pointed the way; but what we need is an even smaller vehicle, powered by electricity, delivered by a powerful storage cell, yet to be invented: the exact opposite of our insolent chariots.

Maneuverability and parkability are the prime urban virtues in cars; and the simplest way to achieve this is by designing smaller cars. These virtues are lacking in all but one of our current American models. But why should our cities be destroyed just so that Detroit's infantile fantasies should remain unchallenged and unchanged?

If we want to make the most of our New Highway program, we must keep most of the proposed expressways in abeyance until we have done two other things. We must replan the inner city for pedestrian circulation, and we must rebuild and extend our public forms of mass transportation. In our entrancement with the motorcar, we have forgotten how much more efficient and how much more flexible the footwalker is. Before there was any public transportation in London, something like fifty thousand people an hour used to pass over London Bridge on their way to work: a single artery. Railroad transportation can bring from forty to sixty thousand people per hour, along a single route, whereas our best expressways, using far more space, cannot move more than four to six thousand cars: even if the average occupancy were more than one and a half passengers, as at present, this is obviously the most costly and inefficient means of handling the peak hours of traffic. As for the pedestrian, one could move a hundred thousand people, by the existing streets, from, say, downtown Boston to the Common, in something like half an hour, and find plenty of room for them to stand. But how many weary hours would it take to move them in cars over these same streets? And what would one do with the cars after they had reached the Common? Or where, for

that matter, could one assemble these cars in the first place?
For open spaces, long distances, and low population densities,
the car is now essential; for urban space, short distances, and
high densities, the pedestrian.

Every urban transportation plan should, accordingly, put
the pedestrian at the center of all its proposals, if only
to facilitate wheeled traffic. But to bring the pedestrian back
into the picture, one must treat him with the respect and
honor we now accord only to the automobile: we should provide him with pleasant walks, insulated from traffic, to take
him to his destination, once he enters a business precinct or
residential quarter. Every city should heed the example of
Rotterdam in creating the Lijnbaan, or of Coventry in creating its new shopping area. It is nonsense to say that this
cannot be done in America, because no one wants to walk.

Where walking is exciting and visually stimulating, whether
it is in a Detroit shopping center or along Fifth Avenue,
Americans are perfectly ready to walk. The legs will come
into their own again, as the ideal means of neighborhood
transportation, once some provision is made for their exercise, as Philadelphia is now doing, both in its Independence
Hall area, and in Penn Center. But if we are to make
walking attractive, we must not only provide trees and wide
pavements and benches, beds of flowers and outdoor cafés,
as they do in Rotterdam: we must also scrap the monotonous
uniformities of American zoning practice, which turns vast
areas, too spread out for pedestrian movement, into single-
district zones, for commerce, industry, or residential purposes.
(As a result, only the mixed zones are architecturally interesting today despite their disorder.)

Why should anyone have to take a car and drive a couple
of miles to get a package of cigarettes or a loaf of bread,
as one must often do in a suburb? Why, on the other hand,
should a growing minority of people not be able again to walk
to work, by living in the interior of the city, or, for that
matter, be able to walk home from the theatre or the concert hall? Where urban facilities are compact, walking still delights the American: does he not travel many thousands of
miles just to enjoy this privilege in the historic urban cores
of Europe? And do not people now travel for miles, of an
evening, from the outskirts of Pittsburgh, just for the pleasure
of a stroll in Mellon Square? Nothing would do more to give
life back to our blighted urban cores than to re-instate the

pedestrian, in malls and pleasances designed to make circulation a delight. And what an opportunity for architecture!

While federal funds and subsidies pour without stint into highway improvements, the two most important modes of transportation for cities—the railroad for long distances and mass transportation, and the subway for shorter journeys— are permitted to languish and even to disappear. This is very much like what has happened to our postal system. While the time needed to deliver a letter across the continent has been reduced, the time needed for local delivery has been multiplied. What used to take two hours now sometimes takes two days. As a whole our postal system has been degraded to a level that would have been regarded as intolerable even thirty years ago. In both cases, an efficient system has been sacrificed to an overfavored new industry, motorcars, telephones, airplanes; whereas, if the integrity of the system itself had been respected, each of these new inventions could have added enormously to the efficiency of the existing network.

If we could overcome the irrational drives that are now at work, promoting shortsighted decisions, the rational case for rebuilding the mass transportation system in our cities would be overwhelming. The current objection to mass transportation comes chiefly from the fact that it has been allowed to decay: this lapse itself reflects the general blight of the central areas. In order to maintain profits, or in many cases to reduce deficits, rates have been raised, services have decreased, and equipment has become obsolete, without being replaced and improved. Yet mass transportation, with far less acreage in roadbeds and rights of way, can deliver at least ten times more people per hour than the private motorcar. This means that if such means were allowed to lapse in our metropolitan centers—as the inter-urban electric trolley system, that complete and efficient network, was allowed to disappear in the nineteen-twenties—we should require probably five to ten times the existing number of arterial highways to bring the present number of commuters into the city, and at least ten times the existing parking space to accommodate them. In that tangled mass of highways, interchanges, and parking lots, the city would be nowhere: a mechanized nonentity ground under an endless procession of wheels.

That plain fact reduces a one-dimensional transportation

system, by motorcar alone, to a calamitous absurdity, as far as urban development goes, even if the number of vehicles and the population count were not increasing year by year. Now it happens that the population of the core of our big cities has remained stable in recent years: in many cases, the decline which set in as early as 1910 in New York seems to have ceased. This means that it is now possible to set an upper limit for the daily inflow of workers, and to work out a permanent mass transportation system that will get them in and out again as pleasantly and efficiently as possible.

In time, if urban renewal projects become sufficient in number to permit the design of a system of minor urban throughways, at ground level, that will bypass the neighborhood, even circulation by motorcar may play a valuable part in the total scheme—provided, of course, that minuscule-size town cars take the place of the long-tailed dinosaurs that now lumber about our metropolitan swamps. But the notion that the private motorcar can be substituted for mass transportation should be put forward only by those who desire to see the city itself disappear, and with it the complex, many-sided civilization that the city makes possible.

There is no purely local engineering solution to the problems of transportation in our age: nothing like a stable solution is possible without giving due weight to all the necessary elements in transportation—private motorcars, railroads, airplanes, and helicopters, mass transportation services by trolley and bus, even ferryboats, and finally, not least, the pedestrian. To achieve the necessary over-all pattern, not merely must there be effective city and regional planning, before new routes or services are planned; we also need eventually—and the sooner the better—an adequate system of federated urban government on a regional scale.

Until these necessary tools of control have been created, most of our planning will be empirical and blundering; and the more we do, on our present premises, the more disastrous will be the results. In short we cannot have an efficient form for our transportation system until we can envisage a better permanent structure for our cities. And the first lesson we have to learn is that a city exists, not for the constant passage of motorcars, but for the care and culture of men.

*1958*